Poetry and Politics

Poetry
and
POLITICS

AN ANTHOLOGY OF ESSAYS

Edited by Richard Jones

WILLIAM MORROW AND COMPANY, INC.

New York

Library of Congress Cataloging in Publication Data
Main entry under title:

Poetry and politics.

1. Political poetry—History and criticism—
Addresses, essays, lectures. 2. Politics in
literature—Addresses, essays, lectures. 3. Politics
and literature—Addresses, essays, lectures. 4. Poets,
American—20th century—Political and social views—
Addresses, essays, lectures. I. Jones, Richard,
1953–
PN1081.P62 1985b   809.1'9358   84-14832
ISBN 0-688-03987-1
ISBN 0-688-03988-X (pbk.)

Printed in the United States of America

First Edition

D#27793

1 2 3 4 5 6 7 8 9 10

BOOK DESIGN BY ELLEN LO GIUDICE

Acknowledgments

My work on this anthology began while editing a volume of *Poetry East* entitled *Art & Guns: Political Poetry at Home and Abroad.* I am, as always, indebted to Kate Daniels, co-editor of *Poetry East,* for her intelligent suggestions, patience, and love.

I would also like to thank those friends and colleagues whose conversations and suggestions were vital to the shaping of this book: Deborah Baker, Robert Bly, Hayden Carruth, Thomas DePietro, Galway Kinnell, Denise Levertov, Philip Levine, Rick Peabody, William Reid, Mark Rudman, James Turner, and Charles Vandersee.

Contents

CONTENTS

Introduction:
The Imprisoned Imagination

Poetry and Politics is a collection of essays written by poets since World War II. The purpose of the anthology is not to assert a political ideology or aesthetic theory that will ultimately define the vague and controversial phrase "poetry and politics"; nor is it intended to be a social history documenting recent trends in contemporary literature. Rather, I hope this book will establish a forum in which basic and commonly held notions regarding the political nature of language may be set forth and discussed. The intention is nonpartisan; that is, I do not seek to promote a particular political point of view. A brief look at the contributors will make this evident: The writers represented range, politically, from T. S. Eliot on the right to Amiri Baraka on the left, with poets like Carolyn Forché and Stanley Kunitz in the center. Nevertheless, I do assume that there is a relationship between poetry and politics and that the two are not inherently antagonistic or exclusive of one another.

From Plato to Marx, questions about the political nature and uses of poetry have been raised. Is poetry meant to please or persuade? Is the language of poetry compatible with the language of politics? Do poems make a difference? What these historical questions point to is an unresolved tension between contemplation and action, between the articulation of an ideal in a work of art and its realization in the polis. These questions have to do with the nature and essence of art, and its function in the world. One possible response is to say that all art is simply "made up," that the articulation of an ideal world (the work of art) is simply that—an abstract concept removed from the flesh-and-blood realities of day-to-day life. But then the question becomes one not only of politics but of simple communication. For if verbal art has nothing to do with what is real, with the politics of existence, then how can it say anything at all?

For many contemporary writers, the answer to this dilemma has been to concentrate on the immediate, the concrete, what the writer can see or feel or touch, and to find, as William Blake suggested, the world in a grain of sand, the mystery and spiritual significance of life in mundane everyday events. This is one reason for the omnipresent first-person voice of contemporary poems. In recent years this predilection for concreteness has been the ruling aesthetic behind both the confessional poem and the neosurrealist poem, as well as the best openly political poems. Today poets go, as Pound justly advised, in fear of abstractions. The political aspect of the successful poem—just like the personal experience of the artist—is not an abstract system of values tacked onto the work; it is organic, as transparent and inseparable from the artist's overall vision as his or her notions of history or psychology or morality, as central to the work as deeply personal feelings of pain or loss, love or anger. It is not the politics of the writer in which we are interested; nor do we hear music in poems filled with political rhetoric, which, as George Orwell noted, is only "designed to make lies sound truthful." We are not interested in being told what to think, in propaganda; we are interested in the story, in its details and images. As readers, we share in the experience and vision of the writer because our own imaginations have been engaged by the vividness or the concreteness of the narrative. Karl Shapiro has said that poetry is a way of seeing, and it is true that we read for the story, not the theory. When it comes to the meaning of the poem, most readers prefer to make up their own minds.

But taken to extremes, this aesthetic of the personal forces new questions about the "proper" arena of the poet: If the ground that the poet works lies exclusively within the sphere of the self, can he or she truly imagine and speak for others' lives and experiences, as has been the tradition in art? The extreme separation of poetry from its social function raises, in a new and urgent form, the questions that had been the concern of Romanticism—questions about the function of contemplation, the territory of the imagination, and the power of language to convey meaning and truth.

10

The danger of assuming this self-imposed boundary that allows the writer to speak *only* about what is immediately and concretely accessible is that the imagination is confined to the personal experience, the private moment, of the artist. The sage maxim "Write about what you know" begins to mean "Write about yourself." Literature forfeits its magical ability to transform the world and settles for documentations of private lives. Occasionally we find poets trying to balance their losses with formal pyrotechnics, as if prosody alone could give a heart to a poem without content. What too often seems lacking in our recent poetry is a larger empathy and sense of history that one finds and admires in a poet such as Whitman, whose imagination could encompass and make vital the great sorrows and triumphs of his time. If one cannot see or feel beyond the immediacies of the self, how can one possibly write about complex and often "invisible" social problems such as the nuclear threat or the Cold War, much less the daily problems of sexism or racism or economics that touch us all, and which constantly inform and determine our lives? Ultimately, these questions challenge our concept of the human imagination, what the artist is capable of imagining, able to feel, and, therefore, allowed to express. This is a new challenge: the idea that the imagination is limited. Even more compelling is the question of why poets have chosen to put themselves in a kind of prison of the self, which is what can only result when an artist is deprived of the power of imagination. Such assessments reflect an extremely rational perspective, as though it were actually possible to determine the exact boundaries of the mind. If we are allowed to believe only what is before us, we deny many poets not only any possibility of social responsibility but also the human ability to empathize with others, to care. The empathic imagination is not merely crippled; it is killed.

Such a rationalistic approach to defining the "boundaries" of the imagination, and, by extension, art, has implications not only for the writer's subject matter but also for the reader, who must ultimately "realize" the poem. When the poet withdraws into solipsism, the reader is abandoned. We no longer share a collective experience with the poet and can do no more than consider what has been written, intellectually, distantly, like a voyeur. We remain impassive as the poet dictates how we must feel, how we must respond, what we must see, and ultimately, what we must *do* in the course of reading a poem. The poem allows no room for involvement, for *choice,* and as readers we are left only with a sort of propaganda of the self.

Traditionally, viewing the great tragedies, audiences became one with the characters in their plights and struggles through empathy. We feel the joy or sorrow of fictional characters (or imagined people) as though their experiences were our own. To put it simply, the liberation and illumination of catharsis are not intellectual processes, but ones of feeling through imagination. Similarly, great political poems do not beat us over the head with what we already know intellectually about the Holocaust or the CIA or the gulags or poverty. Rather, they involve us emotionally in the struggle at hand and allow us the opportunity both to face and acknowledge a crisis and to choose what we would do. When the contemporary writer loses the ability to empathize with others, to let the imagination go out into the world and discover stories that touch us all, he or she loses not only a part of the self, but the traditional ground on which art has always been built.

The general antithesis then is not so much between poetry and politics, but between the personal and the political, or the private and the public. The common argument is that poetry since the Romantics has increasingly become an expression of the individual's personal experience, uttered without regard to or sanction by church or state. Because poetry in our time is personal, it cannot include the political, since the political is outside the individual; in short, politics—the *outside* world— is neither the source nor the focus of the poetic imagination or the language of poetry, but is a domain of public issues to be debated by politicians through reason and rhetoric. The argument is fine, as far as it goes. The problem is that it does not go far enough, and the result is a one-sided view of our inheritance from the Romantics.

The emphasis and concentration on the inner life of the self is only a part of the legacy of the Romantic poets. It is understandable that the Moderns, in their obsessive focus on the needs and concerns of the individual, would emphasize this one element of the Romantic philosophy. But the underlying misinterpretation of Romanticism inherent in our contemporary notions is that the personal world leading to poetry is a *prescribed* world that does not and cannot include the political. What is particularly disturbing about this is the assumption that the Romantics' ideas were in this way limited. In fact, the Romantic idea was liberating in that it enlarged the realm of poetry. Breaking free of the rationalistic rhetoric of the neoclassicists, the poet, through empathy, colloquial language, and imagination, could dramatize and give voice to the human experience. The current criticism that poetry defiles itself and degenerates into vulgar sloganeering everytime it steps outside the private world to enter the public realm of issues seems, if the poems of the Romantics are any example, a wrong-headed generalization. A social consciousness was integral to their advanced ideas regarding language, form, and content. The Romantic aesthetic arose not only out of private visions, but from an awareness of the social conditions of their day. The Romantic poets bore witness to the abuses of industrialization, the squalor and alienation of urban life, the excitement of the French Revolution and the disillusionment that followed. Although most often remembered for their lyrical odes and pastoral idealism, the Romantics also wrote angry poems of social protest, such as William Blake's "London" (1794):

London

I wander through each chartered street,
Near where the chartered Thames does flow,
And mark in every face I meet,
Marks of weakness, marks of woe.

In every cry of every man,
In every infant's cry of fear,
In every voice, in every ban,
The mind-forged manacles I hear.

How the chimney-sweeper's cry
Every blackening church appals;
And the hapless soldier's sigh
Runs in blood down palace walls.

> But most through midnight streets I hear
> How the youthful harlot's curse
> Blasts the newborn infant's tear,
> And blights with plagues the marriage hearse.

The Romantics created a poetry which not only recorded the inward experience but which also was outward-looking, a poetry which could be adamantly democratic in its celebration and application of what Wordsworth called "the real language of men." The Romantic aesthetic, based on a belief in the honesty of emotions, the ability of the senses rather than reason to perceive and interpret experience, and the eloquence of common everyday speech, attests to the balance they sought to achieve between the experience of a personal vision and the articulation and fulfillment of that experience in language.

At the heart of the Romantic philosophy was a faith in the melioristic power of the individual imagination. The Romantics were careful to distinguish between fancy, which they believed took one away from reality (one thinks of today's solipsistic or neosurrealistic poems), and imagination, which they described as the process by which people completed a vision of outside reality through art. Even in their discussion of the imagination (perhaps the most overused, misunderstood, and *abstract* word in contemporary aesthetics), we see the movement was not away from the world—the personal or the political—but toward a poetry that reaffirmed the integrity of the individual voice and purpose of the artist in society, even though the role was often adversarial.

Common to many of the postwar essays collected here is the idea that although there may be a political dimension to poetry, the relationship between poet and politics remains an ambivalent one. In the modern era, the Romantic idea of the individual imagination has been intensified and desocialized: The movement inward has been relentless, like falling into a bottomless well. After the shock of World War I, it is no surprise that the road led on to existentialism, and, ultimately, to a sort of stubborn solipsism, in which the individual became emblematic of the simultaneous fragmentation of the public and homogenization of society. In the thirties, the most politicized period of artistic activity in the United States, the urgent question about

14

poetry was not whether this or that poem had literary merit or "correct" politics, but rather, what was the role of the artist in society. Discussion of political issues of course confronted social and political conditions, from the rise of Fascism abroad to the Depression at home. But the emphasis on the relationship of the artist to society also revealed the self-imposed isolationism of our artists and writers, who found themselves not only without readers but also without any acknowledgment of their authority in the realm of political and moral questions. At least the Romantics were more realistic. As Shelley said in "A Defense of Poetry," "Poets are the *unacknowledged* legislators of the world" (emphasis mine).

Since World War II, the consensus of writers and critics has been that poetry and politics, acknowledged or unacknowledged, simply don't mix. The political role of the poet in society has dwindled, reduced now to that of the occasional spokesperson for this or that issue—civil rights, women's rights, the Vietnam War. Today, a discussion of poetry and politics is often divisive rather than informative. Perhaps the postwar disenchantment with literary radicalism is still with us. Perhaps the political solutions to social problems evade poets as easily as they evade politicians. Aesthetically, we seem comfortable only with discussing the tension between the personal poem and the political poem, applauding apolitical mimesis or denouncing the didacticism and self-aggrandizement inherent in bearing witness. At its worst, contemporary discussion falls into moralistic name calling on one hand and political grandstanding on the other.

What is truly curious, however, is that poets have been largely silent on a crucial issue of the second half of the twentieth century: the bomb. The bomb has made its way into a few poems, but it has only recently been openly discussed by poets. It is indicative of the antipolitics tendency of the last forty years' writing and criticism that we now find ourselves mute in the face of nuclear threat. This is a great challenge to poetry in that it forces poets to live up to their social responsibility, as well as challenging the essential power and spirit of poetry's claim to being the highest artistic expression of our humanity. Each of us, individually, must *imagine* the reality of a nuclear war before we can speak. For poets to write about the bomb is to confront—in the

15

creative act of writing a poem—a subject of immediate urgency, political or otherwise. It is to speak in a voice that goes out from the self to others, acknowledging both personal fears and hopes, as well as the existence of all people. The bomb even raises questions of poetic form. If poetry is meant to "sing" and celebrate, how does one "sing" about the nuclear threat? But, as Galway Kinnell has said, if the free verse poem is to tell the truth and carry a message of hope and humanity in the face of nuclear destruction, then the vessel must be equal to the message.

Although the title of this book is *Poetry and Politics,* it could also have been *Imagination and Tradition,* or some other more agreeable phrase. I have taken to task, in this introductory note, some of the more regrettable aspects of contemporary writing, primarily those tendencies that forever reenact the alienation of the artist from his or her own feelings and from society. What this anthology calls for is not only a new examination of our literary precedents but also a reassessment and reassertion of our belief in the imagination and the power of language to voice a shared vision of the human condition.

Of course, there has been some straightforward political writing among our poets, and those gathered here, some of our best, are no exception. What these poets show us, in their poems as well as in these essays, is that the political dimension in poetry is as open and far-reaching as the individual imagination, which would no more censor the political in art than it would the spiritual. Poetry demands that every writer raise his or her *own* voice. What these essays show us is that we can write about and experience and acknowledge our place in society; through poetry, we can feel the political realities of our existence and reclaim the opportunity to make the choices demanded of us by our lives. There need not be a silence on any level. To go back to the age-old questions of contemplation and realization, we have only to see that we are free to imagine anything, and that it is in the immediacy and physicality of language that what we dream takes the first step toward actualization.

—R.J.

Charlottesville, Virginia
April 1984

The Social Function of Poetry

T. S. ELIOT

The title of this essay* is so likely to suggest different things to different people, that I may be excused for explaining first what I do not mean by it before going on to try to explain what I do mean. When we speak of the "function" of anything we are likely to be thinking of what that thing *ought* to do rather than of what it does do or has done. That is an important distinction, because I do not intend to talk about what I think poetry *ought* to do. People who tell us what poetry ought to do, especially if they are poets themselves, usually have in mind the particular kind of poetry that they would like to write. It is always possible, of course, that poetry may have a different task in the future from what it has had in the past; but even if that is so, it is worth while to decide first what function it has had in the past, both at one time or another in one language or another, and universally. I could easily write about what I do with poetry myself, or what I should like to do, and then try to persuade you that this is exactly what all good poets have tried to do, or ought to have done, in the past—only they have not succeeded completely, but perhaps that is not their fault. But it seems to me probable that if poetry—and I mean *all* great poetry—has had no social function in the past, it is not likely to have any in the future.

When I say *all* great poetry I mean to avoid another way in which I might treat the subject. One might take up the various kinds of poetry, one after another, and discuss the social function of each kind in turn without reaching the general question

*An address delivered at the British–Norwegian Institute in 1943 and subsequently developed for delivery to an audience in Paris in 1945. It later appeared in *The Adelphi*.

of what is the function of poetry as poetry. I want to distinguish between the general and particular functions, so that we shall know what we are not talking about. Poetry may have a deliberate, conscious social purpose. In its more primitive forms this purpose is often quite clear. There are, for example, early runes and chants, some of which had very practical magical purposes—to avert the evil eye, to cure some disease, or to propitiate some demon. Poetry is early used in religious ritual, and when we sing a hymn we are still using poetry for a particular social purpose. The early forms of epic and saga may have transmitted what was held to be history before surviving for communal entertainment only; and before the use of written language a regular verse form must have been extremely helpful to the memory—and the memory of primitive bards, storytellers and scholars must have been prodigious. In more advanced societies, such as that of ancient Greece, the recognized social functions of poetry are also very conspicuous. The Greek drama develops out of religious rites, and remains a formal public ceremony associated with traditional religious celebrations; the pindaric ode develops in relation to a particular social occasion. Certainly, these definite uses of poetry gave poetry a framework which made possible the attainment of perfection in particular kinds.

In more modern poetry some of these forms remain, such as that of the religious hymn which I have mentioned. The meaning of the term *didactic* poetry has undergone some change. *Didactic* may mean "conveying information," or it may mean "giving moral instruction," or it may mean something which comprehends both. Virgil's *Georgics*, for instance, are very beautiful poetry, and contain some very sound information about good farming. But it would seem impossible, at the present day, to write an up-to-date book about farming which should also be fine poetry: for one thing the subject itself has become much more complicated and scientific; and for another, it can be handled more readily in prose. Nor should we, as the Romans did, write astronomical and cosmological treatises in verse. The poem, the ostensible aim of which is to convey information, has been superseded by prose. Didactic poetry has gradually become limited to poetry of moral exhortation, or poetry which aims to *persuade* the reader to the author's point of view about something. It therefore includes a great deal of what can be called *satire*, though satire overlaps with burlesque and parody, the purpose of which is primarily to cause mirth. Some of Dryden's poems, in the seventeenth century, are satires in the sense that they aim to ridicule the objects against which they are directed, and also didactic in the aim to persuade the reader to a particular political or religious point of view; and in doing this they also make use of the allegorical method of disguising reality as fiction: "The Hind and the Panther," which aims to persuade the reader that right was on the side of the Church of Rome against the Church of England, is his most remarkable poem in this kind. In the nineteenth century a good deal of the poetry of Shelley is inspired by a zeal for social and political reforms.

As for *dramatic* poetry, that has a social function of a kind now peculiar to itself. For whereas most poetry today is written to be read in solitude, or to be read aloud in a small company, dramatic verse alone has as its function the making an immediate, collective impression upon a large number of people gathered together to look at an imaginary episode acted upon a stage. Dramatic poetry is different from any other, but as its special laws are those of the drama its function is merged into that of the drama in general, and I am not here concerned with the special social function of the drama.

As for the special function of philosophical poetry, that would involve an analysis and an historical account of some length. I have, I think, already mentioned enough kinds of poetry to make clear that the special function of each is related to some other function: of dramatic poetry to drama, of didactic poetry of information to the function of its subject matter, of didactic poetry of philosophy or religion or politics or morals to the function of these subjects. We might consider the function of any of these kinds of poetry and still leave untouched the question of the function of *poetry*. For all these things can be dealt with in prose.

But before proceeding I want to dismiss one objection that may be raised. People sometimes are suspicious of any poetry that has a particular purpose: poetry in which the poet is advocating social, moral, political or religious views. And they are much more inclined to say that it isn't poetry when they dislike the particular views; just as other people often think that something is real poetry because it happens to express a point of view

19

which they like. I should say that the question of whether the poet is using his poetry to advocate or attack a social attitude does not matter. Bad verse may have a transient vogue when the poet is reflecting a popular attitude of the moment; but real poetry survives not only a change of popular opinion but the complete extinction of interest in the issues with which the poet was passionately concerned. Lucretius' poem remains a great poem, though his notions of physics and astronomy are discredited; Dryden's, though the political quarrels of the seventeenth century no longer concern us; just as a great poem of the past may still give great pleasure, though its subject matter is one which we should now treat in prose.

Now if we are to find the essential social function of poetry we must look first at its more obvious functions, those which it must perform if it is to perform any. The first, I think, that we can be sure about is that poetry has to give pleasure. If you ask what kind of pleasure then I can only answer, the kind of pleasure that poetry gives: simply because any other answer would take us far afield into aesthetics, and the general question of the nature of art.

I suppose it will be agreed that every good poet, whether he be a great poet or not, has something to give us besides pleasure: for if it were only pleasure, the pleasure itself could not be of the highest kind. Beyond any specific intention which poetry may have, such as I have already instanced in the various kinds of poetry, there is always the communication of some new experience, or some fresh understanding of the familiar, or the expression of something we have experienced but have no words for, which enlarges our consciousness or refines our sensibility. But it is not with such individual benefit from poetry, any more than it is with the quality of individual pleasure, that this paper is concerned. We all understand, I think, both the kind of pleasure which poetry can give, and the kind of difference, beyond the pleasure, which it makes to our lives. Without producing these two effects it simply is not poetry. We may acknowledge this, but at the same time overlook something which it does for us collectively, as a society. And I mean that in the widest sense. For I think it is important that every people should have its own poetry, not simply for those who enjoy poetry—such people could always learn other languages and enjoy their poetry—but because it actually makes a difference to the society as a whole, and that means to people who do not enjoy poetry. I include even those who do not know the names of their own national poets. That is the real subject of this paper.

We observe that poetry differs from every other art in having a value for the people of the poet's race and language, which it can have for no other. It is true that even music and painting have a local and racial character: but certainly the difficulties of appreciation in these arts, for a foreigner, are much less. It is true on the other hand that prose writings have significance in their own language which is lost in translation; but we all feel that we lose much less in reading a novel in translation than in reading a poem; and in a translation of some kinds of scientific work the loss may be virtually nil. That poetry is much more local than prose can be seen in the history of European languages. Through the Middle Ages to within a few hundred years ago Latin remained the language for philosophy, theology, and science. The impulse towards the literary use of the languages of the peoples began with poetry. And this appears perfectly natural when we realize that poetry has primarily to do with the expression of feeling and emotion; and that feeling and emotion are particular, whereas thought is general. It is easier to think in a foreign language than it is to feel in it. Therefore no art is more stubbornly national than poetry. A people may have its language taken away from it, suppressed, and another language compelled upon the schools; but unless you teach that people to *feel* in a new language, you have not eradicated the old one, and it will reappear in poetry, which is the vehicle of feeling. I have just said "feel in a new language," and I mean something more than merely "express their feelings in a new language." A thought expressed in a different language may be practically the same thought, but a feeling or emotion expressed in a different language is not the same feeling or emotion. One of the reasons for learning at least one foreign language well is that we acquire a kind of supplementary personality; one of the reasons for not acquiring a new language *instead* of our own is that most of us do not want to become a different person. A superior language can seldom be exterminated except by the extermination of the people who speak it. When one language supersedes another it is usually because that language has

21

advantages which commend it, and which offer not merely a difference but a wider and more refined range, not only for thinking but for feeling, than the more primitive language.

Emotion and feeling, then, are best expressed in the common language of the people—that is, in the language common to all classes: the structure, the rhythm, the sound, the idiom of a language, express the personality of the people which speaks it. When I say that it is poetry rather than prose that is concerned with the expression of emotion and feeling, I do not mean that poetry need have no intellectual content or meaning, or that great poetry does not contain more of such meaning than lesser poetry. But to develop this investigation would take me away from my immediate purpose. I will take it as agreed that people find the most conscious expression of their deepest feelings in the poetry of their own language rather than in any other art or in the poetry of other languages. This does not mean, of course, that true poetry is limited to feelings which everyone can recognize and understand; we must not limit poetry to *popular* poetry. It is enough that in a homogeneous people the feelings of the most refined and complex have something in common with those of the most crude and simple, which they have not in common with those of people of their own level speaking another language. And, when a civilization is healthy, the great poet will have something to say to his fellow countrymen at every level of education.

We may say that the duty of the poet, as poet, is only indirectly to his people: his direct duty is to his *language,* first to preserve, and second to extend and improve. In expressing what other people feel he is also changing the feeling by making it more conscious; he is making people more aware of what they feel already, and therefore teaching them something about themselves. But he is not merely a more conscious person than the others; he is also individually different from other people, and from other poets too, and can make his readers share consciously in new feelings which they had not experienced before. That is the difference between the writer who is merely eccentric or mad and the genuine poet. The former may have feelings which are unique but which cannot be shared, and are therefore useless; the latter discovers new variations of sensibility which can be appropriated by others. And in expressing them he is developing and enriching the language which he speaks.

I have said quite enough about the impalpable differences of feeling between one people and another, differences which are affirmed in, and developed by, their different languages. But people do not only experience the world differently in different places, they experience it differently at different times. In fact, our sensibility is constantly changing, as the world about us changes: ours is not the same as that of the Chinese or the Hindu, but also it is not the same as that of our ancestors several hundred years ago. It is not the same as that of our fathers; and finally, we ourselves are not quite the same persons that we were a year ago. This is obvious; but what is not so obvious is that this is the reason why we cannot afford to *stop* writing poetry. Most educated people take a certain pride in the great authors of their language, though they may never read them, just as they are proud of any other distinction of their country: a few authors even become celebrated enough to be mentioned occasionally in political speeches. But most people do not realize that this is not enough; that unless they go on producing great authors, and especially great poets, their language will deteriorate, their culture will deteriorate and perhaps become absorbed in a stronger one.

One point is, of course, that if we have no living literature we shall become more and more alienated from the literature of the past; unless we keep up continuity, our literature of the past will become more and more remote from us until it is as strange to us as the literature of a foreign people. For our language goes on changing; our way of life changes, under the pressure of material changes in our environment in all sorts of ways; and unless we have those few men who combine an exceptional sensibility with an exceptional power over words, our own ability, not merely to express, but even to feel any but the crudest emotions, will degenerate.

It matters little whether a poet had a large audience in his own time. What matters is that there should always be at least a small audience for him in every generation. Yet what I have just said suggests that his importance is for his own time, or that dead poets cease to be of any use to us unless we have living poets as well. I would even press my first point and say that if a poet gets a large audience very quickly, that is a rather suspicious

23

circumstance: for it leads us to fear that he is not really doing anything new, that he is only giving people what they are already used to, and therefore what they have already had from the poets of the previous generation. But that a poet should have the right, small audience in his own time *is* important. There should always be a small vanguard of people, appreciative of poetry, who are independent and somewhat in advance of their time or ready to assimilate novelty more quickly. The development of culture does not mean bringing everybody up to the front, which amounts to no more than making everyone keep step: it means the maintenance of such an *élite*, with the main, and more passive body of readers not lagging more than a generation or so behind. The changes and developments of sensibility which appear first in a few will work themselves into the language gradually, through their influence on other, and more readily popular authors; and by the time they have become well established, a new advance will be called for. It is, moreover, through the living authors that the dead remain alive. A poet like Shakespeare has influenced the English language very deeply, not only by his influence on his immediate successors. For the greatest poets have aspects which do not come to light at once; and by exercising a direct influence on other poets centuries later, they continue to affect the living language. Indeed, if an English poet is to learn how to use words in our time, he must devote close study to those who have used them best in *their* time; to those who, in their own day, have made the language new.

So far I have only suggested the final point to which I think the influence of poetry may be said to extend; and that can be put best by the assertion that, in the long run, it makes a difference to the speech, to the sensibility, to the lives of all the members of a society, to all the members of the community, to the whole people, whether they read and enjoy poetry or not: even, in fact, whether they know the names of their greatest poets or not. The influence of poetry, at the furthest periphery, is of course very diffused, very indirect, and very difficult to prove. It is like following the course of a bird or an aeroplane in a clear sky: if you have seen it when it was quite near, and kept your eye on it as it flew farther and farther away, you can still see it at a great distance, a distance at which the eye of another person, to whom you try to point it out, will be unable to find it.

So, if you follow the influence of poetry, through those readers who are most affected by it, to those people who never read at all, you will find it present everywhere. At least you will find it if the national culture is living and healthy, for in a healthy society there is a continuous reciprocal influence and interaction of each part upon the others. And this is what I mean by the social function of poetry in its largest sense: that it does, in proportion to its excellence and vigour, affect the speech and the sensibility of the whole nation.

You must not imagine me to be saying that the language which we speak is determined exclusively by our poets. The structure of culture is much more complex than that. Indeed it will equally be true that the quality of our poetry is dependent upon the way in which the people use their language: for a poet must take as his material his own language as it is actually spoken around him. If it is improving, he will profit; if it is deteriorating, he must make the best of it. Poetry can to some extent preserve, and even restore, the beauty of a language; it can and should also help it to develop, to be just as subtle and precise in the more complicated conditions and for the changing purposes of modern life, as it was in and for a simpler age. But poetry, like every other single element in that mysterious social personality which we call our "culture," must be dependent upon a great many circumstances which are beyond its control.

This leads me to a few afterthoughts of a more general nature. My emphasis to this point has been upon the national and local function of poetry; and this must be qualified. I do not wish to leave the impression that the function of poetry is to divide people from people, for I do not believe that the cultures of the several of Europe can flourish in isolation from each other. There have been, no doubt, in the past, high civilizations producing great art, thought and literature, which have developed in isolation. Of that I cannot speak with assurance, for some of them may not have been so isolated as at first appears. But in the history of Europe this has not been so. Even Ancient Greece owed much to Egypt, and something to the Asiatic frontiers; and in the relations of the Greek states to each other, with their different dialects and different manners, we may find a reciprocal influence and stimulus analogous to that of the countries of Europe upon each other. But the history of European

25

literature will not show that any has been independent of the others; rather that there has been a constant give and take, and that each has in turn, from time to time, been revitalized by stimulation from outside. A general *autarky* in culture simply will not work: the hope of perpetuating the culture of any country lies in communication with others. But if separation of cultures within the unity of Europe is a danger, so also would be a unification which led to uniformity. The variety is as essential as the unity. For instance, there is much to be said, for certain limited purposes, for a universal *lingua franca* such as Esperanto or Basic English. But supposing that all communication between nations was carried on in such an artificial language, how imperfect it would be! Or rather, it would be wholly adequate in some respects, and there would be a complete lack of communication in others. Poetry is a constant reminder of all the things that can only be said in one language, and are untranslatable. The *spiritual* communication between people and people cannot be carried on without the individuals who take the trouble to learn at least one foreign language as well as one can learn any language but one's own, and who consequently are able, to a greater or less degree, to *feel* in another language as well as in their own. And one's understanding of another people, in this way, needs to be supplemented by the understanding of those individuals among that people who have gone to the pains to learn one's own language.

Incidentally, the study of another people's poetry is peculiarly instructive. I have said that there are qualities of the poetry of every language, which only those to whom the language is native can understand. But there is another side to this too. I have sometimes found, in trying to read a language which I did not know very well, that I did not understand a piece of prose until I understood it according to the standards of the school teacher: that is, I had to be sure of the meaning of every word, grasp the grammar and syntax, and then I could think the passage out in English. But I have also found sometimes that a piece of poetry, which I could not translate, containing many words unfamiliar to me, and sentences which I could not construe, conveyed something immediate and vivid, which was unique, different from anything in English—something which I could not put into words and yet felt that I understood. And on learning that language better I found that this impression was not an illusion, not something which I had imagined to be in the poetry, but something that was really there. So in poetry you can, now and then, penetrate into another country, so to speak, before your passport has been issued or your ticket taken.

The whole question of the relation of countries of different language but related culture, within the ambit of Europe, is therefore one into which we are led, perhaps unexpectedly, by inquiring into the social function of poetry. I certainly do not intend to pass from this point into purely political questions; but I could wish that those who are concerned with political questions would more often cross the frontier into these which I have been considering. For these give the spiritual aspect of problems the material aspect of which is the concern of politics. On my side of the line one is concerned with living things which have their own laws of growth, which are not always reasonable, but must just be accepted by the reason: things which cannot be neatly planned and put into order any more than the winds and the rains and the seasons can be disciplined.

If, finally, I am right in believing that poetry has a "social function" for the whole of the people of the poet's language, whether they are aware of his existence or not, it follows that it matters to each people of Europe that the others should continue to have poetry. I cannot read Norwegian poetry, but if I were told that no more poetry was being written in the Norwegian language I should feel an alarm which would be much more than generous sympathy. I should regard it as a spot of malady which was likely to spread over the whole Continent; the beginning of a decline which would mean that people everywhere would cease to be able to express, and consequently be able to feel, the emotions of civilized beings. This of course might happen. Much has been said everywhere about the decline of religious belief; not so much notice has been taken of the decline of religious sensibility. The trouble of the modern age is not merely the inability to believe certain things about God and man which our forefathers believed, but the inability to *feel* towards God and man as they did. A belief in which you no longer believe is something which to some extent you can still understand; but when religious feeling disappears, the words in which men have struggled to express it become meaningless. It

27

is true that religious feeling varies naturally from country to country, and from age to age, just as poetic feeling does; the feeling varies, even when the belief, the doctrine, remains the same. But this is a condition of human life, and what I am apprehensive of is death. It is equally possible that the feeling for poetry, and the feelings which are the material of poetry, may disappear everywhere: which might perhaps help to facilitate that unification of the world which some people consider desirable for its own sake.

From *The Life of Poetry*

MURIEL RUKEYSER

In time of crisis, we summon up our strength.

Then, if we are lucky, we are able to call every resource, every forgotten image that can leap to our quickening, every memory that can make us know our power. And this luck is more than it seems to be: it depends on the long preparation of the self to be used.

In time of the crises of the spirit, we are aware of all our need, our need for each other and our need for our selves. We call up, with all the strength of summoning we have, our fullness. And then we turn; for it is a turning that we have prepared; and act. The time of the turning may be very long. It may hardly exist.

I think now of a boat on which I sailed away from the beginning of a war. It was nighttime, and over the deep fertile sea of night the voices of people talking quietly; some lights of the seacoast, faraway; some stars.

This was the first moment of stillness in days of fighting. We had seen the primitive beginnings of the open warfare of this period: men running through the silvery groves, the sniper whose gun would speak, as the bullet broke the wall beside you; a child staring upward at a single plane. More would come; in the city, the cars burned and blood streamed over the walls of houses and the horse shrieked; armies formed and marched out; the gypsies, the priests, in their purity and violence fought. Word from abroad was coming in as they asked us to meet in the summer leafy Square, and told us that they knew. They had seen how, as foreigners, we were deprived; how we were kept from, and wanted, above all things one: our responsibility.

This was a stroke of insight: it was true. "Now you have your responsibility," the voice said, deep, prophetic, direct, "go home: tell your peoples what you have seen."

We had seen a beginning. Much more would come.

I remember how the boys climbed into those trucks, with their ill-matched rifles, as the radio played Beethoven and Bing Crosby and the dances of the country. The machine guns clattered like a loud enormous palm tree, and a baby cried to its mother to come. On the floor of the train were strewn the foreign papers with their pictures printed dark: the possessed man, Nijinsky, giving his first interview from the sanatorium in all those years— the pictures of him, standing as he stood against the great black cross he years before had unrolled on the floor, dancing the insane dance, War and Death.

No darker than this night.

Yes, darker. For the night was living, all of us alive, the living breeze a flaw of coolness over the distant warmth of vineyards, over this central sea. The refugees on the boat were talking. There were people from many countries, thrown abruptly together in time of crisis, and speaking, somehow, the opinions which, later, their countries held.

I did not know this then. But we spoke as if we were shadows on that deck, shadows cast backward by some future fire of explosion.

We were on a small ship, five times past our capacity in refugees, sailing for the first port at peace. On the deck that night, people talked quietly about what they had just seen and what it might mean to the world. The acute scenes were still on our eyes, immediate and clear in their passion; and there were moments, too, in which we were outsiders and could draw away, as if we were in a plane and rose far, to a high focus above that coast, those cities and this sea, with sight and feelings sharper than before. Everything we had heard, some of all we loved and feared, had begun to be acted out. Our realization was fresh and young, we had seen the parts of our lives in a new arrangement. There were long pauses between those broken images of life, spoken in language after language.

Suddenly, throwing his question into talk not at all leading up to it—not seeming to—

a man—a printer, several times a refugee—
asked, "And poetry—among all this—where
is there a place for poetry?"
        Then I began to say what I believe.
        I began to say what I believe.

The identified spirit, man and woman identified, moves toward
further identifications. In a time of long war, surrounded by the
images of war, we imagine peace. Among the resistances, we
imagine poetry. And what city makes the welcome, in what soil
do these roots flourish?

For our concern is with sources.

The sources of poetry are in the spirit seeking completeness. If we look for the definitions of peace, we will find, in history, that they are very few. The treaties never define the peace
they bargain for: their premise is only the lack of war. The languages sometimes offer a choice of words: in the choice is illumination. In one long-standing language there are two meanings
for peace. These two provide a present alternative. One meaning of peace is offered as "rest, security." This is comparable to
our "security, adjustment, peace of mind." The other definition
of peace is this: peace is completeness.

It seems to me that this belief in peace as completeness belongs to the same universe as the hope for the individual as full-
valued.

In what condition does poetry live? In all conditions, sometimes with honor, sometimes underground. That history is in
our poems.

In what climate, poetry? Some will say, the climate of slavery, where the many feed the few, and the few explore their
arts and their sciences. Fashionable now again, the talk of the
elite reaches politics and education.

Some will say, in the wide-open boom times of a patron system: the historic heights of a building Church, the Renaissance
of the small acquisitive states, the times when the bankers
founded their galleries, and the prize of nations is their art.

Some will say, in the pit of suffering, when all is lost but the
central human fire, when the deliverers come, speaking in the
holy symbols of risk and life and everything made sacred.

But we know the partial truth in each of these. We know

31

the slaveholder minds among us, contriving their elite, copying and multiplying natural waste, and believing that meaning can always be put off. These people insist, "He is so great a poet, you need not hear what he says." They are, in their contempt for value, armed. They have whips in their hands. I shall not say they are enemies of poetry; although they are. Only see the effect of their poets on these men: the literature of aversion, guilt, and the longing for forgiveness does its work on the writers and on the witnesses. Its work is tragic; contempt is bred here, and remorse, the dead scatterings. At its best, the poems are those of power and love.

We know the men who need the times of profit; the moment these years fade, they tell us there is no place now for humor, there is no place for poetry. They try to make humor and rage and poetry luxury products. But this cannot be done. At its best, the poems are those of vitality and love.

We know, too, those who are warped until suffering is what they need. We have seen an "occasional verse" grow up of depression and of war. One of the worst things that could happen to our poetry at this time would be for it to become an occasional poetry of war. A good deal of the repugnance to the social poetry of the 1930s was caused by reactionary beliefs; but as much was caused, I think, because there were so many degrees of blood-savagery in it, ranging all the way from self-pity— naked or identified with one victim after another—to actual bloodlust and display of wounds, a rotten sort of begging for attention and sympathy in the name of an art that was supposed to produce action. This was not confined to "social" literature; you may see the style of self-pity in many of the "realistic" novels and confessions of these years. But, fundamentally, this literature is purified to compassion. At its best, the poems are those of offering and love.

We need a background that will let us find ourselves and our poems, let us move in discovery. The tension between the parts of such a society is health; the tension here between the individual and the whole society is health. This state arrives when freedom is a moving goal, when we go beyond the forms to an organic structure which we can in conscience claim and use. Then the multiplicities sing, each in his own voice. Then we understand that there is not meaning, but meanings; not liberty, but liberties. And multiplicity is available to all. Possibility joins the categorical imperative. Suffering and joy are fused in growth; and growth is the universal.

A society in motion, with many overlapping groups, in their dance. And above all, a society in which peace is not lack of war, but a drive toward unity.

Always our wars have been our confessions of weakness. They have not been like the individual's need for action; they have been like our traditional need for confession to another person, but carried further and made grotesque. They have been like the cascades of guilt and self-punishment that certain psychotic criminals have been known to pour out before their judgment.

Those psychiatrists who have been working for more than adjustment in the individual have understood the role of confession. And we all have been aware that action, taken in time, is the child of appropriate response: we then stop fascism as it begins, taproot by taproot in our daily lives, and never need to go to war with each other, pouring out in death our bombs, our plagues, the men and women of our future.

The appropriate release of our decisive forces, and the confession carried to its most human chance. Do these have anything to do with war and peace? Do they have anything to do with poetry?

Confession to another person, to a priest or a psychiatrist, is full of revelation. The self-understanding that comes with the form, with the relation made among memory, conscience, and imagination, brings cure and forgiveness! These are the places where "sooth" and "soothe" meet; places of truth and healing. Confession to divinity, to the essential life of what one loves and hopes, on a level other than the human, is full of revelation. The detachment, here, from conscious and unconscious emotional values, has power to change one's life.

But there is another confession, which is the confession to oneself made available to all. This is confession as a means to understanding, as testimony to the truths of experience as they become form and ourselves. The type of this is the poem; in which the poet, intellectually giving form to emotional and imaginative experience, with the music and history of a lifetime behind the work, offers a total response. And the witness re-

33

ceives the work, and offers a total response, in a most human communication.

Such action does release aggression; or, rather, the making of a poem is the type of action which releases aggression. Since it is released appropriately, it is creation.

For the last time here, I wish to say that we will not be saved by poetry. But poetry is the type of creation in which we may live and which will save us.

The world of this creation, and its poetry, is not yet born.

The possibility before us is that now we enter upon another time, again to choose. Its birth is tragic, but the process is ahead: we must be able to turn a time of war into a time of building.

There are the wounds: they are crying everywhere. There are the false barriers: but they are false. If we believe in the unity and multiplicity of the world, if we believe in the unity and multiplicity of man, then we believe too in the unity and multiplicity of imagination. And we will speak across the barriers, many to many. The great ideas are always emerging, to be available to all men and women. And one hope of our lives is the communication of these truths.

To be against war is not enough, it is hardly a beginning. And all things strive; we who try to speak know the ideas trying to be more human, we know things near their birth that try to become real. The truth here goes farther, there is another way of being against war and for poetry.

We are against war and the sources of war.

We are for poetry and the sources of poetry.

They are everyday, these sources, as the sources of peace are everyday, infinite and commonplace as a look, as each new sun.

As we live our truths, we will communicate across all barriers, speaking for the sources of peace. Peace that is not lack of war, but fierce and positive.

We hear the saints saying: Our brother the world. We hear the revolutionary: Dare we win?

All the poems of our lives are not yet made.

We hear them crying to us, the wounds, the young and the unborn—we will define that peace, we will live to fight its birth, to build these meanings, to sing these songs.

Until the peace makes its people, its forests, and its living cities; in that burning central life, and wherever we live, there is the place for poetry.

And then we will create another peace.

San Francisco
July 1949

The Poet & the City

W. H. AUDEN

It is astonishing how many young people of both sexes, when asked what they want to do in life, give neither a sensible answer like "I want to be a lawyer, an innkeeper, a farmer" nor a romantic answer like "I want to be an explorer, a racing motorist, a missionary, President of the United States." A surprisingly large number say "I want to be a writer," and by writing they mean "creative" writing. Even if they say "I want to be a journalist," this is because they are under the illusion that in that profession they will be able to create; even if their genuine desire is to make money, they will select some highly paid subliterary pursuit like Advertising.

Among these would-be writers, the majority have no marked literary gift. This in itself is not surprising; a marked gift for any occupation is not very common. What is surprising is that such a high percentage of those without any marked talent for any profession should think of writing as the solution. One would have expected that a certain number would imagine that they had a talent for medicine or engineering and so on, but this is not the case. In our age, if a young person is untalented, the odds are in favor of his imagining he wants to write. (There are, no doubt, a lot without any talent for acting who dream of becoming film stars but they have at least been endowed by nature with a fairly attractive face and figure.)

In accepting and defending the social institution of slavery, the Greeks were harder-hearted than we but clearer-headed; they knew that labor as such is slavery, and that no man can feel a personal pride in being a laborer. A man can be proud of being a worker—someone, that is, who fabricates enduring objects, but in our society, the process of fabrication has been so rationalized in the interests of speed, economy and quantity that the part played by the individual factory employee has become too small for it to be meaningful to him as work, and practically all workers have been reduced to laborers. It is only natural, therefore, that the arts which cannot be rationalized in this way—the artist still remains personally responsible for what he makes—should fascinate those who, because they have no marked talent, are afraid, with good reason, that all they have to look forward to is a lifetime of meaningless labor. This fascination is not due to the nature of art itself, but to the way in which an artist works; he, and in our age, almost nobody else, is his own master. The idea of being one's own master appeals to most human beings, and this is apt to lead to the fantastic hope that the capacity for artistic creation is universal, something nearly all human beings, by virtue, not of some special talent, but of their humanity, could do if they tried.

Until quite recently a man was proud of not having to earn his own living and ashamed of being obliged to earn it, but today, would any man dare describe himself when applying for a passport as *Gentleman*, even if, as a matter of fact, he has independent means and no job? Today, the question "What do you do?" means "How do you earn your living?" On my own passport I am described as a "Writer"; this is not embarrassing for me in dealing with the authorities, because immigration and customs officials know that some kinds of writers make lots of money. But if a stranger in the train asks me my occupation, I never

37

answer "writer" for fear that he may go on to ask me what I write, and to answer "poetry" would embarrass us both, for we both know that nobody can earn a living simply by writing poetry. (The most satisfactory answer I have discovered, satisfactory because it withers curiosity, is to say *Medieval Historian.*)

Some writers, even some poets, become famous public figures, but writers as such have no social status, in the way that doctors and lawyers, whether famous or obscure, have.

There are two reasons for this. Firstly, the so-called fine arts have lost the social utility they once had. Since the invention of printing and the spread of literacy, verse no longer has a utility value as a mnemonic, a device by which knowledge and culture were handed on from one generation to the next, and, since the invention of the camera, the draftsman and painter are no longer needed to provide visual documentation; they have, consequently, become "pure" arts, that is to say, gratuitous activities. Secondly, in a society governed by the values appropriate to Labor (capitalist America may well be more completely governed by these than communist Russia) the gratuitous is no longer regarded—most earlier cultures thought differently—as sacred, because, to Man the Laborer, leisure is not sacred but a respite from laboring, a time for relaxation and the pleasures of consumption. In so far as such a society thinks about the gratuitous at all, it is suspicious of it—artists do not labor, therefore, they are probably parasitic idlers—or, at best, regards it as trivial— to write poetry or paint pictures is a harmless private hobby.

In the purely gratuitous arts, poetry, painting, music, our century has no need, I believe, to be ashamed of its achievements, and in its fabrication of purely utile and functional articles like airplanes, dams, surgical instruments, it surpasses any previous age. But whenever it attempts to combine the gratuitous with the utile, to fabricate something which shall be both functional and beautiful, it fails utterly. No previous age has created anything so hideous as the average modern automobile, lampshade or building, whether domestic or public. What could be more terrifying than a modern office building? It seems to be saying to the white-collar slaves who work in it: "For labor in this age, the human body is much more complicated than it need be: you would do better and be happier if it were simplified."

* * *

In the affluent countries today, thanks to the high per capita income, small houses and scarcity of domestic servants, there is one art in which we probably excel all other societies that ever existed, the art of cooking. (It is the one art which Man the Laborer regards as sacred.) If the world population continues to increase at its present rate, this cultural glory will be short-lived, and it may well be that future historians will look nostalgically back to the years 1950–1975 as The Golden Age of Cuisine. It is difficult to imagine a *haute cuisine* based on algae and chemically treated grass.

A poet, painter or musician has to accept the divorce in his art between the gratuitous and the utile as a fact for, if he rebels, he is liable to fall into error.

Had Tolstoi, when he wrote *What Is Art?*, been content with the proposition, "When the gratuitous and the utile are divorced from each other, there can be no art," one might have disagreed with him, but he would have been difficult to refute. But he was unwilling to say that, if Shakespeare and himself were not artists, there was no modern art. Instead he tried to persuade himself that utility alone, a spiritual utility maybe, but still utility without gratuity, was sufficient to produce art, and this compelled him to be dishonest and praise works which aesthetically he must have despised. The notion of *l'art engagé* and art as propaganda are extensions of this heresy, and when poets fall into it, the cause, I fear, is less their social conscience than their vanity; they are nostalgic for a past when poets had a public status. The opposite heresy is to endow the gratuitous with a magic utility of its own, so that the poet comes to think of himself as the god who creates his subjective universe out of nothing—to him the visible material universe *is* nothing. Mallarmé, who planned to write the sacred book of a new universal religion, and Rilke with his notion of *Gesang ist Dasein,* are heresiarchs of this type. Both were geniuses but, admire them as one may and must, one's final impression of their work is of something false and unreal. As Erich Heller says of Rilke:

> In the great poety of the European tradition, the emotions do not interpret; they respond to the interpreted world: in Rilke's mature poetry the emotions do the interpreting and then respond to their own interpretation.

* * *

In all societies, educational facilities are limited to those activities and habits of behavior which a particular society considers important. In a culture like that of Wales in the Middle Ages, which regarded poets as socially important, a would-be poet, like a would-be dentist in our own culture, was systematically trained and admitted to the rank of poet only after meeting high professional standards.

In our culture a would-be poet has to educate himself; he may be in the position to go to a first-class school and university, but such places can only contribute to his poetic education by accident, not by design. This has its drawbacks; a good deal of modern poetry, even some of the best, shows just that uncertainty of taste, crankiness and egoism which self-educated people so often exhibit.

A metropolis can be a wonderful place for a mature artist to live in, but, unless his parents are very poor, it is a dangerous place for a would-be artist to grow up in; he is confronted with too much of the best in art too soon. This is like having a liaison with a wise and beautiful woman twenty years older than himself; all too often his fate is that of *Chéri*.

In my daydream College for Bards, the curriculum would be as follows:

1. In addition to English, at least one ancient language, probably Greek or Hebrew, and two modern languages would be required.
2. Thousands of lines of poetry in these languages would be learned by heart.
3. The library would contain no books of literary criticism, and the only critical exercise required of students would be the writing of parodies.
4. Courses in prosody, rhetoric and comparative philology would be required of all students, and every student would have to select three courses out of courses in mathematics, natural history, geology, meteorology, archaeology, mythology, liturgics, cooking.
5. Every student would be required to look after a domestic animal and cultivate a garden plot.

A poet has not only to educate himself as a poet, he has also to consider how he is going to earn his living. Ideally, he should have a job which does not in any way involve the manipulation of words. At one time, children training to become rabbis were also taught some skilled manual trade, and if only they knew their child was going to become a poet, the best thing parents could do would be to get him, at an early age into some Craft Trades Union. Unfortunately, they cannot know this in advance, and, except in very rare cases, by the time he is twenty-one, the only nonliterary job for which a poet-to-be is qualified is unskilled manual labor. In earning his living, the average poet has to choose between being a translator, a teacher, a literary journalist or a writer of advertising copy and, of these, all but the first can be directly detrimental to his poetry, and even translation does not free him from leading a too exclusively literary life.

There are four aspects of our present *Weltanschauung* which have made an artistic vocation more difficult than it used to be.

1. *The loss of belief in the eternity of the physical universe.* The possibility of becoming an artist, a maker of things which shall outlast the maker's life, might never have occurred to man, had he not had before his eyes, in contrast to the transitoriness of human life, a universe of things, earth, ocean, sky, sun, moon, stars, etc., which appeared to be everlasting and unchanging.

Physics, geology and biology have now replaced this everlasting universe with a picture of nature as a process in which nothing is now what it was or what it will be. Today, Christian and Atheist alike are eschatologically minded. It is difficult for a modern artist to believe he can make an enduring object when he has no model of endurance to go by; he is more tempted than his predecessors to abandon the search for perfection as a waste of time and be content with sketches and improvisations.

2. *The loss of belief in the significance and reality of sensory phenomena.* This loss has been progressive since Luther, who denied any intelligible relation between subjective Faith and objective Works, and Descartes, with his doctrine of

41

primary and secondary qualities. Hitherto, the traditional conception of the phenomenal world had been one of sacramental analogies; what the senses perceived was an outward and visible sign of the inward and invisible, but both were believed to be real and valuable. Modern science has destroyed our faith in the naïve observation of our senses: we cannot, it tells us, ever know what the physical universe is *really* like; we can only hold whatever subjective notion is appropriate to the particular human purpose we have in view.

This destroys the traditional conception of *art* as *mimesis,* for there is no longer a nature "out there" to be truly or falsely imitated; all an artist can be *true* to are his subjective sensations and feelings. The change in attitude is already to be seen in Blake's remark that some people see the sun as a round golden disc the size of a guinea but that he sees it as a host crying Holy, Holy, Holy. What is significant about this is that Blake, like the Newtonians he hated, accepts a division beween the physical and the spiritual, but, in opposition to them, regards the material universe as the abode of Satan, and so attaches no value to what his physical eye sees.
3. *The loss of belief in a norm of human nature which will always require the same kind of man-fabricated world to be at home in.* Until the Industrial Revolution, the way in which men lived changed so slowly that any man, thinking of his great-grandchildren, could imagine them as people living the same kind of life with the same kind of needs and satisfactions as himself. Technology, with its ever-accelerating transformation of man's way of living, has made it impossible for us to imagine what life will be like even twenty years from now.

Further, until recently, men knew and cared little about cultures far removed from their own in time or space; by human nature, they meant the kind of behavior exhibited in their own culture. Anthropology and archaeology have destroyed this provincial notion: we know that human nature is so plastic that it can exhibit varieties of behavior which, in the animal kingdom, could only be exhibited by different species.

The artist, therefore, no longer has any assurance, when he makes something, that even the next generation will find it enjoyable or comprehensible.

He cannot help desiring an immediate success, with all the danger to his integrity which that implies.

Further, the fact that we now have at our disposal the arts of all ages and cultures, has completely changed the meaning of the word tradition. It no longer means a way of working handed down from one generation to the next; a sense of tradition now means a consciousness of the whole of the past as present, yet at the same time as a structured whole the parts of which are related in terms of before and after. Originality no longer means a slight modification in the style of one's immediate predecessors; it means a capacity to find in any work of any date or place a clue to finding one's authentic voice. The burden of choice and selection is put squarely upon the shoulders of each individual poet and it is a heavy one.

4. *The disappearance of the Public Realm as the sphere of revelatory personal deeds.* To the Greeks the Private Realm was the sphere of life ruled by the necessity of sustaining life, and the Public Realm the sphere of freedom where a man could disclose himself to others. Today, the significance of the terms private and public has been reversed; public life is the necessary impersonal life, the place where a man fulfills his social function, and it is in his private life that he is free to be his personal self.

In consequence the arts, literature in particular, have lost their traditional principal human subject, the man of action, the doer of public deeds.

The advent of the machine has destroyed the direct relation between a man's intention and his deed. If St. George meets the dragon face to face and plunges a spear into its heart, he may legitimately say "I slew the dragon," but, if he drops a bomb on the dragon from an altitude of twenty thousand feet, though his intention—to slay it—is the same, his act consists in pressing a lever and it is the bomb, not St. George, that does the killing.

If, at Pharaoh's command, ten thousand of his subjects toil for five years at draining the fens, this means that Pharaoh commands the personal loyalty of enough persons to see that his orders are carried out; if his army revolts, he is powerless. But if Pharaoh can have the fens drained in six months by a hundred men with bulldozers, the situation is changed. He still needs some authority, enough to persuade a hundred men to man the bulldozers, but that is all: the rest of the work is done by machines which know nothing of loyalty or fear, and if his enemy, Nebuchadnezzar, should get hold of them, they will work just as efficiently at filling up the canals as they have just worked at digging them out. It is now possible to imagine a world in which the only human work on such projects will be done by a mere handful of persons who operate computers.

It is extremely difficult today to use public figures as themes for poetry because the good or evil they do depends less upon their characters and intentions than upon the quantity of impersonal force at their disposal.

Every British or American poet will agree that Winston Churchill is a greater figure than Charles II, but he will also know that he could not write a good poem on Churchill, while Dryden had no difficulty in writing a good poem on Charles. To write a good poem on Churchill, a poet would have to know Winston Churchill intimately, and his poem would be about the man, not about the Prime Minister. All attempts to write about persons or events, however important, to which the poet is not intimately related in a personal way are now doomed to failure. Yeats could write great poetry about the Troubles in Ireland, because most of the protagonists were known to him personally and the places where the events occurred had been familiar to him since childhood.

The true men of action in our time, those who transform the world, are not the politicians and statesmen, but the scientists. Unfortunately poetry cannot celebrate them because their deeds are concerned with things, not persons, and are, therefore, speechless.

When I find myself in the company of scientists, I feel like a shabby curate who has strayed by mistake into a drawing room full of dukes.

The growth in size of societies and the development of mass media of communication have created a social phenomenon which was unknown to the ancient world, that peculiar kind of crowd which Kierkegaard calls The Public.

> A public is neither a nation nor a generation, nor a community, nor a society, nor these particular men, for all these are only what they are through the concrete; no single person who belongs to the public makes a real commitment; for some hours of the day, perhaps, he belongs to the public—at moments when he is nothing else, since when he really is what he is, he does not form part of the public. Made up of such individuals at the moments when they are nothing, a public is a kind of gigantic something, an abstract and deserted void which is everything and nothing.

The ancient world knew the phenomenon of the crowd in the sense that Shakespeare uses the word, a visible congregation of a large number of human individuals in a limited physical space, who can, on occasions, be transformed by demagogic oratory into a mob which behaves in a way of which none of its members would be capable by himself, and this phenomenon is known, of course, to us, too. But the public is something else. A student in the subway during the rush hour whose thoughts are concentrated on a mathematical problem or his girl friend is a member of a crowd but not a member of the public. To join the public, it is not necessary for a man to go to some particular spot; he can sit at home, open a newspaper or turn on his TV set.

A man has his distinctive personal scent which his wife, his children and his dog can recognize. A crowd has a generalized stink. The public is odorless.

A mob is active; it smashes, kills and sacrifices itself. The public is passive or, at most, curious. It neither murders nor sacrifices itself; it looks on, or looks away, while the mob beats up a Negro or the police round up Jews for the gas ovens.

The public is the least exclusive of clubs; anybody, rich or poor, educated or unlettered, nice or nasty, can join it: it even toler-

45

ates a pseudo revolt against itself, that is, the formation within itself of clique publics.

In a crowd, a passion like rage or terror is highly contagious; each member of a crowd excites all the others, so that passion increases at a geometric rate. But among members of the public, there is no contact. If two members of the public meet and speak to each other, the function of their words is not to convey meaning or arouse passion but to conceal by noise the silence and solitude of the void in which the public exists.

Occasionally the public embodies itself in a crowd and so becomes visible—in the crowd, for example, which collects to watch the wrecking gang demolish the old family mansion, fascinated by yet another proof that physical force is the Prince of this world against whom no love of the heart shall prevail.

Before the phenomenon of the public appeared in society, there existed naïve art and sophisticated art which were different from each other but only in the way that two brothers are different. The Athenian court may smile at the mechanics' play of Pyramus and Thisbe, but they recognize it as a play. Court poetry and Folk poetry were bound by the common tie that both were made by hand and both were intended to last; the crudest ballad was as custom-built as the most esoteric sonnet. The appearance of the public and the mass media which cater to it have destroyed naïve popular art. The sophisticated "highbrow" artist survives and can still work as he did a thousand years ago, because his audience is too small to interest the mass media. But the audience of the popular artist is the majority and this the mass media must steal from him if they are not to go bankrupt. Consequently, aside from a few comedians, the only art today is "highbrow." What the mass media offer is not popular art, but entertainment which is intended to be consumed like food, forgotten, and replaced by a new dish. This is bad for everyone; the majority lose all genuine taste of their own, and the minority become cultural snobs.

The two characteristics of art which make it possible for an art historian to divide the history of art into periods, are, firstly, a common style of expression over a certain period and, secondly, a common notion, explicit or implicit, of the hero, the kind of human being who most deserves to be celebrated, remembered and, if possible, imitated. The characteristic style of "Modern" poetry is an intimate tone of voice, the speech of one person addressing one person, not a large audience; whenever a modern poet raises his voice he sounds phony. And its characteristic hero is neither the "Great Man" nor the romantic rebel, both doers of extraordinary deeds, but the man or woman in any walk of life who, despite all the impersonal pressures of modern society, manages to acquire and preserve a face of his own.

Poets are, by the nature of their interests and the nature of artistic fabrication, singularly ill-equipped to understand politics or economics. Their natural interest is in singular individuals and personal relations, while politics and economics are concerned with large numbers of people, hence with the human average (the poet is bored to death by the idea of the Common Man) and with impersonal, to a great extent involuntary, relations. The poet cannot understand the function of money in modern society because for him there is no relation between subjective value and market value; he may be paid ten pounds for a poem which he believes is very good and took him months to write, and a hundred pounds for a piece of journalism which costs him but a day's work. If he is a successful poet—though few poets make enough money to be called successful in the way that a novelist or playwright can—he is a member of the Manchester school and believes in absolute *laissez-faire;* if he is unsuccessful and embittered, he is liable to combine aggressive fantasies about the annihilation of the present order with impractical daydreams of Utopia. Society has always to beware of the utopias being planned by artists *manqués* over cafeteria tables late at night.

All poets adore explosions, thunderstorms, tornadoes, conflagrations, ruins, scenes of spectacular carnage. The poetic imagination is not at all a desirable quality in a statesman.

In a war or a revolution, a poet may do very well as a guerilla fighter or a spy, but it is unlikely that he will make a good regular soldier, or, in peace time, a conscientious member of a parliamentary committee.

All political theories which, like Plato's, are based on analogies drawn from artistic fabrication are bound, if put into practice, to turn into tyrannies. The whole aim of a poet, or any other kind of artist, is to produce something which is complete and will endure without change. A poetic city would always contain exactly the same number of inhabitants doing exactly the same jobs forever.

Moreover, in the process of arriving at the finished work, the artist has continually to employ violence. A poet writes:

The mast-high anchor dives through a cleft

changes it to

The anchor dives through closing paths

changes it again to

The anchor dives among hayricks

and finally to

The anchor dives through the floors of a church.

A *cleft* and *closing paths* have been liquidated, and hayricks deported to another stanza.

A society which was really like a good poem, embodying the aesthetic virtues of beauty, order, economy and subordination of detail to the whole, would be a nightmare of horror for, given the historical reality of actual men, such a society could only come into being through selective breeding, extermination of the physically and mentally unfit, absolute obedience to its Director, and a large slave class kept out of sight in cellars.

Vice versa, a poem which was really like a political democracy—examples, unfortunately, exist—would be formless, windy, banal and utterly boring.

There are two kinds of political issues, Party issues and Revolutionary issues. In a party issue, all parties are agreed as to the nature and justice of the social goal to be reached, but differ in their policies for reaching it. The existence of different parties is justified, firstly, because no party can offer irrefutable proof that its policy is the only one which will achieve the commonly desired goal and, secondly, because no social goal can be achieved without some sacrifice of individual or group interest and it is natural for each individual and social group to seek a policy which will keep its sacrifice to a minimum, to hope that, if sacrifices must be made, it would be more just if someone else made them. In a party issue, each party seeks to convince the members of its society, primarily by appealing to their reason; it marshals facts and arguments to convince others that its policy is more likely to achieve the desired goal than that of its opponents. On a party issue it is essential that passions be kept at a low temperature: effective oratory requires, of course, some appeal to the emotions of the audience, but in party politics orators should display the mock-passion of prosecuting and defending attorneys, not really lose their tempers. Outside the Chamber, the rival deputies should be able to dine in each other's houses; fanatics have no place in party politics.

A revolutionary issue is one in which different groups within a society hold different views as to what is just. When this is the case, argument and compromise are out of the question; each group is bound to regard the other as wicked or mad or both. Every revolutionary issue is potentially a *casus belli*. On a revolutionary issue, an orator cannot convince his audience by appealing to their reason; he may convert some of them by awakening and appealing to their conscience, but his principal function, whether he represent the revolutionary or the counterrevolutionary group, is to arouse its passion to the point where it will give all its energies to achieving total victory for itself and total defeat for its opponents. When an issue is revolutionary, fanatics are essential.

Today, there is only one genuine worldwide revolutionary issue, racial equality. The debate between capitalism, socialism and communism is really a party issue, because the goal which all seek is really the same, a goal which is summed up in Brecht's well-known line:

Erst kommt das Fressen, dann kommt die Moral.

I.e., Grub first, then Ethics. In all the technologically advanced countries today, whatever political label they give themselves, their policies have, essentially, the same goal: to guarantee to every member of society, as a psychophysical organism, the right to physical and mental health. The positive symbolic figure of this goal is a naked anonymous baby, the negative symbol, a mass of anonymous concentration camp corpses.

What is so terrifying and immeasurably depressing about most contemporary politics is the refusal—mainly but not, alas, only by the communists—to admit that this is a party issue to be settled by appeal to facts and reason, the insistence that there is a revolutionary issue between us. If an African gives his life for the cause of racial equality, his death is meaningful to him; but what is utterly absurd, is that people should be deprived every day of their liberties and their lives, and that the human race may quite possibly destroy itself over what is really a matter of practical policy like asking whether, given its particular historical circumstances, the health of a community is more or less likely to be secured by Private Practice or by Socialized Medicine.

What is peculiar and novel to our age is that the principal goal of politics in every advanced society is not, strictly speaking, a political one, that is to say, it is not concerned with human beings as persons and citizens but with human bodies, with the precultural, prepolitical human creature. It is, perhaps, inevitable that respect for the liberty of the individual should have so greatly diminished and the authoritarian powers of the State have so greatly increased from what they were fifty years ago, for the main political issue today is concerned not with human liberties but with human necessities.

As creatures we are all equally slaves to natural necessity; we are not free to vote how much food, sleep, light and air we need to keep in good health; we all need a certain quantity, and we all need the same quantity.

Every age is one-sided in its political and social preoccupation and in seeking to realize the particular value it esteems most highly, it neglects and even sacrifices other values. The relation of a poet, or any artist, to society and politics is, except in Africa or still backward semifeudal countries, more difficult than it has ever been because, while he cannot but approve of the importance of *everybody* getting enough food to eat and enough leisure, this problem has nothing whatever to do with art, which is concerned with *singular persons,* as they are alone and as they are in their personal relations. Since these interests are not the predominant ones in his society; indeed, in so far as it thinks about them at all, it is with suspicion and latent hostility—it secretly or openly thinks that the claim that one is a singular person, or a demand for privacy, is putting on airs, a claim to be superior to other folk—every artist feels himself at odds with modern civilization.

In our age, the mere making of a work of art is itself a political act. So long as artists exist, making what they please and think they ought to make, even if it is not terribly good, even if it appeals to only a handful of people, they remind the Management of something managers need to be reminded of, namely, that the managed are people with faces, not anonymous numbers, that *Homo Laborans* is also *Homo Ludens.*

If a poet meets an illiterate peasant, they may not be able to say much to each other, but if they both meet a public official, they share the same feeling of suspicion; neither will trust one further than he can throw a grand piano. If they enter a government building, both share the same feeling of apprehension; perhaps they will never get out again. Whatever the cultural differences between them, they both sniff in any official world the smell of an unreality in which persons are treated as statistics. The peasant may play cards in the evening while the poet writes verses, but there is one political principle to which they both subscribe, namely, that among the half dozen or so things for which a man of honor should be prepared, if necessary, to die, the right to play, the right to frivolity, is not the least.

Notes on Revolutionaries and Reactionaries

STEPHEN SPENDER

I.
REVOLUTIONARIES

In England, the circumstances in which poets intervene in politics are special. In their study of Julian Bell's and John Cornford's tragically broken-off lives, Peter Stansky and William Abrahams* inevitably devote much space to explaining the family background and the personal psychological and intellectual problems which led these young men to anti-Fascism and their deaths in Spain.

If they had been French biographers writing about the young Malraux, Aragon or Eluard, there would have been no need of such explanation. For in France the Thirties was only the most recent episode in the long involvement of the French intellectuals with politics since before the French Revolution. Writers like Romain Rolland, Henri Barbusse, Georges Duhamel and André Gide publicly discussed their attitudes to the Russian Revolution, the League of Nations, war and disarmament, after 1918.

French intellectuals of both the Right and Left had centers, organizations, reviews, newspapers, platforms. In taking sides, the intellectual exploited the legend that, *qua* intellectual, he represented detached intelligence. The "clerc" descended from the clouds of objectivity to make objective yet partisan, seemingly disinterested pronouncements—*Et tu, Julian Benda.*

Journey to the Frontier by Peter Stansky and William Abrahams.

It is true of course that sometimes a Romain Rolland or a Henri Barbusse looked across the Channel and appealed to a Shaw or a Wells as "cher collègue" and asked him to attend some international conference or sign some declaration of human rights. But if and when they responded, these English *maîtres* did not descend as radiant messengers from the realms of pure imagination and impartial intellect. They were already publicists and not quite artists. Wells, although priding himself on being a social prophet, cultivated the manner of a traveling salesman for the scientific culture. Like Shaw, Bennett and Galsworthy he thought of his public personality as anti-aesthetic, lowbrow. He was forever explaining that he was a journalist who breathed a different air from that of characters in the novels of Henry James.

Eliot, Virginia Woolf, D. H. Lawrence saw to it that Wells and Bennett should never be allowed to forget their vulgar public streak—what Lawrence called the "societal." When during the Thirties E. M. Forster appeared on *"front populaire"* platforms he did so because the time demanded that he should assume a role in which he had no confidence and for which he felt little enthusiasm. His presence at congresses of the intellectuals during the anti-Fascist period, and that of young English poets, was an exceptional action produced by exceptional times—like lions walking the streets of Rome on the night preceding the Ides of March. The artist had become denatured by apocalyptic events.

Until the Thirties, the younger generation of Oxford and Cambridge remained influenced by the anti-politics of their parents' generation. Stansky and Abrahams mention in *Journey to the Frontier* that the famous society of Cambridge intellectual undergraduates—the Apostles—which had such a close connection with literary Bloomsbury agreed in the Twenties that "practical politics were beneath discussion." In the early Thirties, the Apostles ceased for some years to exist, as the result of the pressure of "too many conflicting political beliefs" among their members. Yet so different was the atmosphere by then that to Julian Bell, no longer then an undergraduate, and to John Cornford, who was one, this must have seemed like saying that having at last something to discuss, the Apostles had decided to discuss nothing.

To the Cambridge and Bloomsbury generation of their parents, Bell and Cornford seemed changelings, hatched by hens out of ducks' eggs, swimming out on those dirty political waters. Not that Clive and Vanessa Bell and the Cornford parents disagreed with the younger generation's anti-Fascist politics. They sympathized with them. Yet more than this, they regarded politicians as philistine and the artist in politics as betraying the pure cause of pure art. Leftish political sympathies were almost a part of the ethos of literary Bloomsbury, but art had no connection with political action, nor with the good life of personal relations and refined sensations which could only be enjoyed by the individual in separation from society. J. M. Keynes and Leonard Woolf were, it is true, in their different ways, politically involved and influential: but Keynes loved the painter Duncan Grant, and Leonard Woolf was married to Virginia. To both, "Bloomsbury" stood for the values of living.

These attitudes are reflected in Forster's novels, in which the good characters have liberal values but subordinate them to "personal relations." Business, power, government for Forster belong to the world of "telegrams and anger." That Margaret or Helen Schlegel should carry their socialism further than sitting on a few committees, and those personal relations with Henry Wilcox and Leonard Bast which test their principles, seems unthinkable. And although Fielding, Aziz and the other characters who fight on the side of the angels are opposed to the British Raj, it is difficult to think of them taking any effective political action. They attempt to resolve their problems through personal relations between the British and the Indians. Their chief grievance against the Raj is that it makes personal relations impossible.

Forster's anti-politics, anti-power, anti-business attitude is implicit also in the novels of D. H. Lawrence, Virginia Woolf and Aldous Huxley, which have so little else in common. The separation of the world of private values imagined in art from the public values of business, science, politics was an essential part of the victory of the generation for whom "the world changed in 1910" against their elders, Shaw, Wells, Bennett and Galsworthy. The accusation level against the "Georgian" novelists was that they depicted characters who were conditioned by the social circumstances in which they lived. The aim of D. H. Lawrence and Virginia Woolf was to create in their novels isolated creatures of unique awareness with sensibility transcending their material circumstances.

Of course I do not mean that Lawrence had no political sympathies: still less that he had views in common with the liberal ones of Virginia Woolf and E. M. Forster. In his novels those characters like Birkin and Aaron who are representative of the politically searching Lawrence shop around in the political world of action looking for lords of life who are passional, violent and anti-democratic. Bertrand Russell, after some dealings with him during a few months toward the end of the First World War— when Lawrence toyed with the idea of founding some kind of brain (Bertrand Russell) -and-blood (D. H. Lawrence) political movement—came to the conclusion (stated thirty years afterwards) that Lawrence's blood-and-soil view of life was later realized in the horrors of Nazism. What I do mean is that apart from this one disastrous attempt to get together with Russell and the Cambridge intelligentsia, and apart from his general sympathy with what might be termed bloody-bodiedness (in Germany, Italy or Mexico), Lawrence found the world of public affairs, business and any kind of social cooperation utterly antipathetic. He wrote a letter to Forster (in September 1922) charging him with "a nearly deadly mistake in glorifying those *business* people in *Howard's End*," and adding that "business is no good"—a conclusion with which he might have found his correspondent concurred had he bothered to read Forster's novel.

Different as E. M. Forster, Virginia Woolf and D. H. Lawrence were, they all agreed that the novel should be concerned with awareness of life deeper than the conscious mind of the "old novelistic character" and the computable human social unit. Lawrence in his essay on Galsworthy, and Virginia Woolf in her discussion of Arnold Bennett in her famous lecture "Mr. Bennett and Mrs. Brown," attack Galsworthy and Bennett on similar grounds: that the characters in their books are "social units."

Although the Bloomsbury generation (I call them this to make them immediately distinguishable) sympathized with the anti-Fascism of Auden, as also of John Cornford, they were horrified at the idea of poetry being compromised by politics.

Virginia Woolf's *Letter to a Young Poet* (1935) is a sympathizing but troubled protest at the spectacle of sensitive and talented young Oxford and Cambridge poets echoing public matters with a public voice and not writing out of a Wordsworthian isolation, solitary among the solitary reapers. And E. M. Forster, with politeness and forbearance, indicated the underlying grief of Cambridge friends, when he wrote that the future probably lay with Communism but that he did not want to belong to it.

John Cornford was seven years younger than Julian Bell, who was almost contemporaneous with Auden, Day-Lewis, Mac-Neice and myself. In our speeded-up century, those few years marked still another "generation gap." Our earlier Oxford generation, with that which we valued most in ourselves—the poetic imagination—secretly identified with the generation of Forster and Virginia Woolf. And Julian Bell had begun by doing this, but later—being born into Bloomsbury—had rebelled against the parents and aunt, and, in effect, joined Cornford's Cambridge generation.

For John Cornford's generation of anti-Fascist undergraduate agitators at Cambridge, and of the Oxford October Club, did not cherish our generation's sense of the supreme importance of maintaining the distinction between public and private worlds. This difference of generations is also reflected in the seven years' difference between Julian Bell and John Cornford. Cornford became completely politicized, but for Bell, to have to choose between personal loyalties and the public cause was always agonizing. By upbringing anti-political, his choice would have been always for personal values, had he not come to think of anti-Fascism as a human loyalty beyond other public politics. But even so, he remained conscious of entering a new era where private loyalties had to be sacrificed to revolutionary politics. The private ones of poetry and of love for his family had to submit to the public ones of anti-Fascism. Yet when he went to Spain, in joining an ambulance unit rather than the International Brigade, he sacrificed his interest in war and strategy to his parents' pacifism. He chose not to break his mother's heart: and he did not do so until he got to Spain and was killed there.

For Cornford, Julian Bell's junior by seven years, however, there was no question but that personal values had to be sacrificed to the public cause. All that mattered was to defeat Fascism. For him, and for his already "new generation," choices had to be decided by the Marxist interpretation of history. Subjective motives did not count.

In the jargon of the new communist generation all our seven-years-previous-generation's scruples about personal relations and subjective feelings could be consigned to the dustbin of liberal inhibitions. Cornford's conviction of the superiority of Marxist "scientific objectivity" over personal considerations is the dominating theme of his poetry. Leaving the girl who is mother to his child, the objective reason becomes the image of the surgeon's knife cutting away the soft rot of compassion:

> Though parting's as cruel as the surgeon's knife
> It's better than the ingrown canker, the rotten leaf.
> All that I know is I have got to leave.
> There's new life fighting in me to get at the air,
> And I can't stop its mouth with the rags of old love.
> Clean wounds are easiest to bear.

The assurance with which he asserts the superiority of the ideological "new life" struggling in him over the real new life—a child, seen oddly as an "ingrown canker"—struggling in her tells a lot about young human nature dominated by an ideology.

To say that Julian Bell could not, except through changing his nature, have discovered such impersonal grounds for apparent callousness is not to say that he did not behave egotistically towards his mistresses (whom Stansky and Abrahams list as A, B, C, D, etc., far down the alphabet). The difference is that Bell would have found a subjective personal reason for justifying conduct which Cornford justified by an "objective" one.

To most literary-minded readers, Bell will seem more interesting than Cornford because he is the more self-searching and literary character. Certainly his personality and his relations with his relations make fascinating reading. It is part of the excellence of their book that the authors, having put the reader in possession of some of the facts, often leave him wondering. For instance, when Bell wrote that dissertation *The Good and All That*

57

which, it was hoped, would get him a fellowship at Kings, there were plenty of psychological reasons why he should make a hash of it. On the one hand he wished to please his Cambridge mentors by writing an essay on good and evil in the manner of the discussions of the Apostles, but on the other hand "more perhaps than he himself realized, Julian was in full revolt against his Bloomsbury philosophical friends and relations, and their static conception of 'states of mind' as values in themselves, or consequences that might ensue from them." The confusedness was perhaps in part the result of a naive desire not to shock Roger Fry, to whom the dissertation was sent for a report. This was of course a model of tolerance and fair-mindedness. How *liberal!*

Anna Russell in her famous skits on plots of Wagner's operas points out (wrongly) that Siegfried had the misfortune never to have met a lady who was not his aunt. There was something of such a burlesque Siegfried about the burly young Julian Bell, who gives one the impression of always encountering very understanding Bloomsbury aunts. He certainly developed something of an anti-aunt complex. But, as with the other Siegfried, we are also left with a further question on our minds—wasn't this young hero after all a bit obtuse?

John Cornford was priggish but not at all obtuse, and it is this which in the end makes him more interesting than Bell. He was a Greek hero rather than a confused Wagnerian one, his specialty being the cutting through of Gordian knots. He dealt with family, school, Cambridge, love affairs, the problems dividing the poet from the man of action, all in the same way—cut right through them with the surgical knife of objective action. As between poetry and fighting in Spain, he decidedly chose the latter, after he left Cambridge:

> Poetry had become a marginal activity, and a private one. He never discussed his work with his friends in the party; most of them did not even know until after his death that he had been a poet. . . . In the rare moments when he was free to do so, he wrote both personal and political poems. The latter represent a conscious effort to "objectify" his ideas and attitudes as a revolutionary participator, and to transform them into revolutionary poetry.

Instead of being, like Julian Bell, a poet stifled by his need to take action, John Cornford put poetry aside and took part in the Spanish Civil War, but from this, and out of the ideology with which he tempered his will and determination, a hard clear new poetry of the objective will began to emerge. Sketchy, a bit turgid, yet effective, his poetry is dominated by the Communist idea of transforming the dialectic into history—hammered out of his mind and body deliberately "placed" on the side of the proletariat:

> The past, a glacier, gripped the mountain wall,
> And time was inches, dark was all.
> But here it scales the end of the range,
> The dialectic's point of change,
> Crashes in light and minutes to its fall.
>
> Time present is a cataract whose force
> Breaks down the banks even at its source
> And history forming in our hand's
> Not plasticine but roaring sands,
> Yet we must swing it to its final course.

The attempt here is to write a secular Communist poetry corresponding to religious metaphysical poetry. It is blurred because Marxism, in common with other analytic and scientific systems, cannot be taken outside its method and terms, and interpreted imagistically, or converted into a mystique, without in the process losing its mechanical or scientific precision. The precision of science cannot be translated into the precision of poetry. Here the Marxist poet is encountering the difficulty of other modern poets who try to invent a mythology for their poetry in a secular world. Nevertheless, it is clear that Cornford was attempting to write ideological poetry. The ideology—the vision—is materialist. I cannot agree with Stansky and Abrahams that "the abstractions and metaphors proliferate, taking us still further from reality and deeper into the visionary world of the seer." From the Marxist standpoint, what is wrong with such a diagnosis is the idea that "abstractions" (if they are "correct") inevitably lead away from reality instead of penetrating deeper into it. Cornford might, then, have become perhaps a

59

Marxist visionary or seer. And but for Stalin and the Marxists, this would perhaps not be a contradiction in terms.

In the Thirties, anti-Fascism was predominantly a reaction of middle-class young men brought up in a liberal atmosphere, against the old men in power, of their own class, who, while talking about freedom and democracy, were not prepared to denounce Hitler or support the Spanish Republic. This older generation feared that the price of supporting the democratically elected Spanish and Republican government would be that of giving aid and comfort to the Communists, whom they detested considerably more than they did the Fascists. That the old who professed liberal principles did not see the threat of Fascism to democracy, or that, seeing it, they did not take action against the dictators, seemed to the young a betrayal of basic liberal principles by liberals. In the Thirties, "liberal" became a term of contempt. Cornford and Bell were not just young Oedipuses subconsciously wishing to destroy their father's image. They had conscious reasons for attacking it: their father Laius was a liberal.

II
REACTIONARIES

During the decade of the Popular Front the English anti-Fascist writers became, as it were, honorary French intellectuals. This was due to the international tradition of the leftist intelligentsia. But Fascism and the movements of the European Right were not internationalist in the same way. They differed in each country. Thus Yeats, Eliot and Pound seemed to be making a leap in the dark when they attempted to connect their own kind of conservative traditionalism, even when it was called "royalism" and "catholicism," with the politics of a Mussolini or a Hitler.

The political attitudes of Yeats, Eliot, Pound, Wyndham Lewis, D. H. Lawrence, consisted largely of gestures towards some movement, idea or leader that seemed to stand for the writer's deeply held sense of tradition. Such gestures were largely rhetorical. The politics of these writers were projections of their hatred of fragmented modern civilization and the idea of "progress." They were sometimes deeply meditated, sometimes irresponsible, attempts to translate traditionalist attitudes into

60

programs of action. But there was never an international "traditionalist conservative front" corresponding to the "popular front." There were no meetings of the reactionaries in literature. Doubtless Mussolini, Hitler or Franco, if they ever learned that they were supported by W. B. Yeats, T. S. Eliot, Ezra Pound and Wyndham Lewis, would have taken credit for having such distinguished admirers. But they would never have thought of these great figures as part of a single international traditionalist movement with a single conservative ideology.

Whereas the leftist anti-Fascist writers—believing that the overthrow of Fascism was the most important task of their generation—discussed whether their writing should not perhaps be the instrument of a cause which they identified with that of the "people," the reactionaries thought merely that they should perhaps support those leaders and political thinkers who seemed to be occupied in defending the past European tradition. However, they never thought that they should put their talents at the service of the ideas of these politicians and ideologists, or of their parties. On the contrary, they looked to the Fascists as supporters of the traditions which they, the poets and writers, represented. Wyndham Lewis, for instance, never supposed that he should become the mouthpiece of Hitler and the ideas put forward in *Mein Kampf*. He had in fact a rather supercilious attitude towards Hitler whom he patted (metaphorically) on the back for having expressed rather crudely certain ideas already in the mind of Wyndham Lewis. Eliot was even more patronizing towards the Fascists in regard to their ideas, even when he applauded some of their political actions. He regarded the Fascists, Nazis and English Blackshirts as rather inferior exponents of the ideas put forward earlier in the century by Charles Maurras. As an admirer of Maurras, he criticized British Fascism, together with Communism for its lack of intellectual content. On the one occasion when he met Mussolini, Pound was favorably impressed, because he thought that Mussolini, having read a few lines of the *Cantos* and pronounced them "*amusante*," was superior to grudging literary critics in recognizing the genius of Ezra Pound.

There is then this immense difference between the politics of the "reactionary" writers and that of the leftists. The reactionaries never thought that they should put their art at the service

61

of the ideology of the authoritarian fascistic leaders, in the way that many leftists thought that they should put theirs at the service of Marxism and of the political bureaux which laid down the Communist party lines. The reactionary writers never thought that they should "go over" to the most aristocratic and conservative interests in the society, identifying their whole behavior with the pattern of their lives, in the way that leftist writers (and most of all George Orwell) thought that they should "go over" to the proletariat in order, in all their thinking and being and creating, to identify themselves with the working class.

On the contrary, the reactionaries tended to think of the Fascist parties as potential mercenaries who might perhaps be the armies defending the past civilization of which they, the great artists (those whom Wyndham Lewis called "the party of genius"), were the intellectual leaders. If Hitler and Mussolini had cast themselves in the role of Defenders of the European Past, maybe they should be encouraged. That was Wyndham Lewis's attitude and when Yeats for a short time wrote songs for General O'Duffy's Blue Shirts, it was because he too thought that the soldiers of the Right might be the mercenaries of past civilization with its artist-princes.

The reactionaries had a shared vision of the greatness of the European past which implied hatred and contempt for the present. It might be said that all their most important work was an attempt to relate their writing to this central vision. On the secondary level of their attempts to carry forward the vision into politics, there is a good deal of peripheral mess, resulting from their search for politics corresponding to their love of past religion, art, discipline and order. Their politics showed that they cared less for politics than for art.

Mr. John Harrison* takes some remarks of Orwell as his text which he sets out to illustrate with examples drawn from his authors. This text is worth examining:

> The relationship between Fascism and the literary intelligentsia badly needs investigating, and Yeats might well be the starting point. He is best studied by someone like Mr. Menon who knows that a writer's politics and religious be-

The Reactionaries by John Harrison (Gollancz).

liefs are not excrescences to be laughed away, but something that will leave their mark even on the smallest detail of his work.

This sounds plausible enough, though it is perhaps too offhand to bear the weight of Mr. Harrison's thesis. But objections arise. If it were true that a writer's politics and religious beliefs extend from a center outward into every smallest detail of his work, then the converse would also be true: that one could deduce his party loyalties from an analysis of any smallest detail of his work, regardless of whether the writer thought that he supported these politics.

What is questionable is Orwell's loose bracketing of religious and political beliefs, and his assumption that it is comparatively easy to discover what a writer believes politically. But it is not simple, for a writer of genius writes out of his unique vision of life, and not to demonstrate shared attitudes. Orwell appears to think that Yeats's symbolism, mythology, imagery—his poetry, in a word—are projections onto the plane of the imagination of his political and religious beliefs. It is really the other way round. Yeats's religion and politics are attempts to relate his intuitive poetic vision to beliefs and political action. Yeats's Fascism, not his poetry, *was* an excrescence. It grew rather approximately and grossly from the center of his poetic imagination which was neither approximate nor gross. To anyone who reads *A Vision* or his journals and prose, it must be quite clear that his opinions are attempts to rationalize the intuitions of his imagination. They are perhaps irresponsible attempts to be politically responsible.

Add to this that even when they are stated as prose, one cannot discuss Yeats's beliefs without making many qualifications. Outside of believing in art and in some universe of the spirit in which the imaginings of poets become literal truth, Yeats himself was uncertain as to what he believed. He cultivated beliefs and attitudes in himself for the purpose of propping up the symbolism of his poetry. He also had a sharp picture of a materialist world which undermined his world of the poetic imagination: this was Bernard Shaw's Fabian philosophy and belief in material progress. That which to Shaw was superstition and reaction recommended itself as belief and action to Yeats.

* * *

Dr. Conor Cruise O'Brien* has drawn up a formidable list of Yeats's pro-Fascist statements, including one or two sympathetic to Hitler. But to the reader who thinks that Yeats's poems, and not his opinions, matter, it will seem, I think, that he used the political stage properties of the Thirties in the same way that he used the assertions of his esoteric system set out in *A Vision*—as a scenario stocked with symbols and metaphors. To Yeats writing the tragic-gay poetry of his old age, Hitler had the seductive charm of an apocalyptic cat.

What is disturbing about the reactionaries is not that they were occasionally betrayed by intoxication with their own ideas and fantasies into supporting dictators who would, given the opportunity, certainly have disposed very quickly of them, but that in the excess of their hatred of the present and their love of the past, they developed a certain cult of inhumanity. One has to ask, though: Was not their Renaissance vision enormously valuable to us, and could it have been stated without dramatizing the statuesque figures of a visionary past against the twittering ghosts of the disintegrated present?

Eliot's political views, like those of Yeats, are a system hastily thrown out with the intention of defending a spiritual world, deriving strength from the past, against modern materialism. One suspects that Eliot was convinced intellectually, as a critic, and not with his imagination, as a poet, of the necessity of defending traditional values by political actions. Without the example of T. E. Hulme and without some cheerleading from Ezra Pound and some satiric pushing from Wyndham Lewis, Eliot would scarcely have made those remarks about liberalism and progress, which seem casual asides, and which yet set him up as authoritarian, defender of the monarchy and the faith. In his role of political commentator in *The Criterion* he must have baffled readers who did not realize that his mind was moving along lines laid down by Charles Maurras. There is something cloak-and-dagger about the anti-Semitic passages in the Sweeney poems which Mr. Harrison inevitably relies on to demonstrate his thesis:

> The smoky candle end of time

Writers and Politics by Conor Cruise O'Brien.

> Declines. On the Rialto once.
> The rats are underneath the piles.
> The jew is underneath the lot.
> Money in furs.

Of course this is distasteful caricature, more so today than when it was written. But the Jew who is "underneath the lot" is the symbol of a conspiratorial capitalism.

That Eliot, Yeats, Pound and Lawrence were all "exiles" (and Wyndham Lewis a self-declared outsider—"the Enemy") has a bearing on their politics. The exile is particularly apt to dramatize his mind or soul moving through a world of metaphors. Pound and Eliot left what they regarded as barbarous America to come to civilized Europe, where they found, in the First World War:

> There died a myriad,
> And of the best, among them,
> For an old bitch gone in the teeth,
> For a botched civilisation, . . .

Their poetry exalted the past which they had sought among the Georgian poets and found only embalmed in museums, and it derided the present, the decay of standards. They were, politically, Don Quixotes of the new world armed to rescue the Dulcinea of the old—whom they quickly discovered to be an old hag with rotten teeth. The aim of their polemical criticism was to reinvent the past, and convert it into a modern weapon against the arsenals of the dead men stuffed with straw.

They were attracted to those politics whose program presented social and economic conditions as metaphors describing and dealing with the state of civilization. The appeal of politics in the guise of metaphor is curiously shown in the great attraction of Social Credit theories for a number of writers, including not only Eliot and Pound but also Edwin Muir—during the late Twenties and Thirties. Social Credit is easy to visualize. One visualizes property, capital and manufactured goods, listed on one side of a column and on the other side money—credit—being printed equal to the wealth created. Since Schacht and

Mussolini actually made adjustments to the German and Italian economies along Social Credit lines, Social Credit seemed to be an element which could be abstracted from Fascism and applied to other systems. For reactionaries who could not swallow violence, it was a kind of Fascism without tears.

Students of Ezra Pound's *Cantos* will observe how metaphors drawn from economics thus visualized and then applied to explain the moral state of the civilization are used sometimes to justify inhuman attitudes. A famous example is the passage about usury in which Pound explains that the introduction of usury into the economic system falsifies the line drawn by the painter, causes his hand to err.

The Left also of course had their metaphors, which, by making history appear a poetic act, tended to regard human beings as words to be acted upon, deleted if necessary, so that the poem might come right. The word *liquidate* applied to killing all the members of some social class is, after all, a poetic metaphor.

On a level of false rhetoric, so far from there being a separation of politics from poetry, there is a dangerous convergence. Marxism, because it regards history as malleable material to be manipulated by the creative will of the Marxist, is rich in raw material of poetry. Marx concretized the language of economics.

The temptation for the poet is to take over the rhetoric of political will and action and translate it into the rhetoric of poetry. If there is a sin common to Auden's *Spain*, the anti-Semitic passages in Eliot's Sweeney poems, the political passages in Pound's *Cantos*, Wyndham Lewis's adulation of what he calls "the party of genius" (meaning Michelangelo and Wyndham Lewis), Lawrence's worship of the dynamic will of nature's aristocrats (in *The Plumed Serpent*), it is that the poet has allowed his scrupulous poet's rhetoric of the study of "minute particulars" to be overwhelmed by his secret yearning for a heroic public rhetoric of historic action. Sensibility has surrendered to will, the Keatsian concept of poetic personality to the dominating mode of political character.

In a period when poets seemed imprisoned in their private worlds, their occasional acts of surrender to the excitement of a public world of action in the service of what they could pretend to themselves was a civilizing cause is understandable. But the reactionariness of the "reactionaries" is the weakness, not the strength, of their work. William Empson writes in his odd, sympathetic preface to Mr. Harrison's book that he doubts whether the political issues of "their weakness for Fascism [was] the central one." He adds:

> Now that everything is so dismal we should look back with reverence on the great age of poets and fundamental thinkers, who were so ready to consider heroic remedies. Perhaps their gloomy prophecies have simply come true.

We (and here by "we" I mean the Thirties' writers) not only looked back on Yeats, Eliot, Pound and Lawrence with reverence, but we also revered them at the time. It is important to understand that we thought of them as a greater generation of artists more dedicated and more gifted than ourselves. They made us reflect that we were a generation less single-minded in our art, but which had perhaps found a new subject—the social situation. We did not think this could lead to better work; however, we did see that young poets could not go on writing esoteric poetry about the end of civilization. In their end-games were our game-beginnings. Our generation reacted against the same conventions of Georgian poetry and the novel as did the generation of T. S. Eliot, Virginia Woolf, D. H. Lawrence and E. M. Forster. They were indeed our heroes.

Pound, Wyndham Lewis and Roy Campbell were the only reactionaries whose public attitudes we sometimes attacked: with the mental reservation that we thought them zanies anyway. As for Eliot, Yeats and Lawrence, if we minimized their statements about politics, there was much in their deepest political insights with which we agreed.

> Things fall apart; the center cannot hold;
> Mere anarchy is loose upon the world . . .

This describes our situation. By comparison the fact that Yeats went out and supported General O'Duffy seemed scarcely relevant. He was being just "silly, like us." No poem could show better than "The Second Coming" how wrong Orwell was to approach Yeats's poetry as a symptom of his Fascism. To us, his Fascism seemed a misconception, but nevertheless it rose from deep political (and here the word seems quite inadequate) insight.

It is a pity that Mr. Harrison, instead of accepting at their face value labels like "Left" and "reactionary," did not compare at a deeper level than that of political parties the social vision of the poets of the Thirties and the older generation. He might have found then that the two generations often agreed in their diagnoses: they came to opposite conclusions with regard to remedies. He might also have found that the younger generation, in coming to their revolutionary conclusions, owed their view that we were living in a revolutionary situation to the insights of the reactionaries.

Stansky and Abrahams point out that John Cornford, while he was still a schoolboy, was led to Communism by reading, *The Waste Land.* "He believed it to be a great poem, read it not as a religious allegory . . . but as an anatomy of capitalist society in decay; it shaped his style, but more important, it was a preface to his politics."

To the imagination the poetry does not preach party programs. It penetrates into the depths of an external situation and shows what is strange and terrible. Eliot drew conclusions from his own poetic insight with his intellect. Cornford disagreed not with the poetic insight but with the secondary political conclusions when he wrote:

> *The Waste Land* . . . is of great importance not for the pleasure it gives, but for its perfect picture of the disintegration of a civilization. . . . But something more than description, some analysis of the situation is needed. And it is here that Eliot breaks down. He refuses to answer the question that he has so perfectly formulated. He retreats into the familiar triangle—Classicism, Royalism, Anglo-Catholicism. He has not found an answer to the question in resignation. Rather he has resigned himself to finding no answer.

Eliot's imagination which can give the "perfect picture of disintegration" is seen by Cornford as posing the question to which his intellect gives the answer—the wrong answer, according to Cornford (just as Yeats gave the wrong answers to his insights), but even he, the convinced Communist undergraduate about to go to Spain, cared more that the question should have been posed than that the answer should be "correct," for the question suggests what was to him the "correct" answer—which the subsequent history of Stalinist Russia also showed to have been wrong.

What was common to modern poets between 1910 and 1930 was their condemnation of a society which they saw as the disintegration of civilization. Given this agreed-on line, it was possible to be on the reactionary or the revolutionary side of it. The reactionaries, on their side, asked: "How can there be new life?" The awesome achievement of the earlier generation was to have created for their contemporaries a vision of the whole past tradition which had a poignant immediacy: giving shattered contemporary civilization consciousness of its own past greatness, like the legendary glimpse of every act of his past life in the eyes of a man drowning. Without the awareness of drowning, of the end of the long game, the apprehended moment could not have been so vivid. Thus the gloomy prophecies of the future, and the consequent weakness for reactionary politics, were the dark side of an intensely burning vision.

The liberals, the progressives, the anti-Fascists, could not invest their writing with a vision of the values of future civilization as great as the reactionaries' vision of past values. Perhaps, though, they secretly agreed with the reactionaries that the genius of our civilization which had flickered on since the Renaissance was soon to be extinguished. E. M. Forster, whose work stands midway between the idea of past and present, sees the greatness of England and Europe as over. The past commands his love, though the causes which should ultimately make people better off—freedom of the peoples of the world from the old imperialisms, greater social justice, etc.—command his loyalty. But his loyalty inspires him with no new love, and he has no enthusiasm for the liberated materially better world which he feels morally bound to support.

The anti-Fascists in the end accepted or were influenced by the idea that the struggle for the future meant abandoning nostalgia for a past civilization. They had now to emphasize "new life," a new culture not obsessed with the past. Julian Bell and John Cornford came to feel that in putting the cause before everything they must be prepared even to jettison their own poetry. And they found themselves relieved to do so. In 1932, when he started becoming interested in politics, John Cornford wrote to his mother: "I have found it a great relief to stop pretending to be an artist" and in the same letter he told her that he had bought *"Kapital* and a good deal of commentary, which I hope to find time to tackle this term. Also *The Communist Manifesto.*" In renouncing being an artist he is also turning his back on the world of his mother, Frances Cornford, the Georgian poet. Julian Bell experienced an immense sense of relief when he decided to abandon literature and go to Spain. In doing so he is turning his back on his mother, Vanessa Bell, the painter. If Auden and Isherwood had written a play on the theme of Cornford and Bell, one can well imagine that the deaths of these heroes on the battlefield would have been seen as the finale of a dialogue with a chorus of artistic mothers and Bloomsbury aunts.

Feelings and motives involved here are complex. Uncertainty about their vocations, rebellion against their mothers and against the values of the literary world of Cambridge, Oxford and London, a suppressed anti-intellectualism and an expression of the tendency of the young in that decade to interpret all current issues as a conflict between principles of "life" and "death," and "real" and the "unreal," enter in. The reader of Stansky and Abrahams cannot help noting that in a decade when people were always being reproached for "escapsim" the immersion into the life of action and political choice filled Bell and Cornford with an elation remarkably like that of escape— escape from having to be poets. Escape is wrong if it means escape from high standards to lower or more relaxed ones. In their renunciation of those standards of their parents which were, perhaps, too aesthetic, Cornford and Bell shared a tendency to escape into accepting means which were perilously close to those of their Fascist enemies. Thus Bell writes:

> The disgraceful part of the German business is not that the Nazis kill and torture their enemies; it is that Socialists and Communists let themselves be made prisoners instead of first killing as many Nazis as they can.

Bell's reaction is all the more striking because it is so much a renunciation of that pacifism which was one of his deepest ties with his parents:

> Most of my friends are unutterably squeamish about means; they feel that it would be terrible to use force or fraud against anyone. . . . Even most Communists seem to me to have only a hysterical and quite unrealistic notion about violent methods. . . . I can't imagine anyone of *The New Statesman* doing anything "unfair" to an opponent. . . . Whereas for my own part . . . I can't feel the slightest qualms about the notion of doing anything effective, however ungentlemanly and unchristian, nor about admitting to myself that certain actions would be very unfair indeed. . . .

and he ends the same letter with a sentence that is surely very revealing:

> I don't feel, myself, as if I could ever be satisfied to do nothing but produce works of art, or even really nothing but leading a private life and producing works in the intervals.

I do not quote these passages because I think them characteristic of Cornford and Bell (in fact they are out of character) but because of the light which—paradoxically—they throw on the relationship of the Thirties' generation with an older one. This balances the violence of the reactionaries supporting Fascism in the name of art, against the violence of the leftists prepared to sacrifice art to the cause of anti-Fascism.

The reactionaries cared passionately for past values. Their nostalgia misled them into sympathizing with whatever jackbooted corporal or demagogue set himself up in defense of order. As the history of Ezra Pound shows, the results of this could be tragic. But in their own lives, their own behavior and activity, their work, they did put literature before politics, and their first concern was to preserve the civilization without which, as they thought, neither past nor future literature could survive. They did not, as the anti-Fascist writers did, abandon or postpone their literary tasks. For the anti-Fascists allowed them-

71

selves, rightly or wrongly, to be persuaded that civilization could only be saved by action: the logical consequence of this attitude was to put writing at the service of necessity as dictated by political leaders.

There was, then, the paradox that the reactionaries who were on the side of the past, the dead, lived, in spite of everything, for the sake of literature, whereas circumstances drove the most sincere anti-Fascists—men like Cornford, Bell, Fox and Caudwell—to death for the sake of a public cause which they had made absolute. The reactionaries wrote out of their tragic sense of modern life. The Cornfords and Bells lived and died the tragedy.

Poetry and the Primitive: Notes on Poetry as an Ecological Survival Technique

GARY SNYDER

BILATERAL SYMMETRY

"Poetry" as the skilled and inspired use of the voice and language to embody rare and powerful states of mind that are in immediate origin personal to the singer, but at deep levels common to all who listen. "Primitive" as those societies which have remained nonliterate and nonpolitical while necessarily exploring and developing in directions that civilized societies have tended to ignore. Having fewer tools, no concern with history, a living oral tradition rather than an accumulated library, no overriding social goals, and considerable freedom of sexual and inner life, such people live vastly in the present. Their daily reality is a fabric of friends and family, the field of feeling and energy that one's own body is, the earth they stand on and the wind that wraps around it; and various areas of consciousness.

At this point some might be tempted to say that the primitive's real life is no different from anybody else's. I think this is not so. To live in the "mythological present" in close relation to nature and in basic but disciplined body/mind states suggests a wider-ranging imagination and a closer subjective knowledge of one's own physical properties than is usually available to men living (as they themselves describe it) impotently and inadequately in "history"—their mind-content programmed, and their caressing of nature complicated by the extensions and abstractions which elaborate tools are. A hand pushing a button may wield great power, but that hand will never learn what a hand can do. Unused capacities go sour.

Poetry must sing or speak from authentic experience. Of all the streams of civilized tradition with roots in the paleolithic, poetry is one of the few that can realistically claim an unchanged function and a relevance which will outlast most of the activities that surround us today. Poets, as few others, must live close to the world that primitive men are in: the world, in its nakedness, which is fundamental for all of us—birth, love, death; the sheer fact of being alive.

Music, dance, religion, and philosophy of course have archaic roots—a shared origin with poetry. Religion has tended to become the social justifier, a lackey to power, instead of the vehicle of hair-raising liberating and healing realizations. Dance has mostly lost its connection with ritual drama, the miming of animals, or tracing the maze of the spiritual journey. Most music takes too many tools. The poet can make it on his own voice and mother tongue, while steering a course between crystal clouds of utterly incommunicable nonverbal states—and the gleaming daggers and glittering nets of language.

In one school of Mahayana Buddhism, they talk about the "Three Mysteries." These are Body, Voice and Mind. The things that are what living *is* for us, in life. Poetry is the vehicle of the mystery of voice. The universe, as they sometimes say, is a vast breathing body.

With artists, certain kinds of scientists, yogins, and poets, a kind of mind-sense is not only surviving but modestly flourishing in the twentieth century. Claude Lévi-Strauss (*The Savage Mind*) sees no problem in the continuity: ". . . it is neither the mind of savages nor that of primitive or archaic humanity, but rather mind in its untamed state as distinct from mind cultivated or domesticated for yielding a return. . . . We are better able to understand today that it is possible for the two to coexist and interpenetrate in the same way that (in theory at least) it is possible for natural species, of which some are in their savage state and others transformed by agriculture and domestication, to coexist and cross . . . whether one deplores or rejoices in the fact, there are still zones in which savage thought, like savage species, is relatively protected. This is the case of art, to which our civilization accords the status of a national park."

MAKING LOVE WITH ANIMALS

By civilized times, hunting was a sport of kings. The early Chinese emperors had vast fenced hunting reserves; peasants were not allowed to shoot deer. Millennia of experience, the proud knowledge of hunting magic—animal habits—and the skills of wild plant and herb gathering were all but scrubbed away. Much has been said about the frontier in American history, but overlooking perhaps some key points: the American confrontation with a vast wild ecology, an earthly paradise of grass, water, and game—was mind shaking. Americans lived next to vigorous primitives whom they could not help but respect and even envy, for three hundred years. Finally, as ordinary men supporting their families, they often hunted for food. Although marginal peasants in Europe and Asia did remain part-time hunters at the bottom of the social scale, these Americans were the vanguard of an expanding culture. For Americans, "nature" means wilderness, the untamed realm of total freedom—not brutish and nasty, but beautiful and terrible. Something is always eating at the American heart like acid: it is the knowledge of what we have done to our continent, and to the American Indian.

Other civilizations have done the same, but at a pace too slow to be remembered. One finds evidence in T'ang and Sung poetry that the barren hills of central and northern China were once richly forested. The Far Eastern love of nature has become fear of nature: gardens and pine trees are tormented and controlled. Chinese nature poets were too often retired bureaucrats living on two or three acres of trees trimmed by hired gardeners. The professional nature-aesthetes of modern Japan, tea-teachers and flower arrangers, are amazed to hear that only a century ago dozens of species of birds passed through Kyoto where today only swallows and sparrows can be seen; and the aesthetes can scarcely distinguish those. "Wild" in the Far East means uncontrollable, objectionable, crude, sexually unrestrained, violent; actually ritually polluting. China cast off my-

75

thology, which means its own dreams, with hairy cocks and gaping pudenda, millennia ago; and modern Japanese families participating in an "economic miracle" can have daughters in college who are not sure which hole babies come out of. One of the most remarkable intuitions in Western thought was Rousseau's Noble Savage: the idea that perhaps civilization has something to learn from the primitive.

Man is a beautiful animal. We know this because other animals admire us and love us. Almost all animals are beautiful and paleolithic hunters were deeply moved by it. To hunt means to use your body and senses to the fullest: to strain your consciousness to feel what the deer are thinking today, this moment; to sit still and let your self go into the birds and wind while waiting by a game trail. Hunting magic is designed to bring the game to you—the creature who has heard your song, witnessed your sincerity, and out of compassion comes within your range. Hunting magic is not only aimed at bringing beasts to their death, but to assist in their birth—to promote their fertility. Thus the great Iberian cave paintings are not of hunting alone—but of animals mating and giving birth. A Spanish farmer who saw some reproductions from Altamira is reported to have said, "How beautifully this cow gives birth to a calf!" Breuil has said, "The religion of those days did *not* elevate the animal to the position of a god . . . but it was *humbly entreated* to be fertile." A Haida incantation goes:

> "The Great One coming up against the current
>   begins thinking of it.
> The Great One coming putting gravel in his mouth
>   thinks of it
> You look at it with white stone eyes—
>   Great Eater begins thinking of it."

People of primitive cultures appreciate animals as other people off on various trips. Snakes move without limbs, and are like free penises. Birds fly, sing, and dance; they gather food for their babies; they disappear for months and then come back. Fish can breathe water and are brilliant colors. Mammals are like us, they fuck and give birth to babies while panting and purring; their young suck their mothers' breasts; they know terror and delight, they play.

Lévi-Strauss quotes Swanton's report on the Chickasaw, the tribe's own amusing game of seeing the different clans as acting out the lives of their totemic emblems: "The Raccoon people were said to live on fish and wild fruit, those of the Puma lived in the mountains, avoided water of which they were very frightened and lived principally on game. The Wild Cat clan slept in the daytime and hunted at night, for they had keen eyes; they were indifferent to women. Members of the Bird clan were up before daybreak: 'They were like real birds in that they would not bother anybody . . . the people of this clan have different sorts of minds, just as there are different species of birds.' They were said to live well, to be polygamous, disinclined to work, and prolific . . . the inhabitants of the 'bending-post-oak' house group lived in the woods . . . the High Corncrib house people were respected in spite of their arrogance: they were good gardeners, very industrious but poor hunters; they bartered their maize for game. They were said to be truthful and stubborn, and skilled at forecasting the weather. As for the Redskunk house group: they lived in dugouts underground."

We all know what primitive cultures don't have. What they *do* have is this knowledge of connection and responsibility which amounts to a spiritual ascesis for the whole community. Monks of Christianity or Buddhism, "leaving the world" (which means the games of society), are trying, in a decadent way, to achieve what whole primitive communities—men, women, and children—live by daily; and with more wholeness. The Shaman-poet is simply the man whose mind reaches easily out into all manners of shapes and other lives, and gives song to dreams. Poets have carried this function forward all through civilized times: poets don't sing about society, they sing about nature—even if the closest they ever get to nature is their lady's queynt. Class-structured civilized society is a kind of mass ego. To transcend the ego is to go beyond society as well. "Beyond" there lies, inwardly, the unconscious. Outwardly, the equivalent of the unconscious is the wilderness: both of these terms meet, one step even farther on, as *one*.

One religious tradition of this communion with nature which has survived into historic Western times is what has been called Witchcraft. The antlered and pelted figure painted on the cave wall of Trois Frères, a shaman-dancer-poet, is a prototype of both Shiva and the Devil.

Animal marriages (and supernatural marriages) are a common motif of folklore the world around. A recent article by Lynn White puts the blame for the present ecological crisis on the Judaeo-Christian tradition—animals don't have souls and can't be saved; nature is merely a ground for us to exploit while working out our drama of free will and salvation under the watch of Jehovah. The Devil? "The Deivill apeired vnto her in the liknes of ane prettie boy in grein clothes . . . and at that tyme the Deivil gaive hir his markis; and went away from her in the liknes of ane blak dowg." "He wold haw carnall dealling with ws in the shap of a deir, or in any vther shap, now and then, somtyme he vold be lyk a stirk, a bull, a deir, a rae, or a dowg, etc, and haw dealling with us."

The archaic and primitive ritual dramas, which acknowledged all the sides of human nature, including the destructive, demonic, and ambivalent, were liberating and harmonizing. Freud said *he* didn't discover the unconscious, poets had centuries before. The purpose of California Shamanism was "to heal disease and resist death, with a power acquired from dreams." An Arapaho dancer of the Ghost Dance came back from his trance to sing:

> "I circle around, I circle around
>
> The boundaries of the earth,
> The boundaries of the earth
>
> Wearing the long wing feathers as I fly
> Wearing the long wing feathers as I fly."

THE VOICE AS A GIRL

"Everything was alive—the trees, grasses, and winds were dancing with me, talking with me; I could understand the songs of the birds." This ancient experience is not so much—in spite of later commentators—"religious" as it is a pure perception of beauty. The phenomenal world experienced at certain pitches is totally living, exciting, mysterious, filling one with a trembling awe, leaving one grateful and humble. The wonder of the mystery returns direct to one's own senses and consciousness: inside and outside; the voice breathes, "Ah!"

Breath is the outer world coming into one's body. With pulse—the two always harmonizing—the source of our inward sense of rhythm. Breath is spirit, "inspiration." Expiration, "voiced," makes the signals by which the species connects. Certain emotions and states occasionally seize the body, one becomes a whole tube of air vibrating; all voice. In mantra chanting, the magic utterances, built of seed-syllables such as OM and AYNG and AH, repeated over and over, fold and curl on the breath until—when most weary and bored—a new voice enters, a voice speaks through you clearer and stronger than what you know of yourself; with a sureness and melody of its own, singing out the inner song of the self, and of the planet.

Poetry, it should not have to be said, is not writing or books. Nonliterate cultures with their traditional training methods of hearing and reciting, carry thousands of poems—death, war, love, dream, work, and spirit-power songs—through time. The voice of inspiration as an "other" has long been known in the West as the Muse. Widely speaking, the muse is anything other that touches you and moves you. Be it a mountain range, a band of people, the morning star, or a diesel generator. Breaks through the ego-barrier. But this touching-deep is as a mirror, and man in his sexual nature has found the clearest mirror to be his human lover. As the West moved into increasing complexities and hierarchies with civilization, Woman as nature, beauty, and The Other came to be an all-dominating symbol; secretly striving through the last three millennia with the Jehovah or Imperator God-figure, a projection of the gathered power of antinature social forces. Thus in the Western tradition the Muse and Romantic Love became part of the same energy, and woman as nature the field for experiencing the universe as sacramental. The lovers' bed was the sole place to enact the dances and ritual dramas that link primitive people to their geology and the Milky Way. The contemporary decline of the cult of romance is linked to the rise of the sense of the primitive, and the knowledge of the variety of spiritual practices and paths to beauty that cultural anthropology has brought us. We begin to move away now, in this interesting historical spiral, from monogamy and monotheism.

Yet the Muse remains a woman. Poetry is voice, and according to Indian tradition, voice, vāk (vox)—is a Goddess. Vāk is also called Sarasvati, she is the lover of Brahma and his actual creative energy; she rides a peacock, wears white, carries a book-scroll and a vīna. The name Sarasvati means "the flowing one." "She is again the Divine in the aspect of wisdom and learning, for she is the Mother of Veda; that is of all knowledge touching Brahman and the universe. She is the Word of which it was born and She is that which is the issue of her great womb, Mahāyoni. Not therefore idly have men worshipped Vāk, or Sarasvati, as the Supreme Power."

As Vāk is wife to Brahma ("wife" means "wave" means "vibrator" in Indo-European etymology) so the voice, in everyone, is a mirror of his own deepest self. The voice rises to answer an inner need; or as BusTon says, "The voice of the Buddha arises, being called forth by the thought of the living beings." In esoteric Buddhism this becomes the basis of a mandala meditation practice: "In their midst is Nayika, the essence of *Ali*, the vowel series—she possesses the true nature of Vajrasattva, and is Queen of the Vajra-realm. She is known as the Lady, as Suchness, as Void, as Perfection of Wisdom, as limit of Reality, as Absence of Self."

The conch shell is an ancient symbol of the sense of hearing, and of the female; the vulva and the fruitful womb. At Koptos there is a bas-relief of a four-point buck, on the statue of the god Min, licking his tongue out toward two conches. There are many Magdalenian bone and horn engravings of bear, bison, and deer licking abstract penises and vulvas. At this point (and from our most archaic past transmitted) the mystery of voice becomes one with the mystery of body.

How does this work among primitive peoples in practice? James Mooney, discussing the Ghost Dance religion, says "There is no limit to the number of these [Ghost Dance] songs, as every trance at every dance produces a new one, the trance subject after regaining consciousness embodying his experience in the spirit world in the form of a song, which is sung at the next dance and succeeding performances until superseded by other songs originating in the same way. Thus a single dance may easily result in twenty or thirty new songs. While songs are thus born and die, certain ones which appeal especially to the Indian heart, on account of their mythology, pathos, or peculiar sweetness, live and are perpetuated."

Modern poets in America, Europe, and Japan, are discovering the breath, the voice, and trance. It is also for some a discovery to realize that the universe is not a dead thing but a continual creation, the song of Sarasvati springing from the trance of Brahma. "Reverence to Her who is eternal, Raudrī, Gaurī, Dhātri, reverence and again reverence, to Her who is the Consciousness in all beings, reverence and again reverence. . . . Candī says."

HOPSCOTCH AND CATS CRADLES

*The clouds are "Shining Heaven" with his different
bird-blankets on.*

Haida

The human race, as it immediately concerns us, has a vertical axis of about 40,000 years and as of A.D. 1900 a horizontal spread of roughly 3,000 different languages and 1,000 different cultures. Every living culture and language is the result of countless cross-fertilizations—not a "rise and fall" of civilizations, but more like a flowerlike periodic absorbing—blooming—bursting and scattering of seed. Today we are aware as never before of the plurality of human life-styles and possibilities, while at the same time being tied, like in an old silent movie, to a runaway locomotive rushing headlong toward a very singular catastrophe. Science, as far as it is capable of looking "on beauty bare" is on our side. Part of our being modern is the very fact of our awareness that we are one with our beginnings—contemporary with all periods—members of all cultures. The seeds of every social structure or custom are in the mind.

The anthropologist Stanley Diamond has said, "The sickness of civilization consists in its failure to incorporate (and only then) to move beyond the limits of the primitive." Civilization is, so to speak, a lack of faith, a human laziness, a willingness to accept the perceptions and decisions of others in place of your own—to be less than a full man. Plus, perhaps, a primate inheritance of excessive socializing; and surviving submission/dominance traits (as can be observed in monkey or baboon bands) closely related to exploitative sexuality. If evolution has any meaning at all we must hope to slowly move away from such biological limitations, just as it is within our power to move away from the self-imposed limitations of small-minded social systems. We all live within skin, ego, society, and species boundaries. Consciousness has boundaries of a different order, "the mind is free." College students trying something different because "they do it in New Guinea" is part of the real work of modern man: to uncover the inner structure and actual boundaries of the mind. The third Mystery. The charts and maps of this realm are called mandalas in Sanskrit. (A poem by the Sixth Dalai Lama runs "Drawing diagrams I measured/Movement of the stars/Though her tender flesh is near/Her mind I cannot measure.") Buddhist and Hindu philosophers have gone deeper into this than almost anyone else but the work is just beginning. We are now gathering all the threads of history together and linking modern science to the primitive and archaic sources.

The stability of certain folklore motifs and themes—evidences of linguistic borrowing—the deeper meaning of linguistic drift—the laws by which styles and structures, art forms and grammars, songs and ways of courting, relate and reflect each other are all mirrors of the self. Even the uses of the word "nature," as in the seventeenth-century witch Isobel Gowdie's testimony about what it was like to make love to the Devil—"I found his nature cold within me as spring-well-water"—throw light on human nature.

Thus nature leads into nature—the wilderness—and the reciprocities and balances by which man lives on earth. Ecology: "eco" (*oikos*) meaning "house" (cf. "ecumenical"): Housekeeping on Earth. Economics, which is merely the housekeeping of various social orders—taking out more than it puts back—must learn the rules of the greater realm. Ancient and primitive cultures had this knowledge more surely and with almost as much empirical precision (see H. C. Conklin's work on Hanunoo plant-knowledge, for example) as the most concerned biologist today. Inner and outer: the Brihadāranyaka Upanishad says, "Now this Self is the state of being of all contingent beings. In so far as a man pours libations and offers sacrifice, he is in the sphere of the gods; in so far as he recites the Veda he is in the sphere of the seers; in so far as he offers cakes and water to the ancestors, in so far as he gives food and lodging to men, he is of the sphere of men. In so far as he finds grass and water for domestic animals, he is in the sphere of domestic animals; in so far as wild beasts and birds, even down to ants, find something to live on in his house, he is of their sphere."

The primitive world view, far-out scientific knowledge, and the poetic imagination are related forces which may help if not to save the world or humanity, at least to save the Redwoods. The goal of Revolution is Transformation. Mystical traditions within the great religions of civilized times have taught a doctrine of Great Effort for the achievement of Transcendence. This must have been their necessary compromise with civilization, which needed for its period to turn man's vision away from nature, to nourish the growth of the social energy. The archaic, the esoteric, and the primitive traditions alike all teach that beyond transcendence is Great Play, and Transformation. After the mind-breaking Void, the emptiness of a million universes appearing and disappearing, all created things rushing into Krishna's devouring mouth; beyond the enlightenment that can say "these beings are dead already; go ahead and kill them, Arjuna" is a loving, simple awareness of the absolute beauty and preciousness of mice and weeds.

Tsong-kha-pa tells us of a transformed universe:

"1. This is a Buddha-realm of infinite beauty
2. All men are divine, are subjects
3. Whatever we use or own are vehicles of worship
4. All acts are authentic, not escapes."

Such authenticity is at the heart of many a primitive world view. For the Anaguta of the Jos plateau, Northern Nigeria, North is called "up"; South is called "down." East is called "morning" and West is called "evening." Hence (according to Dr. Stanley Diamond in his *Anaguta Cosmography*), "Time flows past the permanent central position . . . they live at a place called noon, at the center of the world, the only place where space and time intersect." The Australian aborigines live in a world of ongoing recurrence—comradeship with the landscape and continual exchanges of being and form and position; every person, animals, forces, all are related via a web of reincarnation—or rather, they are "interborn." It may well be that rebirth (or interbirth, for we are actually mutually creating each other and all things while living) is the objective fact of existence which we have not yet brought into conscious knowledge and practice.

It is clear that the empirically observable interconnectedness of nature is but a corner of the vast "jewelled net" which moves from without to within. The spiral (think of nebulae) and spiral conch (vulva/womb) is a symbol of the Great Goddess. It is charming to note that physical properties of spiral conches approximate the Indian notion of the world-creating dance, "expanding form"—"We see that the successive chambers of a spiral Nautilus or of a straight Orthoceras, each whorl or part of a whorl of a periwinkle or other gastropod, each additional increment of an elephant's tusk, or each new chamber of a spiral foraminifer, has its leading characteristic at once described and its form so far described by the simple statement that it constitutes a *gnomon* to the whole previously existing structure" (D'Arcy Thompson).

The maze dances, spiral processions, cats cradles, Micronesian string star charts, mandalas and symbolic journeys of the old wild world are with us still in the universally distributed children's game. Let poetry and Bushmen lead the way in a great hop forward:

> In the following game of long hopscotch, the part marked H is for Heaven: it is played in the usual way except that when you are finishing the first part, on the way up, you throw your tor into Heaven. Then you hop to 11, pick up your tor, jump to the very spot where your tor landed in Heaven,
> and say, as fast as you can,
> the alphabet forwards and backwards,
> your name, address and telephone number (if you have one),
> your age,
> and the name of your boyfriend or girl friend (if you have one of those).
>
> Patricia Evans, "Hopscotch"

Absolute Poetry and Absolute Politics

MICHAEL HAMBURGER

I

As long as Romantic-Symbolist attitudes prevailed in poetry—
and they have attracted poets right up to our time, even though
the practice of these poets may have had little to do with Symbolism—there has been a tendency towards extreme political
views, more often conservative or reactionary than progressive.
The reasons for this are so complex that it is best not to attempt
a general explanation here, but to examine a few outstanding
cases. Yet the following general observations must be made.

Romantic-Symbolist attitudes presuppose a high degree of
isolation or alienation from society. Ever since Baudelaire poets
have felt themselves to be pariahs or aristocrats—if not both at
once—in societies dominated by bourgeois values and institutions. Baudelaire's gibes at "democratization" and "syphiliza-
tion" are typical reactions of an aristocrat-pariah who is excluded
from the benefits of capitalist industry as much as from solidarity with the working classes. That, of course, is a simplification,
since it implies that Baudelaire's attitudes were determined by
his economic and social status, whereas a moral and aesthetic
revulsion from modern commercialism may well have been a
more powerful motive. Yeats, who could identify himself with
the Protestant Anglo-Irish gentry and with the Catholic peasantry, but not with the urban middle and working classes, defined the gentleman as "a man whose principal ideas are not
connected with his personal needs and his personal success."[1]

85

We may assume that Baudelaire was a gentleman in that sense, though the case of Yeats himself shows that conscious attitudes are one thing, the subconscious pressure of "personal needs" and personal ambition another.

What Laura Riding and Robert Graves wrote about the generation of early twentieth-century modernists applies to their Romantic-Symbolist predecessors also:

> As a generation writing in the limelight of modernism it has an over-developed historical sense and professional self-consciousness. It is mentally uncomfortable—shrewd, nervous, suspicious of itself. It rejects philosophy and religion in the old drivelling romantic sense, but would make an intellectual system—a permanently accessible mental cocktail—that would be a stiff, sane, steadying combination of both. It cares so much that in all matters where the plain reader is accustomed to meet with earnest conviction of one kind or another in the poet, it is hysterically, gruesomely "I-don't-care-ish." It is like a person between life and death: everything that would ordinarily seem serious to him now seems a tragic joke. This nervousness, this superior sort of stage-fright, is aggravated by the fact that in the new synthesis of values—even in the system that he is attempting to realize for himself—the historically-minded modernist poet is uncertain whether there is any excuse for the existence of poets at all. He finds himself in a defensive position; and in sympathy with his position; but also with the system that has put him in this position.[2]

The same writers also point out:

> Genuine professional modernism inclines rather toward the two extremes of radicalism and conservatism, or aristocraticness and rough-neckedness; not so much out of militant opposition to bourgeois liberalism as out of peripatetic avoidance of a crowded thoroughfare—bourgeois liberalism, being a position of compromise between all extremes, is the breeding place of settled, personally secure convictions.

The two extremes may assert a simultaneous pull on the same poet. Baudelaire succumbed to revolutionary frenzy at the time

of the 1848 barricades. Yeats was the spokesman both for "aristocraticness" and for "rough-neckedness." Nor was it Irish nationalism alone that Yeats celebrated in the uprising of 1916,
writing: "A terrible beauty is born." Violent upheaval itself has
fascinated and excited the imagination of Romantic-Symbolist
poets almost regardless of their political sympathies. Alexander
Blok was one of many such poets who became victims of the
revolutions which they glorified.

The one thing constant in the attitude of Romantic-Symbolist poets is the rejection of the very fabric of modern civilization; and even Robert Graves, a poet whose formative years were
spent in the trenches, has been unable to reconcile his poetic
creed with the utilitarianism dominant in every advanced country, whether capitalist, Socialist or Communist. Whatever Graves's
political views—and they are known to be moderate and liberal—the creed professed in his Foreword to *The White Goddess*
could not be more profoundly romantic, and therefore reactionary:

> The function of poetry is religious invocation of the Muse;
> its use is the experience of musical exaltation and horror
> that her presence excites. But "nowadays"? Function and
> use remain the same; only the application has changed.
> This was once a warning to man that he must keep
> in harmony with the family of living creatures among which
> he was born, by obedience to the wishes of the lady of the
> house; it is now a reminder that he has disregarded the
> warning, turned the house upside down by capricious ex-
> periments in philosophy, science and industry, and brought
> ruin on himself and his family. "Nowadays" is a civilization
> in which the prime emblems of poetry are dishonoured.
> In which serpent, lion and eagle belong to the circus-tent;
> ox, salmon and boar to the cannery; race-horse and grey-
> hound to the betting-ring; and the sacred grove to the
> sawmill. In which the Moon is despised as a burnt-out sat-
> ellite of the Earth and woman reckoned as "auxiliary state
> personnel." In which money will buy almost anything but
> the truth, and almost anyone but the truth possessed poet.[3]

Robert Graves is mundane and scrupulous enough to be
aware that a creed so deeply incompatible with the aims and
pursuits of the majority cannot be related to political realities at

all. He has been a non-political poet ever since he arrived at that poetic creed; and he has been fortunate enough not to be forced into the position of having to commit himself politically. In a sense all the poets with Romantic-Symbolist attitudes have been non-political, in as much as their values have sprung from the imagination, and the imagination is too radical and utopian to adjust to political issues proper. Yet ever since Thomas Mann's *Reflections of a Non-Political Man* (1917), and his later reversal of its anti-democratic argument, it has been clear that to be non-political or anti-political at a time when "the destiny of a man presents its meaning in political terms" is almost inevitably to be conservative or reactionary—at least under régimes that perpetuate an established structure of power and privilege. The imagination, in our time, has also tended to be primitivist, out of a reaction against the complexities and pluralism of a culture which it cannot assimilate. Yeats's "ceremony of innocence," which is "drowned" in our time, is one instance of the many lost Edens invoked or created by the poetic imagination; Robert Graves's matriarchal order is another. The temptation for poets, therefore—a temptation which Graves resisted, but Yeats did not—has been to succumb to political movements that spring from a related primitivism, a related reaction against cultural pluralism. Italian and Spanish Fascism, German National Socialism, the Action Française, are a few right-wing movements of that kind; but so is Anarcho-Syndicalism, a left-wing movement that appealed not only to Spanish intellectuals but to English poets such as Herbert Read. If that left-wing movement has declined, it is because its primitivism—that is, its opposition to modern industrialism and urbanization—was so radical and consistent as to make it incapable of using the existing machinery of power, as right-wing primitivism did with a ruthlessness and duplicity that need no exemplification here.

The politics of poets would be of limited interest if their temptations were utterly different from those of other people; but a revolt of the imagination or of the instincts against an ever more intricately organized civilization is general enough. A sociologist, Professor Michael Polanyi, has written about "the tension between a positivist scepticism and a modern moral perfectionism in our time" which "has erupted with vast consequences."[4]

It has erupted in two directions, towards art and philosophy and towards politics. The first was a move towards extreme individualism, the second, on the contrary, towards modern totalitarianism. These two movements may appear diametrically opposed, yet they are but alternative solutions of the equation which required *the joint satisfaction of a belief in moral perfection with a complete denial of moral motives.*

A man looking at the world with complete scepticism can see no grounds for moral authority or transcendent moral obligations; there may seem to be no scope then for his moral perfectionism. Yet he can satisfy it by turning his scepticism against existing society, denouncing its morality as shoddy, artificial, hypocritical, and a mere mask for lust and exploitation. Though such combination of his moral scepticism with his moral indignation is inconsistent, the two are in fact fused together by the joint attack on the same target. The result is a moral hatred of existing society and the alienation of the modern intellectual. The effect on his inner life goes deep. His scepticism-cum-perfectionism scorns any expression of his own traditional morality. . . . Divided against himself, he seeks an identity safe against self-doubt. Having condemned the distinction between good and evil as dishonest, he can still take pride in the honesty of such condemnation. Since ordinary decent behaviour can never be safe against the suspicion of sheer conformity or downright hypocrisy, only an absolutely a-moral meaningless act can assure man of his complete authenticity. All the moral fervour which scientific scepticism has released from religious control and then rendered homeless by discrediting its ideals, returns then to imbue an a-moral authenticity with intense moral approval. . . . This theme has prevailed in Continental thought since a century ago Dostoevsky first described murder as an experiment in moral scepticism and, soon after, Nietzsche repudiated all traditional conceptions of good and evil as hypocritical. . . . These are some individualistic solutions of the conflict between scepticism and perfectionism. They unite the two opposites in a moral nihilism charged with moral fury. This paradoxical combination is new in history and deserves a new name; I have called it *moral inversion.* In public life moral inversion leads to totalitarianism.

MICHAEL HAMBURGER

The work of W. B. Yeats abounds in instances of a "moral nihilism charged with moral fury"; and his sympathy with right-wing totalitarian movements was shared by poets as various as Rainer Maria Rilke, Wallace Stevens, Ezra Pound, Gottfried Benn and the Futurist F. T. Marinetti. The conservatism of Hugo von Hofmannsthal and T. S. Eliot was less nihilistically based, less "charged with moral fury"; but Hofmannsthal took up the dangerous slogan "conservative revolution"—a concept also dear to the various nationalist factions that prepared the way for Nazism in Germany and Austria—and Eliot's "idea of a Christian society" was so absolute and utopian as to be irreconcilable with liberal democracy. Stefan George's cult of "Caesarism" had obvious affinities with the Caesarist antics of Mussolini, though George did not succumb to the advances of the National Socialist leaders, whose plebeian "rough-neckedness" was uncongenial to his fastidious "aristocraticness."* (Hofmannsthal found George's "aristocraticness" altogether "too bourgeois"; and it is true that the whole trend towards sectarian cultural élites was a bourgeois phenomenon. Yet it was an aristocratic disciple of Stefan George, Count Stauffenberg, who tried to assassinate Hitler.) In every case these sympathies were qualified by important reservations. In most cases they were of short duration, contradicted by other statements or decisions, or positively withdrawn if and when knowledge of political realities came to outweigh the attraction of political gestures. Yet there is no getting away from the fact that the "moral perfectionism" of all these poets could not come to terms with "bourgeois liberalism," that their imagination rejected its assumptions and institutions even where their reason acknowledged that it gave them what they needed most, the freedom to dissent, assert their own values and despise "the common dream."

II

Yeats's attitude to Irish and European Fascism has ben examined by Conor Cruise O'Brien,[5] who not only documented it in detail but related it to Yeats's poetry.

This attitude was complicated both by Yeats's ambiguous

*See the chapter, *Stefan George: Perilous Prophet*, in Peter Viereck: *Dream and Responsibility*, Washington, D.C., 1953, pp. 25–35.

position as a Protestant in the Irish nationalist movement—politically anti-British, but with strong linguistic, cultural and social ties to England—and by vacillations due to periodical retreats into non-political privacy. "And always," O'Brien comments, "in the long phases of withdrawal, he tended to write of all politics with a kind of contempt, a plague-on-both-your-houses air. (Contempt for politics is of course a characteristic Conservative stance.)" As O'Brien points out, "the two main currents in Yeats's active politics" were "his Anglophobe Irish nationalism and his authoritarianism." Yet, with very few exceptions, even Yeats's directly political poems render much more than those currents. At times his apocalyptic imagination could transform a political occasion into a universal myth, as in the case of *Leda and the Swan,* cited by O'Brien. Only Yeats's own note on the poem recalls the circumstances of its inception, the invitation by the editor of a political review to contribute a poem: ". . . Then I thought 'Nothing is now possible but some movement from above preceded by some violent annunciation.' My fancy began to play with Leda and the Swan for metaphor, and I began this poem: but as I wrote, bird and lady took such possession of the scene that all politics went out of it, and my friend tells me his 'conservative readers would misunderstand the poem.' "

O'Brien shows how the forces in Yeats "that responded to the hatred, cruelty and violence welling up in Europe" produced prophetic poems like *The Second Coming* and the last part of *Nineteen Hundred and Nineteen.* Yeats's opinions and sympathies, like his "active politics," have become irrelevant to those poems. What matters is their powerful evocation of forces which few of his contemporaries recognized (though Hofmannsthal, who died in 1929, ten years before Yeats, did recognize them in his late play *Der Turm:* Hofmannsthal noted that the "imagination is conservative," but his own imagination could be as prophetic and apocalyptic as Yeats's). O'Brien's comments on *Leda and the Swan* say all that needs to be said about the way in which the poems profited by Yeats's "fanatic heart," by the capacity for hatred that makes Yeats's politics unacceptable to O'Brien and the majority of Yeats's readers.

In the poetry, however, the raw intimations of what is impending—the telepathetic waves of violence and fear—

91

make themselves known, not in the form of calculated practical deductions, but in the attempt to reveal, through metaphoric insight, what is actually happening and even, in a broad sense, what is about to happen. The poet, like the lady, is

> so caught up,
> So mastered by the brute blood of the air

that he does indeed take on the knowledge of what is happening with the power to make it known. The political man had his cautious understanding with fascism, the diplomatic relation to a great force; the poet conveyed the nature of the force, the dimension of the tragedy. The impurities of his long and extraordinary life went into his devious and sometimes sinister political theories and activities. The purity and integrity—including the truth about politics as Yeats apprehended it—are in the poetry concentrated in metaphors of such power that they thrust aside all calculated intent: the bird and lady take possession of the scene.

Yeats is one of the writers whom Frank Kermode has called "the new apocalyptics."[6] Kermode, too, is worried by the discrepancy between Yeats's moral relativism and the beliefs, or half-beliefs, of which he made use for his poetry. "At bottom," Kermode writes, "he was sceptical about the nonsense with which he satisfied what we can call his lust for commitment. Now and again he believed some of it, but in so far as his true commitment was to poetry he recognized his fictions as heuristic and dispensable, 'consciously false.' 'They give me metaphors for poetry,' he noted." Yet the discrepancy remains; and we shall see how later poets came to distrust metaphor itself, because it lends itself to a kind of double-dealing, unacknowledged shifts and transferences from one order of reality to another. Kermode writes of Yeats's "retreat to myth and to the rituals of the occult; on the one side were the shopkeeping logicians, on the other the seductive and various forms of unreason." O'Brien has shown how that very retreat to myth could thwart the poet's original intentions, and redeem the poem from its occasion. Elsewhere, as Kermode observed, the very reverse occurred: pragmatic reality asserted itself in Yeats's diction, deflating his fury and replacing apocalypse with experience: "What saved him in the end was a confidence basic to the entire European tradition, a confidence in the common language, the vernacular by means of which from day to day we deal with reality as against justice. Everything depends upon a power

> To compound the imagination's Latin with
> The lingua franca et jocundissima.

In the same way, Yeats, though he entertained the fictions of apocalypse, renovation, transition, saw the need to compound them with the *lingua franca* of reality."

This, however, applies only to the poetry, as Kermode goes on to say. "The dreams of apocalypse, if they usurp waking thought, may be the worst dreams," he writes, and quotes Dewey's remark that "even aesthetic systems may breed a disposition towards the world and take overt effect." In Yeats Kermode sees one instance of "totalitarian theories of form matched or reflected by totalitarian politics"; and "the only reason why this is unimportant is that he had no influence upon those who might have put his beliefs to an operational test."

From whatever angle we look at it, Yeats's case is paradoxical, not least because he made his poetry out of a quarrel with himself, rather than resolutions of that quarrel—though the resolutions, too, matter, since they account for Yeats's extraordinary progression from melancholy romantic reverie to prophetic or starkly realistic encounters with "the Savage God," so that in his old age he could write lines as new, intense, yet seemingly effortless as

> A barnacle goose
> Far up in the stretches of night; night splits and the dawn breaks
>   loose;
> I, through the terrible novelty of light, stalk on, stalk on;
> Those great sea-horses bare their teeth and laugh at the
>   dawn.[7]

Yeats's capacity to change, to learn even from younger men like Ezra Pound, also makes it likely that he would have revised his political sympathies had he lived long enough to experience the cataclysms which he invoked. Despite his use of masks, Yeats did not allow an aesthetic system or any other to insulate him against shocks and disturbances and breakdown. "To speak of one's emotions without fear or moral ambition, to come out from under the shadow of other men's minds, to forget their needs, to be utterly oneself, that is all the Muses care for."[8] Beneath all Yeats's masks we sense the need to be "utterly oneself," though it was only the masks that enabled him to render the multiplicity of that self without loss of intensity and concentration, or the universality which he owed to tradition and found in the great lyric and tragic poets before him: "That shaping joy has kept the sorrow pure, as it had kept it were the emotion love or hate, for the nobleness of the arts is in the mingling of contraries, the extremity of sorrow, the extremity of joy, perfection of personality, the perfection of its surrender, overflowing turbulent energy, and marvellous stillness. . . ." Since "we believe only in the thoughts which have been conceived not in the brain but the whole body," at least as far as poetry is concerned, Yeats's opinions obtrude far less than do those of other poets more consistently modern than he, such as Ezra Pound. Yeats himself wrote in his late *General Introduction for My Work,* "I hated and still hate with an ever growing hatred the literature of the point of view." Apart from a few conspicuous lapses, Yeats's poetry conveys to us not only the moral fury but the tragic insight of the poet who wrote before the Second World War:

> Civilization is hooped together, brought
> Under a rule, under the semblance of peace
> By manifold illusion; but man's life is thought,
> And he, despite his terror, cannot cease
> Ravening through century after century,
> Ravening, raging, and uprooting that he may come
> Into the desolation of reality. . . .[9]

Whatever our point of view, and whatever Yeats's when he wrote those lines, even so general and undramatized a statement must convince us, not only because the modulation and control of the blank verse are masterly, but because the statement is true; and events which Yeats did not live to experience have made its truth not less but more apparent.

If we do consult Yeats's opinions, we find that all of them have a corrective or complement in his own writings. His pro-Fascist leanings, for instance, are modified by the admission, "I am no nationalist, except in Ireland for passing reasons," and those "passing reasons" must not be left out of account; also by his psychological observation: "All empty souls tend to extreme opinion. It is only in those who have built up a rich world of memories and habits of thought that extreme opinions affront the sense of probability. Propositions, for instance, which set all the truth upon one side can only enter sick minds to dislocate and strain, if they enter at all, and sooner or later the mind expels them by instinct."[10] Most of the extreme opinions and attitudes in Yeats's work are those of his anti-self. The Yeats who confessed, "I have no solution, none," was the reasonable man who despaired of "perfection of the life," knowing that the kind of perfection that he wanted for his work could not be obtained without the help of his "circus animals," of that mask of style which even the prose writer could rarely bring himself to discard.

III

Yeats's participation both in the Irish literary revival and in the political developments that were so closely linked with it exacerbated his moral and artistic dilemmas. Yet the choice between "perfection of the life" and "perfection of the work" was familiar to poets who had less opportunity than Yeats to let the apocalyptic imagination encroach on active politics. Paul Valéry, too, remarked: "Whoever says Work says Sacrifice. The crucial question is to decide what one is going to sacrifice: one needs to know *who, who is going to be devoured.*"[11] As a French intellectual, however, Valéry was saved from apocalyptic proclivities by the tradition of sceptical, analytical and psychologically probing intelligence—a tradition going back to the French moralists of the seventeenth century and beyond them, to Montaigne—which his prose works continued, despite his "exercises" in absolute poetry. Yeats could never have written: "A political or artistic opinion should be something so vague that under the same semblance the same individual can always accommodate it to his moods and his interests; justify his action; explain his vote."[12]

Yeats's definition of the gentleman—one instance of his indebt-
edness to English culture and morality—forbade so deliberate a
relativism.

In the same way, Valéry's very French reluctance to make a
fool of himself prevented him from indulging in prophecy when,
in writings like *La Politique de l'esprit* or *Regards sur le monde actuel*, he dealt with public and general issues, the "crisis" in European civilization of which his poetry has so little to say, as
compared with Yeats's apocalyptic awareness that "things fall
apart, the centre cannot hold." Pronouncements of the same
order by Hugo von Hofmannsthal, but especially his lecture *Das
Schrifttum als geistiger Raum der Nation* (1927), show how prudent
it was of Valéry to exercise this kind of restraint. Hofmannsthal's theme has a great deal in common with Valéry's. As social
critics and cultural politicians both men were profoundly disturbed by the changes not only in the institutions but in the
mentality of Europe between the two wars. Indeed, Valéry's
analysis, in *La Politique de l'esprit*, of what technology and con-
formism were doing to that mentality is more devastating than
Hofmannsthal's fears, in his lecture, about the centrifugal *hubris*
of his contemporaries. Yet Valéry's "horror of prophecies"
prompted him to conclude his analysis with an admission that
he had "no solution, none," did not know what would become
of the human species, and could only advise his audience to be
prepared for anything, "or almost anything." Hofmannsthal attempted a synthesis; and in doing so he used the words "conservative revolution," crossing the dangerous borderline between
cultural analysis and active politics, between diagnosis and prescription. Hofmannsthal was not a Fascist or sympathizer with
Fascism, and the National Socialists were to ban his works because of one Jewish, or "non-Aryan," grandparent; but "conservative revolution" became the slogan of a number of extreme
nationalist and near-Fascist groups in Austria and Germany.
Hofmannsthal's exasperated conservatism, quite different in spirit
and intent from the programme of any political faction of that
or a later period, was modified by irony, self-criticism and liberalism in his imaginative works. In the public address, his poetic imagination proposed a solution more rhetorical and more
drastic, because the poetic imagination tends towards utopia,
apocalypse and prophecy when it is not engaged with the kind

of realities that engaged Hofmannsthal as a story-teller and dramatist.

Valéry knew his limitations. He knew that literary men are well qualified to offer social and cultural criticism, but tend to have "no solution, none," when it comes to the choice of evils inseparable from practical politics. Besides, Valéry's pervasive scepticism and his individualism always on the verge of solipsism made it difficult for him to take politics seriously. "All politics," he wrote, "are founded on the indifference of the majority of those involved; otherwise, no politics would be possible."[13] At best he could be a cynical observer of events to which he attached less importance than to changes in the intellectual habits and processes of his contemporaries: "Great events, perhaps, are only such for little minds. To more attentive minds it is the imperceptible and continuous events that count." Valéry, therefore, has next to nothing to say about the political movements and conflicts that were sweeping away his own individualist and bourgeois culture, though he excelled at the analysis of "more attentive minds." For all their political indiscretions, both Yeats and Hofmannsthal were on more intimate terms with the *Zeitgeist*, more responsive to the tremors and rumblings of a violent age. One reason is that both men were less inclined to solipsism than Valéry, more involved in the human condition generally, and more concerned with particular societies, their own.

IV

The German critic and philosopher Walter Benjamin, who became a Marxist in his later years, once remarked that Fascism "aestheticizes politics," whereas Communism "politicizes art."[14] He cites the Italian Futurist Marinetti as an instance of the Fascist apocalyptic who finds his satisfaction in war, proclaiming "*fiat ars—pereat mundus*"; and he comments: "That, clearly, is the consummation of l'art pour l'art."

There is enough truth in that generalization to make one wonder whether there is any middle way between the "aestheticization" of politics and the "politicization" of art. In the period that extends from the initiation of the "art for art's sake" principle to the 1920s—and *l'art pour l'art* was proclaimed as early as the 1830s by Théophile Gautier—that middle way was often

97

found in practice, though rarely in theory. From the start there was a tendency for poets to confuse the autonomy of art with the autonomy of the artist, a confusion that came easily to an age in which the artist was worshipped as a hero and "representative man." Paradoxically, that "representative man" insisted on his uniqueness, indeed, on all that separated and isolated him from humanity as a whole. Hence the pervasive uneasiness of poets about their "empirical selves" and the cult of masks or of impersonality which turned their uneasiness into a new imaginative and moral freedom. Without this freedom, used in a great variety of ways by a great variety of poets throughout Europe and America, there would have been no modern poetry of the kind that flourished internationally in the first half of the twentieth century. All the best poems of C. P. Cavafy, for instance, are historical *persona* poems that owe their subtlety and vividness to that freedom—so much so that Cavafy's empirical self is present only in its disguises, fulfilled itself only in its transformations. To a lesser degree this applies to most of the outstanding modern Greek poets, with their special ability to merge a modern sensibility in the figures and landscapes of history or myth. In the work of George Seferis personal experience—including political experience, doubts and fears about the state of his country, exile, loss, deprivation and recovery—is transformed with such delicacy into the figures and images that are its "objective correlative" that only irrelevant biographical information could prompt one to separate his empirical from his poetic self. So seemingly effortless and complete a transposition demands something other than a readiness to put on masks; in the case of Seferis the rival claims of aesthetics and experience have been truly reconciled, by an impersonality that is not an artistic device, but a conviction that the whole is greater than the part, the individual consciousness less important than what it contains. A similar conviction informs the work of T. S. Eliot, but the traditions to which he looked for sustenance of his impersonality were less easy to take for granted, less close at hand, more diversified, and more problematical. Eliot's early preoccupation with the work of Laforgue and Corbière, the self-questioners *par excellence,* indicates some of his difficulties.

Paul Valéry said that "tradition and progress are two great enemies of the human race"[15]—an example of his ingenious and mischievous humour—but went on to investigate the ambivalent, if not positively hostile, attitudes of nineteenth-century poets to progress in the sciences and technology. Edgar Allan Poe is cited as a writer of the Romantic period who opposed such progress, but made use of new discoveries in his works. In Poe's succession, Villiers de l'Isle-Adam, that out-and-out aesthete, was also one of the fathers of modern science fiction, in his novel *L'Eve future.* Romantic-Symbolist poetry, on the other hand, could not make even such ambiguous use of the sciences, because its specialization was an aesthetic one which inevitably conflicted with the increasing specialization of scientific enquiry and with a technology felt to be as materialistic as it was ruthlessly antagonistic to "the ceremony of innocence." Valéry's own work shows the extent of the rift between intellectual curiosity in prose and mythopoeic atavism in verse.

That rift could be satisfactorily closed or mended by those poets who worked in the more technically backward areas of Europe and America, or could draw without too much strain on memories of such a background. The Spanish poet Juan Ramón Jiménez, for instance, was still able to believe that "any one who progresses in one discipline (poetry, for example, religion, art or science, etc.) will inevitably progress in all others even though he may not consider them individually to be his."[16] The same poet attempted to reconcile the anti-progressive bias of Romantic-Symbolist poets with a humanist affirmation of liberal democracy; and so did his contemporary Antonio Machado and most of the next generation of Spanish poets, the generation of Lorca, Alberti, Aleixandre, Alonso, Guillén and Cernuda. In 1941, Jiménez redefined the terms "democracy" and "aristocracy" in such a way as to minimize their social and political incompatibilities. Yet the poetic imagination is revealed in his identification of "aristocracy" with the peasantry, because "there is no more exquisite form of aristocracy than living out of doors."[17] It is difficult to imagine any poet with a metropolitan background making that pronouncement in 1941 without hearing the mocking cackle of the sociologists at his back. Even Yeats's preference for the peasantry is regarded as a reactionary gesture—and Yeats was an Irishman. Jiménez, true, made it clear that his aristocracy was not the aristocracy of birth, which Yeats also glorified; but like Yeats he believed that "always and in

99

everything one must end with poetry, which is the unequalled expression of aristocracy."

These are the words of a poet who proved his preference for liberal democracy by leaving his country after the Civil War. That political and moral choice is one thing, the premises of Romantic-Symbolist poetry are another. As a poet, Jiménez could not conceive of a civilization without roots in nature and tradition. In another essay of that period he specifically distinguished poetry from literature. "The literary man scarcely ever makes a mistake," he noted; "he nearly always catches the plates he has tossed into the air, and if one falls it falls on somebody else's head. The poet customarily loses some plates, but they do not fall on any head, they are lost in the infinite because he is a good friend of space." The literary man, in other words, knows what he is doing and what he wants to do; but "poetry is never realized by everyone, it always escapes and the true poet, who is usually an honourable person because he has the habit of living with truth, knows how to let it escape. . . ." Jiménez concludes that "literature is a state of culture, poetry a state of grace, before and after culture."

Jiménez was perfectly right in implying that the primacy of the imagination in poetry forbids the total integration and assimilation of poetic values into any social or cultural order that exists in the modern world; and he was equally right to keep his political and moral choices separate from his knowledge that this is so. "The imagination is autonomous," he wrote, "and I am an imaginative autonomist."[18] Unlike so many of his fellow poets, however, he recognized the bounds of the autonomous imagination and refrained from aggressive sallies beyond its bounds. That was the purpose of his distinction between poetry and literature, the art exercised for its own sake, instinctively, and the craft "obsessed by the external world which it has to incorporate." Because poetry is "a state of grace"—"the poet, when mute or when writing, is an abstract dancer, and if he writes, it is out of an everyday weakness, for to be truly consistent he ought not to write. He who ought to write is the literary man."[19]

Yeats, Valéry and Hofmannsthal were a few of the many poets in the Romantic-Symbolist tradition who were fascinated by the mute arts, aspiring not so much to "the condition of music" as to the condition of silence; and "dance," as Frank Kermode has written, "is the most primitive, non-discursive art, offering a pre-scientific image of life, an intuitive truth. Thus it is the emblem of the Romantic image. Dance belongs to a period before the self and the world were divided, and so achieves naturally that 'original unity' which modern poetry can reproduce only by a great and exhausting effort."[20] Jiménez suggests that it is literature, not poetry, which ought to make that "great and exhausting effort." As a Spaniard it was easier for him than for most of the poets with whom Frank Kermode dealt in *Romantic Image* to preserve "the ceremony of innocence," and attain the simplicity and nakedness celebrated and enacted in his poem from *Eternidades* (1918) about poetry that begins

> Vino, primero, pura
> vestido de inocencia
>
> (Pure at first, she came,
> Clothed in innocence),

traces an intermediary stage of sophistication and adornment, but ends in praise of a poetry that has learnt to undress again, wholly this time, a "naked poetry." In a poem from the same collection Jiménez asks for that "intelligence" which provides "the exact names of things," and asks that his word may be "the thing itself," so that through him those who have no knowledge of things may reach them. As Rilke, Williams and Ponge did in very different ways, Jiménez puts himself at the disposal of things, losing himself in order to find himself. This transposition, too, required a "great and exhausting effort" on the part of poets confronted with things that were artifacts of the new technology. Jiménez had the advantage of not being provoked to pseudo-political gestures by the things that confronted him, since they were part of nature or of a way of life still largely pre-industrial. He could leave it to "literature" to accept or reject those other things, products of the machine age.

V

At the heart of every Romantic-Symbolist poet's aesthetic, then, there is a private religion, a *religio poetae* irreconcilable with the exigencies of the public world. In the case of Jiménez, his image of the "abstract dancer" betrays it. Essentially and inescapably, the abstract dance is non-political, solitary and anachronistic; but since it cannot be mute, because the poet's medium is words, the abstract dancer interrupts his dance to engage in "literature," if only by explaining himself to himself and looking for the link, never doubted though invisible, between his solitary performance and the needs of humanity as a whole.

At that point he must be prepared to "go out of himself," to meet others half-way and understand that in the social and political spheres imaginative values are not, and cannot be, absolute without a clash of autonomous imaginations. If he fails to make the adjustment he will align himself with absolute political creeds, mistaking their monomania for a dedication akin to his own, and seduced by promises of order.

Again and again readers of modern poetry are dismayed by revelations, often posthumous, that their favourite poets, "gentle" and retiring and "sensitive" persons, admired the most violent and ruthless politicians of their time. Yeats, at least, did not pretend to be gentle, and neither did D. H. Lawrence or Gottfried Benn. The strangest case of all is that of Rainer Maria Rilke, because Rilke's extreme eclecticism, apparent in the many successive phrases of his work, as in the multiplicity of his masks and *personae*, did rest on an explicit profession of gentleness, sensitiveness and compassion. Unlike his slightly older contemporary Stefan George, Rilke began not with a rigid aesthetic canon and a stance of rigorous exclusiveness, but a readiness to respond to almost any experience and avail himself of almost any literary model that came his way. After the Romantic practice of much of his early verse he followed the Naturalists— George's chief aversion—in a poetry of pity that drew on the megalopolitan scene of his time, mainly by a self-identification with its outcasts, the poor, the sick and the oppressed. Then came the pseudo-Christian and pseudo-mystical lyricism of the *Stundenbuch*, anticipated, it's true, by a good many of the more personal poems in *Das Buch der Bilder*—and the reaction against its subjectivity in the "thing poems" of *Neue Gedichte*, written under the influence of Rodin and Cézanne as a deliberate attempt to apply the disciplines of the visual arts to poetry. In the critical years between 1908 and the completion of the *Duineser Elegien* and *Sonette an Orpheus* in 1922, Rilke proved receptive to many

new trends in poetry, in the other arts and in society, a seemingly cosmopolitan mind at home in the palaces and slums of
Europe, in touch with aristocrats and working men, open to the
"pure" poetry of Valéry as to the less "pure" poetry of Super-
vielle and to the decidedly committed poetry of the politically
revolutionary German Expressionists. It is in the poems written, but not collected, in this period that Rilke's diverse exper-
iments made him a decidedly modernist poet, far in advance of
his near-coevals, George and Hofmannsthal. (Hofmannsthal, in
any case, had turned to drama and various forms of imaginative or expository prose in his desperate endeavours to bridge
the gap between Romantic-Symbolist art and society.)

It was not till 1956, thirty years after Rilke's death, that his
Lettres milanaises, 1921–1926,[21] written in French to the Italian
Duchess Aurelia Gallarati-Scotti, showed him to have been as
ambiguous about the new nationalism in Europe as he had been
about the First World War. His notorious rootlessness did not
prevent him from telling the Duchess that "internationalism" and
"humanism" are no more than abstract ideas—and this is the
context of defence of Mussolini's Fascism. To the same correspondent he wrote:

> It would have been difficult for me to be a soldier any-
> where else, but I could have been one with conviction and
> enthusiasm in one of those countries, if I had been born
> there: an Italian soldier, a French soldier, yes, I could have
> been one, confraternally, to the point of the supreme sac-
> rifice: to such an extent does nationality in those two
> countries seem to us bound up with gesture, with action,
> with the visible example. Amongst you, even more than in
> France, blood truly is *one* and, at some moments, the idea,
> borne along by this blood, can also be *one*.[22]

In his admiration for Mussolini Rilke was in good company,
including Yeats, Wallace Stevens, Ezra Pound and D. H. Lawrence; but these writers had not flirted with Romain Rolland's
pan-European pacifist movement, as Rilke had, or made semi-
autobiographical fiction out of the sufferings of a sensitive pupil
in a military academy, as Rilke had done in his story *Die Turns-
tunde,* as well as glorifying military honour and self-sacrifice in

103

his most popular prose work, *Die Weise von Liebe und Tod des Cornets Christoph Rilke* (1899). That same early work had announced the theme of a mystique of blood and race which Rilke expounds in the letter with a vicarious and devious patriotism which may well have made the Duchess smile, if she did not share the high religious seriousness characteristic of most of Rilke's female correspondents.

There is a recurrent vacillation in all Rilke's work between the *personae* of aristocrat and pariah, a vacillation especially apparent in the Parisian episodes of *Die Aufzeichungen des Malte Laurids Brigge,* as in the section headed *Bibliothèque Nationale.* The vacillation goes back to Baudelaire, whose presence is so conspicuous in those episodes. In *Malte Laurids Brigge,* too, Rilke writes of the need for masks: "I had never seen masks before, but I realized at once that there must be masks,"[23] and the mask that Brigge puts on takes possession of him, driving out his familiar self, though the identity and character of the mask are dubious and undefined. Rilke's extraordinary richness as a lyrical poet is inseparable from a "negative capability," a gift of empathy, which, outside his poems, led him into almost every conceivable absurdity. No other poet of his time had so fluid a personality, so wide a range of masks and styles; but also of sympathies and attitudes which exclude and contradict one another as soon as we look at them from a pragmatic or logical point of view. That is why inestimable harm has been done to Rilke's work by the posthumous publication of his letters and private documents.

VI

Early in 1927, not many months after Rilke's death, his daughter wrote to Hugo von Hofmannsthal to tell him of plans for the posthumous publication of work by Rilke and ask Hofmannsthal's advice and cooperation. Hofmannsthal, who believed that the era of bourgeois individualism was over, and who had evolved a doctrine of impersonality not unlike that of T. S. Eliot, replied:

> . . . If I felt my death drawing very close, I should leave
> instructions in a sense almost diametrically opposed. I

should do all I could—in so far as anything can be done in this disconnected world of ours—to suppress all those tiresome and often indiscreet statements about a productive individual and his works, all that diluting chatter, or at least to deprive it of nourishment as far as possible by the removal of private letters and notes, by putting difficulties in the way of that inane biography-mania and all indecencies of that kind. My idea would be to really entrust the hardly explicable phenomenon that once existed here, R.M.R. or H.H., to death, even to oblivion if need be (except in the hearts of a few loyal men and women), and leave the works to engage unaided in their hard secret struggle with the next hostile decades. . . .[24]

It may look as though Rilke's reputation had not only withstood these hostile decades, but reversed the usual process by turning hostility into unstinted homage. Editions of his poems, prose works and letters, translations into countless languages, biographies, memoirs, critical studies and academic theses have jostled one another at a rate that must be almost unique in modern literature. To many of his readers Rilke was not a poet, but *the* poet, the reincarnation in his time of the archetypal Orpheus whose myth he revived and celebrated in the *Sonnets.* Yet his work appealed to many different kinds of readers and satisfied many different needs. It was as exquisitely musical and pictorial as the poetry of the French Symbolists and their German successor, Stefan George, yet without being deliberately recondite and exclusive; and though firmly based on an aesthetic akin to theirs, it was open to that order of reality which had been the province of the opposing school, the Naturalists. It ranged from the intense self-communion of the *Stundenbuch* to the seemingly social preoccupations of the *Buch der Bilder* and the seeming absorption in things of the *Neue Gedichte.* During the critical years that followed, Rilke came to terms with the new styles and energies that might so easily have left him stranded. Like Yeats, and unlike Valéry, George or Hofmannsthal, he entered yet another new phase as a distinctly "modern"—post-1914—poet. Most important of all, as far as his reputation is concerned, he annexed so much "life" to a basically autonomous art, so much of the language of religious mystical communion to a basically individualistic outlook, that like no other

105

poet of his time he seemed to offer a new existential philosophy and a new morality. This philosophic and didactic function can be discounted as one of those misunderstandings on which, as he said, the fame of artists rests; but it has become as difficult to separate from Rilke's fame as our knowledge of his person from his poetry.

Hofmannsthal knew that his own choice entailed other difficulties and dangers, and foresaw the eclipse which his own work was to suffer during those hostile decades; but, now that Rilke's struggle has begun in earnest, it will soon be all too clear that Hofmannsthal's warning was apt and right. Four decades after Rilke's death the spate of publications continues as though nothing had happened; but more and more readers of poetry turn from Rilke's poetry with a feeling little short of disgust. The myth so beautifully sustained in his later poetry has been blasted by a barrage of biographical "indecencies"; the philosophy well and truly debunked by critical examinations.

If poetry, as well as poets, were subject to the moral criteria which one applies to the actions and decisions of public figures, it would be reasonable to blame Rilke for some of the posthumous indignities which his work has suffered. It was he who wrote those copious letters with an unmistakable squint at posterity. It was he who sowed the seeds of the philosophical and theological criticism that has discredited his most ambitious work, in confessions and manifestos like his *Letters to a Young Poet, Letter from a Young Artisan* and his letters to his Polish translator about the *Duino Elegies*. Almost from the start Rilke claimed an absolute authority. His early autobiographical story *Ewald Tragy* contains this casual remark: "I am my own legislator and King; there is no one above me, not even God." Yet as far as his poetry is concerned this question of responsibility is simply irrelevant. The truth of poetry is of a different order. If we cannot dissociate the poetry from the pretensions and vanities—let alone the harmless foibles—of the man, it is we who are the losers; and only a small part of Rilke's poetry calls for a "suspension of disbelief." The part in question—mainly sections of the *Duino Elegies* and *Sonnets to Orpheus*—is that in which Rilke made the mistake of formulating his private *religio poetae*, instead of using it to write poetry. That private religion was an auxiliary religion with little relevance or validity outside and beyond Rilke's poetry. The angels of the *Duino Elegies,* for instance, are not to be confused with the angels of theology, since they were secular angels, the functionaries not of faith but of imagination. Like the angel of Wallace Stevens, they were "necessary angels of the earth" within an imaginative system, but nowhere else; and indeed there is an extraordinary accordance between the private religions of Rilke and Wallace Stevens, both of whom were theologians of the poetic imagination, hierophants of the earthly, but especially of things and places. "Life is an affair of people and places," Stevens wrote. "But for me life is an affair of places and that is the trouble."[25]

That was Rilke's trouble, too, though he could never have said so as bluntly and straightforwardly. Rilke's crisis poems of the years 1912 to 1914, particularly the poems *Wendung, Klage, Narziss* and *Waldteich,* render his awareness of what he had lost by being unable to relate himself to people—people as independent agents, not as *personae* to be filled with his own "inwardness"—as completely as he had related himself to landscapes, plants, animals and artifacts. In other words, Rilke knew that his relation to people had been no different from his relation to those things which do not and cannot answer back. His Narcissus poem contains the line

Er liebte, was ihm ausging, wieder ein

(Back into himself he loved that which went out of him)

an admirably precise description of the whole process by which Rilke assimilated the world to his imagination without ever giving any part of himself away in a more than imaginative involvement. The woodland pond of *Waldteich* is an image of the same seeming reciprocity of world and mind, a reciprocity threatened or broken by the awareness that there are storms and oceans beyond the woodland pond's stillness, "turned in upon itself." In a poem of the same period, *To Hölderlin,*[26] Rilke adds this comment to his Narcissus, pond and mirror images:

Seen
Sind erst im Ewigen. Hier ist Fallen
das Tüchtigste.

(Lakes
don't exist till eternity. Here
falling's the best we can do.)

And the poem *Wendung* (Turning-Point)[27] hinges on the distinction between the active contemplation by which things or places can be assimilated and transformed, and human relations that demand a measure of self-sacrifice, a love that gives as well as takes:

> Werk des Gesichts ist getan,
> tue nun Herz-Werk
> an den Bildern in dir, jenen gefangenen; denn du
> überwältigtest sie: aber nun kennst du sie nicht.

> (Work of seeing is done,
> now practise heart-work
> upon those images captive within you, for you
> overpowered them only; but now do not know them.)

VII

Rilke's political inconsistencies and absurdities may seem to have nothing to do with that personal crisis, a crisis that was never resolved in his life, as distinct from his work. Yet the failure to love others instead of projecting himself into them, "overpowering" them and exploiting them imaginatively, is not really distinct from Rilke's failure to see the political world as anything other than a screen on which to project his private feelings and attitudes. Both failures were those of an "imaginative autonomist," a maker of "supreme fictions" who could not get himself to believe in those realities which defy the creative imagination.

The term "supreme fictions" is another borrowing from Wallace Stevens, whose *religio poetae* was almost identical with Rilke's. "What makes the poet the potent figure that he is, or was, or ought to be," Stevens wrote, "is that he creates the world to which we turn incessantly and without knowing it, and that he gives to life the supreme fictions without which we are unable to conceive of it."[28] The poet "has had immensely to do with giving life whatever savour it possesses. He has had to do with whatever the imagination and the senses have made of the world." "The world about us would be desolate except for the world within us." "Besides, unreal things have a reality of their own, in poetry as elsewhere." Poetry "is an interdependence of the imagination and reality as equals." "It comes to this, that poetry is a part of the structure of reality." All these statements from Wallace Stevens's *The Necessary Angel* are part of what he called "poetry's mystical theology," the formulation of which in Rilke's *Duino Elegies* has given so much offence to his Christian and humanist critics alike. "The major poetic idea in the world is and always has been the idea of God," Wallace Stevens also wrote;[29] and: "After one has abandoned a belief in God, poetry is the essence which takes its place as life's redemption." The poet becomes "the priest of the invisible," words that recall Rilke's to his Polish translator about the "bees of the invisible." In both cases the imagination has taken the place of that transcendent order on whose existence outside the imagination most of the great religions insist.

This "mystical theology," then, is at once materialistic—since its starting point is empirical—and irrational, if not antirational. For all his emphasis on thinking in poetry—an emphasis just as marked in Rilke—Stevens said that "rational beings are canaille,"[30] and: "The poem reveals itself only to the ignorant man," because "poetry must resist the intelligence almost successfully." Above all, the "real" must not be confused with the rational or even with the realistic mode in the arts. Reality has to be transformed by the imagination before it is truly perceived. That is what Stevens meant in saying that "in the long run, the truth does not matter." This truth is a fixed truth, the truth held on to once and for all either by reason or by faith. Poetry, on the other hand, is a perpetual two-way traffic between experience and imagination. Poets like himself, Stevens said repeatedly, are "thinkers without final thoughts,"

> In an always incipient cosmos,
> The way, when we climb a mountain,
> Vermont throws itself together.[31]

There are also poets with final thoughts, of course, and Stevens distinguished between "adherents of the imagination" and "adherents of the central," whose ambition is "to press away from mysticism toward that ultimate good sense which we term civilization."[32] T. S. Eliot and Hofmannsthal were "adherents of the central," Rilke and Stevens, on the other hand, cannot be tied down by a philosophically anchored criticism. Every overall interpretation of Rilke's or Stevens's thought—rather than of their thinking—must treat it as though it were definitive, as though their discoveries were codifications, their flashes of recognition (within a particular context) the articles of a creed. The result is like using a lasso to catch a humming-bird.

"Poetry is a satisfying of the desire for resemblance,"[33] Stevens wrote. The satisfying of this desire is rarely contained within the bounds of a poet's beliefs, even if he is a poet who holds beliefs. The imagination picks up its resemblances wherever it can find them. If it needs angels it will take them from a religion which the poet cannot accept, or actively opposes, as Rilke opposed Christianity. Unscrupulous as such habits may seem, not only Christian mystics but sober apologists and preachers are equally apt to borrow metaphors and analogies from worldly pursuits which they have no intention of glorifying. The medium of language is to blame.

Granted that Stevens's and Rilke's thinking scarcely "works" outside the sphere in which poetic processes, or their analogues, apply, we are forced every day of our lives to allow for specializations of this order. Railway tickets can't be cashed at the bank, though they represent money. To write great poetry is quite enough for one man to achieve in "this disconnected world of ours." That the truths of some poetry are partial and provisional truths does not make them less valuable. It is up to the reader of poetry not to approach it with expectations and demands which it cannot, by its nature, fulfil.

VIII

In taking issue with the "politicization of art," in the form of what he took to be a Marxist rejoinder to his poem *The Idea of Order at Key West*, Stevens remarked parenthetically: "(I am pro-Mussolini personally)."[34] This casual admission is almost irrelevant to Stevens's poetry, not excluding the poem *Mr Burnshaw and the Statue*[35] that was his answer to political criticism. In that poem Stevens sees Communism as directed towards an unreal and unrealizable future, as a utopian religion that denies the thing in favour of the idea. Stevens's mysticism, like Rilke's, begins with the visible world:

> the apple in the orchard, round
> And red, will not be redder, rounder then
> Than now . . .

Fascist ideology does not enter into the poem. Yet a predilection for the past is as much a premise of Stevens's poetry as it is of Yeats's, Rilke's, Eliot's and Ezra Pound's; and one could well argue that all these poets' treatment of the past is no less utopian than the Marxist ideology which Stevens opposed in the poem. This, again, has to do with the poetic imagination, which is "conservative," as Hofmannsthal said, because the past is less abstract than the future. However elusive as a whole, the past is a repository of fragments that are palpable to the imagination and can therefore be "shored against one's ruins."

Rilke's opposition to the machine, which "threatens all we have acquired as long as it does not obey but lays claim on the mind,"[36] belongs to the same Romantic-Symbolist complex; and so does the anti-capitalism of a sonnet in the same sequence, No. XIX of Part II of the *Sonnets to Orpheus,* in which Rilke shows his ability, also apparent in passages of the *Duino Elegies,* to incorporate the idioms and phenomena of contemporary civilization into a kind of poetry that is radically antagonistic to them. The money that "lives somewhere in the pampering bank, acting familiar with thousands," is contrasted with the figure of the blind beggar, a figure that recalls Rilke's early *Buch der Bilder:*

> In den Geschäften entlang ist das Geld wie zuhause
> und verkleidet sich scheinbar in Seide, Nelken und Pelz.
> Er, der Schweigende, steht in der Atempause
> alles des wach oder schlafend atmenden Gelds.

> (In the length of those shops money's as though in its place,
> at home, and seems to dress up in silk, carnations and furs.
> He, the silent, stands in the breathing-space
> of all that money which breathes as it sleeps or stirs.)

111

Here we come up against the dilemma of all the many poets who thought if only briefly that Fascism offered an alternative to the primacy of economics in both capitalism and Marxism, a primacy obscured in Fascist ideology by emotionally primitivist gestures. Rilke did not live to see how far Fascism would go in its mechanization of the mind. Wallace Stevens did; and in a later letter[37] he wrote: "For a long time, I have thought of adding other sections to the *Notes [toward a Supreme Fiction]* and one in particular: *It Must Be Human.*"

> The heaven of Europe is empty, like a Schloss
> Abandoned because of taxes . . .

Stevens had written in *The Greenest Continent* (1945), and in the tenth of Rilke's *Duino Elegies* there are related images of desolation characterizing modern Europe, like the "market of consolations," bounded by the church "bought ready made,"

reinlich und zu und enttäuscht wie ein Postamt am Sonntag

(clean, disappointed and shut like the post office on a Sunday).

This is the negative use of modernity also to be found in T. S. Eliot and Ezra Pound's *Mauberley* sequence, as in much modern poetry, other than that by Communists and Futurists, written up to the Second World War. There is no complete agreement as to what the imaginations of the different poets of this period wanted to conserve; but all looked to past, all were preoccupied with tradition as something alive and precious, more alive and more precious than the paraphernalia of contemporary civilization. In a late poem, *Recitation after Dinner*,[38] Stevens found this metaphor for tradition (which means "carrying over," an active sense that is often forgotten by those who use words less attentively and scrupulously than the poets):

> It has a clear, a single, a solid form,
> That of the son who bears upon his back
> The father that he loves, and bears him from
> The ruins of the past, out of nothing left,
> Made noble by the honour he receives,

As if in a golden cloud. The son restores
The father. He hides his ancient blue beneath
His own bright red. But he bears him out of love,
His life made double by his father's life,
Ascending the humane . . .

In their concern with things on the one hand, a supreme
(and aesthetically satisfying) fiction on the other, these poets were
inclined to forget Stevens's addendum, *It Must Be Human,* if that
is taken to mean that every kind of human need, not only the
aesthetic and imaginative, must be taken into account. Commenting on the work of St-John Perse, a poet who has continued to write imaginatively "absolute" poetry even after the Second
World War, Kathleen Raine has pointed to "an element entirely
absent from the writings of St-John Perse—the human as such.
The poet stops short, in his account of man, precisely with what
is (in terms of all the higher religions) precisely human in man,
his individual being. The gods whom he invokes are old pan-
theistic gods. . . ."[39] I shall have more to say elsewhere of the
longing for primordially uncomplicated ways of life in certain
poets who put up a desperate fight against complexities intrac-
table to the imagination; but Stevens's words could also mean
that the supreme fiction cannot be other than human, because
the imagination is a human faculty, however little use it may have
for human manifestations like those listed in E. E. Cummings's
love-hate poem about humanity:

> humanity i love you because you
> are perpetually putting the secret of
> life in your pants and forgetting
> it's there and sitting down
>
> on it
> and because you are
> forever making poems in the lap
> of death Humanity
>
> i hate you[40]

The same ambivalence pervades other poems by Cummings, like the one beginning

113

> pity this busy monster, manunkind,
> not[41]

or the one beginning "what if a much of a which of a wind," in which every sort of destruction—even of the universe—is cheerfully accepted because

> the most who die, the more we live.[42]

These are playful poems, intended to disturb and make fun of the solemn humanitarian commonplaces. That, too, is one of the useful functions of poetry, though to the puritanical and literal-minded the playfulness of Cummings will seem as irresponsible as Rilke's and Stevens's delight in the rich resources of both formal and informal language, simply as the material for intricate inventions.

As even Yeats recognized, the "politicization of art" in this century has placed too great a burden of responsibility on the poetic imagination. Rilke, that almost monomaniacally dedicated poet, at one time considered giving up poetry to become a country doctor. And Yeats wrote:

> I think it better that in times like these
> A poet's mouth be silent, for in truth
> We have no gift to set a statesman right.[43]

The more heavily their social conscience came to weigh on poets, the more difficult it became for them to produce a body of work as consistent in quality as that of Yeats, Rilke, Stevens or St-John Perse. Such major work required the kind of specialization to which many poets no longer feel they have a right, a specialization not only of craft but of vision; "One of the essential conditions to the writing of poetry," Stevens wrote in a letter,[44] "is impetus. That is a reason for thinking that to be a poet at all one ought to be a poet constantly. It was a great loss to poetry when people began to think that the professional poet was an outlaw or an exile. Writing poetry is a conscious activity. While poems may very well occur, they had very much better be caused." Only very few poets opposed to the Romantic-Symbolist aesthetic—usually on conscientious grounds—have found it possible to be poets constantly; many more have lost impetus not only because of economic or political pressures, but because of a deep distrust of the autonomous imagination and its ataistic affinities.

NOTES

1. Yeats, in *Autobiographies*, London, 1955, p. 487; American edition, p. 297.
2. Riding and Graves, ibid., pp. 227, 254–55.
3. *The White Goddess*, London, 1951, p. 14.
4. *On the Modern Mind*, in *Encounter*, Vol. XXIV, No. 5, p. 18.
5. *Yeats and Fascism*, in *The New Statesman*, 26 February 1965; reprinted in *Excited Reverie*, London, 1965.
6. In *Partisan Review*, Vol. XXXIII, No. 3, pp. 339–61.
7. From *High Talk. Last Poems and Plays*, London, 1940, p. 73; *The Collected Poems of William Butler Yeats*, New York, 1956, p. 331.
8. *Essays and Introductions*, pp. 203, 225, 339, 511, 526.
9. From *Meru. A Full Moon in March*, London, 1935, p. 70; *The Collected Poems*, New York, 1956, p. 287.
10. *Autobiographies*, p. 469; American edition, pp. 284 f.
11. *Tel Quel II*, Paris, 1943, p. 65.
12. Ibid., p. 43.
13. *Regards sur le monde actuel*, Paris, 1931, pp. 95, 101; *History and Politics*, p. 248.
14. Walter Benjamin: *Das Kunstwerk im Zeitalter seiner technischen Reproduzierbarkeit*, in *Schriften*, Frankfurt, 1955, Vol. I, p. 397; English version by Harry Fohn, in Benjamin: *Illuminations*, New York, 1968, pp. 243 f.
15. *Regards sur le monde actuel*, p. 174; *History and Politics*, p. 394.
16. *The Selected Writings of Juan Ramón Jiménez*, translated by H. R. Hays, New York, 1957, p. 214.
17. Ibid., pp. 188, 196, 200, 202.
18. Ibid., p. 251.
19. Ibid., p. 199.
20. Frank Kermode: *Puzzles and Epiphanies*, London, 1962, p. 4.
21. Paris, 1956.
22. Translated by Eudo C. Mason in *Rilke, Europe and the English-Speaking World*, Cambridge, 1961, p. 13. The same writer gives a full account of Rilke's political attitudes, their complexities and contradictions.
23. R. M. Rilke: *Gesammelte Werke*, Leipzig, 1927, Vol. III, p. 127.
24. From a letter dated Rodaun, 24 April 1927, unpublished as far as I know, given to me in a typed transcription by Hofmannsthal's widow, Gerty von Hofmannsthal, who copied it from the original.
25. Wallace Stevens: *Opus Posthumous*, New York, 1957, p. 158.
26. English version by David Luke in *Modern German Poetry: 1910–60*, London and New York, 1962, pp. 29–31.
27. Ibid., pp. 25–27.
28. Wallace Stevens: *The Necessary Angel*, New York, 1951, pp. 4, 30, 31, 81, 169.
29. *Opus Posthumous*, pp. xv, 158.
30. Ibid., pp. 160, 171, 227.
31. Ibid., p. 115.
32. *The Necessary Angel*, p. 116.
33. Ibid., p. 77.
34. Letter to R. L. Latimer, 31 October 1935; *Letters*, New York, 1966, p. 289.

35. *Opus Posthumous*, pp. 46–52.
36. *Sonette an Orpheus*, Leipzig, 1923, pp. 44, 53.
37. To Robert Pack, 28 December 1954. *Letters*, p. 863.
38. *Opus Posthumous*, pp. 86–88.
39. Kathleen Raine: *Defending Ancient Springs*, Oxford, 1967, p. 186.
40. *Poems 1923–54*, New York, 1954, p. 152; *Selected Poems 1923–58*, London, 1960, p. 11.
41. Ibid., New York, p. 397; London, p. 56.
42. Ibid., New York, p. 401; London, p. 58.
43. From *On Being Asked for a War Poem*, in *Later Poems*, London, 1931, p. 287.
44. To R. L. Latimer, 8 January 1935; *Letters*, p. 274.

Poet and State*

STANLEY KUNITZ

> *Geniuses are like a storm; they come up against*
> *the wind; terrify men; clean the atmosphere.*
> SØREN KIERKEGAARD

> *"It is impossible to remake the country." Quite*
> *so, but it is not impossible to remake the country in*
> *the* imagination. . . . *I want to place a value on*
> *everything I touch.* . . .
> WILLIAM CARLOS WILLIAMS

I begin with a parable. When Andrei Voznesensky was a young man, he aspired to be an architect. One day a terrible thing happened. The Moscow Architectural Institute, where he was enrolled, went up in smoke, abruptly terminating his studies. Voznesensky celebrated the event in a poem that created something of a sensation. My version of it reads:

> *Fire in the Architectural Institute!*
> *through all the rooms and over the blueprints*
> *like an amnesty through the jails . . .*
> *Fire! Fire!*

> *High on the sleepy façade*
> *shamelessly, mischievously*
> *like a red-assed baboon*
> *a window skitters.*

> *We'd already written our theses,*
> *the time had come for us to defend them.*

*Based on a lecture delivered at the Cooper Union School of Art and Architecture, New York, April 22, 1970.

117

They're crackling away in a sealed cupboard:
all those bad reports on me!

The drafting paper is wounded,
it's a red fall of leaves;
my drawing boards are burning,
whole cities are burning.

Five summers and five winters shoot up in flames
like a jar of kerosene.
Karen, my pet,
Oi! we're on fire!

Farewell architecture:
it's down to a cinder
for all those cowsheds decorated with cupids
and those rec halls in rococo!

O youth, phoenix, ninny,
your dissertation is hot stuff,
flirting its little red skirt now,
flaunting its little red tongue.

Farewell life in the sticks!
Life is a series of burned-out sites.
Nobody escapes the bonfire:
if you live—you burn.

But tomorrow, out of these ashes,
more poisonous than a bee
your compass point will dart
to sting you in the finger.

Everything's gone up in smoke,
and there's no end of people sighing.
It's the end? *It's only the beginning.*
*Let's go to the movies!**

Why is the poet so in love with that fire? A good citizen should deplore the destruction of property, especially of state property. The poet is drawn to that fire because it reveals itself

*From *Antiworlds,* by Andrei Voznesensky, edited by Patricia Blake and Max Hayward, Basic Books, New York, 1966, p. 57.

to him as a metaphor for rage, for a passion burning beyond control, for a new and beautiful disorder that will make a shambles of the old Establishment. Those flames are fanned by a fresh wind blowing through the mind. In this poem, early in his career, Voznesensky affiliates himself with the great art of the West, which persists in opposing the solitary conscience to the overwhelming power of the corporate state.

So too, but with an opposite emphasis, the central theme of both Greek and Elizabethan tragedy is the irreconcilable conflict between individual will, passion, or genius and the dictates of a higher authority, whether sacred or secular. Shakespeare's major tragedies characteristically show us a state in the throes of convulsion induced by human weakness or error in high places. Those whose behavior threatens the security or stability of the kingdom must be beaten down. The stage is piled high with their corpses. In the end, when the turmoil has subsided, the new emblem of authority—Fortinbras or his equivalent—appears on the scene, to a flourish of trumpets. By the sacrifice of the hubristic ego, order has been restored.

The connection between good government and right words—of which poetry is the paradigm—has several facets. Confucius was once asked what he would do first if it were left for him to administer a country. As recorded in the *Analects,* the Master said: "It would certainly be to correct language." His listeners were surprised. "Surely," they said, "this has nothing to do with the matter. Why should language be corrected?" The Master's answer was: "If language is not correct, then what is said is not what is meant; if what is said is not meant, then what ought to be done remains undone; if this remains undone, morals and arts will deteriorate; if morals and arts deteriorate, justice will go astray; if justice goes astray, the people will stand in helpless confusion. Hence there must be no arbitrariness in what is said. This matters above everything."

Plato, on the other hand, felt that the right words for the poet might be the wrong words for the state. In justifying his proposal to expel "the makers" from his ideal Republic, he specifies that he has nothing against poets who know their place and are content to exercise their craft by writing hymns to the gods and praises of famous men. The poets to guard against are those who nourish the passions and desires. These are the sons of Dionysus, the god of wine and ecstasy, as opposed to the rulers of the state, who are sons of Apollo, a relatively moderate divinity. And he asks, in effect, the same sort of question that has issued from the vicinity of the White House in modern times: "How can you hope to preserve law and order if you permit these enemies of reason and decorum to run wild in the streets and disturb the population with their obscenities? Sometimes they get drunk. Sometimes they even get inspired. The reckless god turns them on."

I must have had Plato's animadversions in mind when I wrote in a poem some years ago, before the cracks in the public marble became visible:

> *Perhaps there's too much order in this world.*
> *The poets love to haul disorder in,*
> *Braiding their wrists with her long mistress hair.*

But that is only part of the picture, and I am ready to concede that in certain of his aspects the poet—including the Shakespearian archetype—is a fairly conservative fellow, who has earned whatever grants and honors the establishment chooses to heap on him. For one thing, no matter how iconoclastic he may profess to be, he realizes that he comes of a long line, and that his art is the momentary product of an ancient tradition, which will ultimately claim his words, if they have enough juice in them, and pass them on to the next generation.

Indeed, the poet is a Confucian of a sort, for he reveres his ancestors and acknowledges his debt to them. If, through personal or cultural privation, he is uncertain of his ancestors, he will spend his life, if need be, in search of them. Long before Frantz Fanon advised "the wretched of the earth" that if they were to have a future they must first create a past, poets were busy with their myth-making. And the posterity that poets keep in mind, and for which some of them foolishly write, is one that understands their language and inherits their values.

Form itself may be construed as a means of diverting subversive energies into productive channels. Even a rejection of "the System" gets incorporated into a system. If the poet celebrates, according to his temper, the life of the senses; if his mind is enchanted by the splendor and purity of forms; if he loves, in Keats's phrase, "the principle of beauty in all things," he serves to make existence more tolerable for others. At the least he is "the solitary who makes others less alone."

Since the poet's defense of order is unwitting and disguised, he should not expect to be thanked for it. I can recall how shocked I was early in my teaching experience, when the president of a girls' college told me that my course in "Creative Writing"—obnoxious term!—was exerting a pernicious influence on his charges. "All it does," he said, "is stir up the little bitches." I could not in good conscience reply that I was instructing them in an art designed to comfort, tranquilize, or console. Certainly the modern poets I cherish most are disturbing spirits: they do not come to coo.

The revolutionary is concerned with changing others; the poet wants to change himself. This does not make him less of a radical force. I recall Christopher Caudwell's shrewd observation, in *Illusion and Reality,* that the poet in his search for perfection inadvertently keeps alive the image of an ideal condition. In particular, the Romantic poet is inspired by love for a lost Eden, or for a Paradise not yet made. And a curious circumstance explains why the guardians of the state are right not to put their trust in him. Those kingdoms of his imagination become the reality of others. The news that breaks from them foments discontent with things as they are.

Hypothetically the state approximates the condition of the poem in its ability to maintain a precarious balance of order and freedom, tradition and change, tension and release. "The art of a free society," wrote Alfred North Whitehead, "consists, first, in the maintenance of the symbolic code; and secondly, in fearlessness of revision. . . . Those societies which cannot combine reverence to their symbols with freedom of revision must simultaneously decay." In Whitehead's formula, politics and poetry are made subject to the same law. Their vigor depends on an unremitting reciprocity between pastness and possibility. When the connecting syntax breaks down, the poles fly apart. Tradition deteriorates into orthodoxy or conformity, possibility into futurism or novelty.

The mind lives by its contradictions. And the poetic imagination must oppose any form of oppression, including the oppression of the mind by a single idea. Petty bureaucrats, party

121

hacks, poetasters, all those who have failed, in Chekhov's phrase, to squeeze the serf out of their veins, can be counted on to do the oppressor's dirty work for him.

In a revolutionary period the activists are understandably disappointed in artists who do not overtly serve their movement. The Irish fighters for freedom despised Yeats for his failure to give them his unqualified support, not realizing that it was he who would immortalize their names and their cause:

> *I write it out in verse—*
> *MacDonagh and MacBride*
> *And Connolly and Pearse*
> *Now and in time to be,*
> *Wherever green is worn,*
> *Are changed, changed utterly:*
> *A terrible beauty is born.*

I can recall how vehemently the theologians of the left denounced American writers in the thirties who refrained from producing agitprop tracts. Those who were most abusive were the very ones who later felt that they had been betrayed by their dogma. Some of them turned eventually into reactionary scolds. The Weathermen of the sixties—idealists, most of them, intoxicated by their faith in the holiness of violence—were, in their turn, incapable of grasping that a society bereft of the graces and values that the arts perpetuate would not be a society worth inheriting.

I think of the poet as the representative free man of our time. Since the Industrial Revolution anyone who works for himself and alone has become a rarity. The writer is more different from others than ever because of his immediate, whole, and solitary relation to his work in the midst of a society where men labor in packs or gangs and are productive only in bits and pieces. Among writers the poet is freer than his brothers the novelist and playwright, because his work, unlike theirs, is practically worthless as a commodity. He is less subject than they to the pressure to modify the quality of his work in order to produce an entertainment. Nothing he can do will make his labor profitable. He might as well yield to the beautiful temptation to strive towards the purity of an absolute art. How much more fortunate he is than the contemporary painter or sculptor, whose work has become preeminently a thing to be bought and sold on the auction block at the whim of hustling speculators and custodians!

The modern crisis in poetry is older than most of us think. It goes back in time to a pair of related phenomena, the triumph of reason and the Industrial Revolution. With the Enlightenment, when rationalism became king, the church could no longer offer itself as a chalice in which to pour the wine of transcendence. Art divined itself as a substitute for religion, whereby men could satisfy their old need to belong to eternity as well as to time. The Industrial Revolution threatened people by proposing to turn them into wage-slaves—which indeed it did! It threatened the natural universe, that broad perspective of images, by polluting the landscape, by defiling Eden. Into the gardens of the West crept Satan, in the form of the wily entrepreneur. This is what the English poets at the dawn of the nineteenth century were trying to say, with varying degrees of awareness of what it was that alarmed them. "We have given our hearts away, a sordid boon!" cried Wordsworth. Blake, whose voice gets clearer every year, cursed the "dark Satanic Mills" and promised not to "cease from Mental Fight/ . . . Till we have built Jerusalem/ In England's green and pleasant Land." In Victorian England, when the battle was all but lost, the Jesuit Hopkins, who still clung to his faith that "nature is never spent;/ There lives the dearest freshness deep down things," protested, for an audience not yet born:

> *Generations have trod, have trod, have trod;*
> *And all is seared with trade; bleared, smeared with toil;*
> *And wears man's smudge and shares man's smell; the soil*
> *Is bare now, nor can foot feel, being shod.*

The poet knows that his roots, the roots of being, strike deep into the biosphere; that the entire living creation is sacred to him; that whoever cuts him off from his source withers him; that whoever despoils, defoliates, hates, kills, is his enemy. In Blake's lacerating words: "Each outcry of the hunted hare/ A fibre from the brain doth tear." Coleridge felt man's inhumanity so strongly that he risked blemishing his masterpiece by ap-

123

pending to it a moral tag: "He prayeth well who loveth well/ Both Man and bird and beast."

The God whom Coleridge invokes is the God "of all things, both great and small." But in the distribution of souls the Church subscribes to a restrictive covenant. The prime offense of Christianity against nature is that it has concerned itself with the salvation of man at the expense of all other creatures. Only now is it becoming evident that a gospel confined to the human parish—and in practice to only a fraction of its inhabitants—is a prescription for annihilation.

"A conversation about trees is almost a crime," wrote Bertolt Brecht, "because it involves keeping silent about so many misdeeds"—as if to imply, by his unfortunate example, that there are no sins against nature worth talking about. Even a Communist genius can fall into Christian error. And why not? Marxist dogma is no less man-centered than its adversary.

The frontier where man must defend his life, the principle of life itself, is at the very edge of creation, where existence and nonexistence are scarcely distinguishable, where we confront the anonymous and minimal, among the plankton and protozoa. Man will perish unless he learns that the web of the universe is a continuous tissue. Touch it at any point, and the whole web shudders.

The arts, like that web, comprise a far-flung network, a psychic membrane, along whose filaments communication is almost instantaneous. All arts, all artists, are somehow connected. Cézanne paints a new picture in his studio in Aix. Overnight, through the rest of France, thousands of paintings begin to fall off the walls. And all at once poets, waking, look out of their windows at a landscape that they had never seen before. One of them, inventor of the color of vowels, announces: *"Il faut être absolument moderne."* It keeps happening all the time.

The poet knows that revolutions of sensibility are not won at the barricades. He also knows that there is no way in which he can escape history, even if he should want to. Stephen Dedalus's arrogant cry, *"Non serviam,"* still echoes in his ear, flattering his conviction that genius does not stoop to causes. At the same time he realizes that the hour is late now, and that some refusals are no longer permitted him, lest he wither at the heart. "The writer's function," said Camus in his acceptance of the

Nobel Prize, "is not without arduous duties. By definition, he cannot serve those who make history; he must serve those who are subject to it." To whom can one pledge one's allegiance except to the victims?

A generation ago it was possible—though I still find it hardly credible—to be both a reactionary and a poet, even a major poet. Yeats adored the aristocracy; Eliot was a snob and sometimes worse; Stevens in some of his letters sounds like a proto-Bircher; and we all know the sad truth about Pound. But I do not go to them for their politics. And besides, if I try hard enough, I can rationalize their defections. These were the last voices of an élitist society—though Pound's case was complicated by an odd infusion of populism. The fruits of Progress dismayed them. They saw a world cheapened and brutalized. So they fought, each in his own way, to preserve a kind of life that was sweeter and nobler to them than the new barbarism that threatened to engulf them.

If poetry teaches us anything about our feelings, it must be that we can have several feelings about the same thing at the same time. These feelings are not necessarily compatible; and if we try to solidify them into a certainty, they become other feelings. When I think of Ezra Pound, I do not try to ignore the shameful fugue of his Fascism and anti-Semitism; but I also remember his generosity to other poets, the wide range of his sympathy and intelligence, his lovely gift for friendship, his seminal influence, and—above all—those poems of his, defying an age that "demanded an image of its accelerated grimace":

> *There died a myriad,*
> *And of the best, among them,*
> *For an old bitch gone in the teeth,*
> *For a botched civilization.*
>
> *Charm, smiling at the good mouth,*
> *Quick eyes gone under earth's lid,*
>
> *For two gross of broken statues,*
> *For a few thousand battered books.*

I value that man in the act of writing that poem.

In a politicized world the labels we pin on people—Communist or Fascist, Democrat or Republican, liberal or conservative—are thought to betoken constant and irrevocable values, of paramount significance. Most of us believe that the shape of the future will be determined politically. When priorities are discussed, it is usually assumed that art is somehow "less relevant" than politics, though both are structures concerned with the quality of life—politics for the short term, art for the long. In Russia, where poets are subject to political censorship, they are regarded as heroes; in our own country, where they write what they please, they are generally treated, outside of academic circles, with indifference, and not infrequently with contempt. Even so fine a critical intellect as Edmund Wilson could ask, "Does it really constitute a career for a man to do nothing but write lyric poetry?" To put me in my place I keep a copy of that impolite query on my desk. But I am fortified by an impolite retort, which I will not repeat here.

Thomas Mann once remarked that history might have been changed if Karl Marx had read the poet Friedrich Hölderlin—Hellenist, enthusiast, pantheist, and madman. The notion of such a pairing is infinitely provocative. I could wish that Nixon had been capable of reading Berryman's *Dream Songs*. But that would be like hoping for him to recover a childhood he lost or never owned. Can any American politician since Lincoln be said to have possessed the quality that Yeats defined as "radical innocence," a root-purity of wonder?

Among poets the exaltation of the innocents springs from their kinship with the natural life force. A patch of bluebells brought Hopkins "news of God." The effort of a plant cutting to sprout led Roethke to exclaim: "What saint strained so much,/ Rose on such lopped limbs to a new life?" Pasternak's dear friend, the poet Marina Tsvetaeva, said of him: "He anticipated Adam, and was still living in the fourth day of creation." Even the Revolution, she noted, entered his consciousness "like everything in his life, through nature. In the summer of 1917, he kept in step with it: he listened." What was he listening for? For whatever the roots could tell him of life, of hope, of rebirth. As Anna Akhmatova wrote in a poem about him: "It means he is tiptoeing over pine needles,/ So as not to startle the light sleep of space." And the last stanza of her tribute begins: "He has been rewarded by a kind of eternal childhood."

Not all the great writers of the century have been so fortunate. Neither Joyce, nor Proust, nor Eliot, nor Frost, nor Stevens—I could name others—can be said to have cultivated their humanity, to have fulfilled themselves outside their art. Pasternak, as he says in one of his poems, remained "alive to the very end."

Among modern American poets I think of William Carlos Williams as belonging to that blessed category. Who else had enough love and life and buoyancy in him to write?:

> *He has on*
> *an old light grey Fedora*
> *She a black Beret*
>
> *He a dirty sweater*
> *She an old bue coat*
> *that fits her tight*
>
> *Grey flapping pants*
> *Red skirt and*
> *broken down black pumps*
>
> *Fat Lost Ambling*
> *nowhere through*
> *the upper town they kick*
> *their way through*
> *heaps of fallen maple leaves*
>
> *still green—and*
> *crisp as dollar bills*
> *Nothing to do. Hot cha!**

Of Pasternak and Williams it can be said that they did more than merely care about their art: they cared about others. If they were ruthless on occasion in friendship or love, they were consistently more ruthless with themselves. For these reasons their work gives off a special kind of radiance.

To preserve that shining innocence, that irrepressible élan, and yet to know evil, to be the steady vessel of a rage—how many are great enough for such a task? No bolder challenge con-

---

*"Late for Summer Weather," in *The Complete Collected Poems of William Carlos Williams 1906–1938*, New Directions, 1938, p. 214.

fronts the modern artist than to stay healthy in a sick world. Humanity these days, in the view of Claude Lévi-Strauss, recalls the behavior of maggots in a sack of flour. "When the population of these worms increases," he observes, "even before they meet, before they become conscious of one another, they secrete certain toxins that kill at a distance—that is, they poison the flour they are in, and they die." And he presents the ominous drama inside that self-contaminated bag of maggots as a metaphor for the human predicament.

The conscience of the artist constrains him to remain sensitive to the psychological and moral toxins that mankind secretes. He does so at the risk of sounding like a redundant alarm bell. One of the dangers of poetry, certainly, is grandiosity. Let us not deceive ourselves: a poet isn't going to change the world with even the most powerful of his poems. The best he can reasonably hope for is to conquer a piece of himself. Wallace Stevens said, in a modest tone of voice, that poetry was a way of getting the day in order.

Leaping up into Political Poetry

ROBERT BLY

I

Poems touching on American history are clearly political poems. Most educated people advise that poetry on political subjects should not be attempted. For an intricate painting, we are urged to bring forward our finest awareness. At the same time, we understand that we should leave that awareness behind when we go to examine political acts. Our wise men and wise institutions assure us that national political events are beyond the reach of ordinary, or even extraordinary, human sensitivity.

That habit is not new: Thoreau's friends thought that his writings on nature were very good, but that he was beyond his depth when he protested against the Mexican War. The circumstances surrounding the Austrian Franz Jagerstätter, whose life ended thirty years ago, during the Second World War, are very interesting in this connection. Jagerstätter was a farmer, with the equivalent of a high school education, though he possessed a remarkable intelligence. He decided that the Nazis were incompatible with the best he had seen or read of life, and made this decision before the Nazis took over in Austria; he cast the only "no" ballot in his village against the Anchluss. Jagerstätter's firm opposition to the Nazi regime is particularly interesting because he did not act out a doctrinaire position of a closely knit group, like the Jehovah's Witnesses, nor was he a member of a group being systematically wiped out, like the Jews: he simply made up his mind on a specific political situation, relying on his own judgment, and what he was able to piece together from the Bible, and using information available to everyone.

When drafted by the Nazis after the Anchluss, he refused to serve. The military judges sympathized, but told him they would have to cut off his head if he did not change his mind. Gordon Zahn's book, *In Solitary Witness*, recounts the meetings Jagerstätter had with various authorities shortly before his execution. All persons in authority who interviewed Jagerstätter, including bishops of the Austrian Catholic Church, psychiatrists, lawyers, and judges, told him that his sensibility was advising him wrongly. He was not responsible for acts he might take as a soldier: that was the responsibility of the legal government. They told him that he should turn his sensibility to the precarious situation of his family. He was advised, in effect, not to be serious. It was recommended that he be Christian in regard to his domestic life, but not to his political life. By study Jagerstätter had increased the range of his sensibility, and now this sensibility looked on acts he would have to take under orders by the government with the same calm penetration with which it would look on wasting time, or deciding on the quality of a book. He had extended his awareness farther than society wanted him to, and everyone he met, with the exception of a single parish priest, tried to drive it back again. Jagerstätter, however, refused to change his mind, would not enter the army despite disturbed appeals by the authorities, and was executed.

Most Americans have serious doubts about the morality of the Vietnam War. We are all aware of the large number of spirited and courageous young Americans in the Resistance who are refusing induction and are risking and being given lengthy prison sentences.

The majority of American draftees, however, go into the Army as they are told. Their doubt is interrupted on its way, and does not continue forward to end in an act, as Jagerstätter's doubt did or as the objector's and resister's doubt does. This failure to carry through means essentially that American culture has succeeded in killing some sensibilities. In order to take the rebellious and responsible action, the man thinking must be able to establish firm reasons for it; and in order to imagine those reasons, his awareness must have grown, over years, finer and finer. The "invisible organs of government," schools, broadcasting houses, orthodox churches, move to kill the awareness. The schools emphasize competitiveness over compassion; television and advertising do their part in numbing the sensibilities. Killing awareness is easier than killing the man later for a firm act.

II

The calculated effort of a society to kill awareness helps explain why so few citizens take rebellious actions. But I'm not sure it explains why so few American poets have written political poems. A poem can be a political act, but it has not been so far at least an illegal act. Moreover, since much of the poet's energy goes toward extending his awareness, he is immune to the more gross effects of brainwashing. Why then have so few American poems penetrated to any reality in our political life? I think one reason is that political concerns and inward concerns have always been regarded in our tradition as opposites, even incompatibles. *Time* is very upset that Buddhists should take part in political activity: the *Time* writers are convinced that the worlds are two mutually exclusive worlds, and if you work in one, you are excused from working in the other. English and American poets have adopted this schemata also, and poets in the Fifties felt that in *not* writing anything political, they were doing something meritorious. It's clear that many of the events that create our foreign relations and our domestic relations come from more or less hidden impulses in the American psyche. It's also clear I think that some sort of husk has grown around that psyche, so that in the Fifties we could not look into it or did not. The Negroes and the Vietnam War have worn the husk thin in a couple of places now. But if that is so, then the poet's main job is to penetrate that husk around the American psyche, and since that psyche is inside *him* too, the writing of political poetry is like the writing of personal poetry, a sudden drive by the poet inward.

As a matter of fact, we notice that it has been inward poets, Robert Duncan, Denise Levertov, and Galway Kinnell, who have written the best poems about the Vietnam War.

When a poet succeeds in driving part way inward, he often develops new energy that carries him on through the polished husk of the inner psyche that deflects most citizens or poets. Once

131

inside the psyche, he can speak of inward and political things with the same assurance. We can make a statement then that would not have been accepted in the Thirties, namely, that what is needed to write good poems about the outward world is inwardness. The political activists in the literary world are wrong—they try to force political poetry out of poets by pushing them more deeply into events, making them feel guilt if they don't abandon privacy. But the truth is that the political poem comes out of the deepest privacy.

III

Let me continue a minute with the comparison of the political poem with the personal poem. I'll use Yeats's marvelous word *entangle;* he suggested that the symbolist poem entangles some substance from the divine world in its words. Similarly a great personal poet like Villon entangles some of the private substance of his life in his language so well that hundreds of years later it still remains embedded. The subject of personal poetry is often spiritual growth, or the absence of it.

The dominant poem in American literature has always been the personal poem. John Crowe Ransom, for instance, wrote an elegant version of the personal poem, Randall Jarrell a flabby version, Robert Lowell a harsh version, Reed Whittemore a funny version, W. D. Snodgrass a whining version, and Robert Creeley a laconic one, etc. I love the work of many of these poets, but they choose, on the whole, not to go beyond the boundaries of the personal poem. Many poets say flatly—and proudly—that they are "not political." If a tree said that, I would find it more convincing than when a man says it. I think it is conceivable that a tree could report that it grew just as well in the Johnson administration as in the Kennedy administration or the Lincoln administration. But a modern man's spiritual life and his growth are increasingly sensitive to the tone and content of a regime. A man of draft age will find that his life itself depends on the political content of an administration. So these poets' assertion of independence, I think, is a fiction.

The only body of political poetry written with any determination in the U.S. were those written during the Thirties by Edwin Rolfe, Sol Funaroff, Kenneth Fearing, among others. It is interesting that their poems were usually political in *opinions*. For example, the poet might declare that he had discovered who the phonies in the world are, something he didn't know before. But changes of opinion are steps in the growth of the poet's personality, they are events in his psychic history. These "political" poems of the Thirties then were not really political poems at all, but personal poems appearing under another guise.

We find many political poems composed entirely of opinions; they are political but not poems. Here is an example from a Scandinavian anthology:

> Poor America
> so huge, so strong, so afraid.
> afraid in Guatemala,
> afraid in Congo, Panama,
> afraid in Cuba, in Santo Domingo,
> afraid in Vietnam . . .
> America, take your hands off Vietnam!
> The poor are rising
> You are through stealing now
> Your face is distorted with hate . . .

These lines have boiled off the outermost layer of the brain. The poem is not inside the poet's own life, let alone inside this nation's life.

The life of the nation can be imagined also not as something deep inside our psyche, but as a psyche larger than the psyche of anyone living, a larger sphere, floating above everyone. In order for the poet to write a true political poem, he has to be able to have such a grasp of his own concerns that he can leave them for a while, and then leap up into this other psyche. He wanders about there a while, and as he returns he brings back plantseeds that have stuck to his clothes, some inhabitants of this curious sphere, which he then tries to keep alive with his own psychic body.

Some poets try to write political poems impelled by hatred, or fear. But these emotions are heavy, they affect the gravity of the body. What the poet needs to get up that far and bring back something are great leaps of the imagination.

A true political poem is a quarrel with ourselves, and the

rhetoric is as harmful in that sort of poem as in the personal poem. The true political poem does not order us either to take any specific acts: like the personal poem, it moves to deepen awareness.

Thinking of the rarity of the political poem in the United States, another image comes to mind. We can imagine Americans inside a sphere, like those sad men in Bosch's "Garden of Earthly Delights." The clear glass is the limit of the ego. We float inside it. Around us there are worlds of energy, but we are unable to describe them in words, because we are unable to get out of our own egos.

IV

The political poem needs an especially fragrant language. Neruda's "The Dictators" has that curious fragrance that comes from its words brushing unknown parts of the psyche. It seems to me a masterpiece of the political poem:

> An odor has remained among the sugar cane:
> A mixture of blood and body, a penetrating
> Petal that brings nausea.
> Between the coconut palms the graves are full
> Of ruined bones, of speechless death-rattles.
> A delicate underling converses
> With glasses, braid collars, and cords of gold.
> The tiny palace gleams like a watch
> And the rapid laughs with gloves on
> Cross the corridors at times
> And join the dead voices
> And the blue mouths freshly buried.
> The weeping is hidden like a water-plant
> Whose seeds fall constantly on the earth
> And without light make the great blind leaves to grow.
> Hatred has grown scale upon scale,
> Blow on blow, in the ghastly water of the swamp,
> With a snout full of ooze and silence.

The poem's task is to entangle in the language the psychic substance of a South American country under a dictator. The

Spanish original, of course, is much more resonant. But even in the translation it is clear that Neruda is bringing in unexpected images: "The tiny palace gleams like a watch"—images one would expect in an entirely different sort of poem: "rapid laughs with gloves on." Suddenly a blind plant appears, that reproduces itself by dropping seeds constantly on the ground, shaded by its own huge leaves. This image is complicated, created by a part of the mind inaccessible to hatred, and yet it carries the reality of hatred radiating from dictators into the consciousness with a kind of massive intelligence.

Describing dictators in "The United Fruit Company," Neruda uses for them the image of ordinary houseflies. By contrast, the journalistic mind would tend to describe them as huge and cunning. Whitman was the first true political poet we had in North America. His short poem "To the States" has great fragrance in its language as well. "(With gathering murk, with muttering thunder and lambent shoots we all duly awake)."

William Vaughn Moody in 1898 wrote some powerful lines:

Are we the eagle nation Milton saw
Mewing its mighty youth,
Soon to possess the mountain winds of truth,
And be swift familiar of the sun
Where aye before God's face his trumpets run?
Or have we but the talons and the maw,
And for the abject likeness of our heart
Shall some less lordly bird be set apart?
Some gross-billed wader where the swamps are fat?
Some gorger in the sun? Some prowler with the bat?

His poem was written against United States policy the first time we invaded Cuba. The language at times is remarkably swift and intense, particularly when compared to the hopelessly foggy language of political poetry being written by others at that time.

The political poem in the U.S. after Whitman and Moody lay dormant until the inventive generation of 1917 came along. It revived with mixed results. Pound demanded that American history enter his Cantos, Eliot wrote well, though always of a generalized modern nation, rather than of the U.S.; Jeffers wrote marvelously, but really was not interested in the U.S. as a nation at all. In the next generation, Cummings wrote of this country using a sense of superiority as his impulse; he almost never escaped from himself. After Cummings the New Critical mentality, profoundly opposed to any questioning of the white power structure, took over, and the language and strength of political poetry survived only in three men, in Kenneth Rexroth, Thomas McGrath, and a slightly younger man, David Ignatow. During the Forties and Fifties most poets kept away from the political poem. In his "Ode for the American Dead in Korea," Thomas McGrath wrote:

> And God (whose sparrows fall aslant his gaze,
> Like grace or confetti) blinks, and he is gone,
> And you are gone . . . But, in another year
> We will mourn you, whose fossil courage fills
> The limestone histories: brave: ignorant: amazed:
> Dead in the rice paddies, dead on the nameless hills.

Rexroth has written beautiful political poems, among them "A Christmas Note for Geraldine Udell." His great common sense and stubborn intelligence helped immensely in keeping the political poem alive.

The new critical influence in poetry began to dim in the middle 1950's, just at the time America's fantastic capacity for aggression and self-delusion began to be palpable like rising water to the beach walker. William Carlos Williams' refusal to ignore political lies was passed on to Allen Ginsberg; Neruda's example began to take hold; Rexroth, McGrath and Ignatow continued to write well; Ferlinghetti separately wrote his "A Tentative Description of a Dinner Given to Promote the Impeachment of President Eisenhower." Many black poets began to be visible. As the Vietnam War escalated, Robert Duncan wrote several powerful poems on the War. His "Uprising" ends:

> this specter that in the beginning Adams and
>   Jefferson feared and knew
> would corrupt the very body of the nation
>   and all our sense of our common human-
>   ity . . .
> now shines from the eyes of the President
> in the swollen head of the nation.

America is still young herself, and she may become something magnificent and shining, or she may turn, as Rome did, into a black dinosaur, the enemy of every nation in the world who wants to live its own life. In my opinion, that decision has not yet been made.

When We Dead Awaken: Writing as Re-Vision (1971)

ADRIENNE RICH

The Modern Language Association is both marketplace and funeral parlor for the professional study of Western literature in North America. Like all gatherings of the professions, it has been and remains a "procession of the sons of educated men" (Virginia Woolf): a congeries of old-boys' networks, academicians rehearsing their numb canons in sessions dedicated to the literature of white males, junior scholars under the lash of "publish or perish" delivering papers in the bizarrely lit drawing rooms of immense hotels: a ritual competition veering between cynicism and desperation.

However, in the interstices of these gentlemanly rites (or, in Mary Daly's words, on the boundaries of this patriarchal space),* some feminist scholars, teachers, and graduate students, joined by feminist writers, editors, and publishers, have for a decade been creating more subversive occasions, challenging the sacredness of the gentlemanly canon, sharing the rediscovery of buried works by women, asking women's questions, bringing literary history and criticism back to life in both senses. The Commission on the Status of Women in the Profession was formed in 1969, and held its first public event in 1970. In 1971 the Commission asked Ellen Peck Killoh, Tillie Olsen, Elaine Reuben, and myself, with Elaine Hedges as moderator, to talk on "The Woman Writer in the Twentieth Century." The essay that follows was written for that forum, and later published, along

---

*Mary Daly, *Beyond God the Father* (Boston: Beacon, 1971), pp. 40–41.

with the other papers from the forum and workshops, in an issue of *College English* edited by Elaine Hedges ("Women Writing and Teaching," vol. 34, no. 1, October 1972). With a few revisions, mainly updating, it was reprinted in *American Poets in 1976*, edited by William Heyen (New York: Bobbs-Merrill, 1976). That later text is the one published here.

The challenge flung by feminists at the accepted literary canon, at the methods of teaching it, and at the biased and astigmatic view of male "literary scholarship," has not diminished in the decade since the first Women's Forum; it has become broadened and intensified more recently by the challenges of black and lesbian feminists pointing out that feminist literary criticism itself has overlooked or held back from examining the work of black women and lesbians. The dynamic between a political vision and the demand for a fresh vision of literature is clear: without a growing feminist movement, the first inroads of feminist scholarship could not have been made; without the sharpening of a black feminist consciousness, black women's writing would have been left in limbo between misogynist black male critics and white feminists still struggling to unearth a white woman's tradition; without an articulate lesbian/feminist movement, lesbian writing would still be lying in that closet where many of us used to sit reading forbidden books "in a bad light."

Much, much more is yet to be done; and university curricula have of course changed very little as a result of all this. What *is* changing is the availability of knowledge, of vital texts, the visible effects on women's lives of seeing, hearing our wordless or negated experience affirmed and pursued further in language.

Ibsen's *When We Dead Awaken* is a play about the use that the male artist and thinker—in the process of creating culture as we know it—has made of women, in his life and in his work; and about a woman's slow struggling awakening to the use to which her life has been put. Bernard Shaw wrote in 1900 of this play:

> [Ibsen] shows us that no degradation ever devized or permitted is as disastrous as this degradation; that through it women can die into luxuries for men and yet can kill them;

139

that men and women are becoming conscious of this; and
that what remains to be seen as perhaps the most interesting of all imminent social developments is what will happen "when we dead awaken."[1]

It's exhilarating to be alive in a time of awakening consciousness; it can also be confusing, disorienting, and painful.
This awakening of dead or sleeping consciousness has already
affected the lives of millions of women, even those who don't
know it yet. It is also affecting the lives of men, even those who
deny its claims upon them. The argument will go on whether
an oppressive economic class system is responsible for the oppressive nature of male/female relations, or whether, in fact,
patriarchy—the domination of males—is the original model of
oppression on which all others are based. But in the last few
years the women's movement has drawn inescapable and illu-
minating connections between our sexual lives and our political
institutions. The sleepwalkers are coming awake, and for the first
time this awakening has a collective reality; it is no longer such
a lonely thing to open one's eyes.

Re-vision—the act of looking back, of seeing with fresh eyes,
of entering an old text from a new critical direction—is for
women more than a chapter in cultural history: it is an act of
survival. Until we can understand the assumptions in which we
are drenched we cannot know ourselves. And this drive to self-
knowledge, for women, is more than a search for identity: it is
part of our refusal of the self-destructiveness of male-domi-
nated society. A radical critique of literature, feminist in its impulse, would take the work first of all as a clue to how we live,
how we have been living, how we have been led to imagine ourselves, how our language has trapped as well as liberated us, how
the very act of naming has been till now a male prerogative, and
how we can begin to see and name—and therefore live—afresh.
A change in the concept of sexual identity is essential if we are
not going to see the old political order reassert itself in every
new revolution. We need to know the writing of the past, and
know it differently than we have ever known it; not to pass on
a tradition but to break its hold over us.

For writers, and at this moment for women writers in particular, there is the challenge and promise of a whole new psychic

geography to be explored. But there is also a difficult and dangerous walking on the ice, as we try to find language and images for a consciousness we are just coming into, and with little in the past to support us. I want to talk about some aspects of this difficulty and this danger.

Jane Harrison, the great classical anthropologist, wrote in 1914 in a letter to her friend Gilbert Murray:

> By the by, about "Women," it has bothered me often—why do women never want to write poetry about Man as a sex— why is Woman a dream and a terror to man and not the other way around? . . . Is it mere convention and propriety, or something deeper?[2]

I think Jane Harrison's question cuts deep into the myth-making tradition, the romantic tradition; deep into what women and men have been to each other; and deep into the psyche of the woman writer. Thinking about that question, I began thinking of the work of two twentieth-century women poets, Sylvia Plath and Diane Wakoski. It strikes me that in the work of both Man appears as, if not a dream, a fascination and a terror; and that the source of the fascination and the terror is, simply, Man's power—to dominate, tyrannize, choose, or reject the woman. The charisma of Man seems to come purely from his power over her and his control of the world by force, not from anything fertile or life-giving in him. And, in the work of both these poets, it is finally the woman's sense of *herself*—embattled, possessed—that gives the poetry its dynamic charge, its rhythms of struggle, need, will, and female energy. Until recently this female anger and this furious awareness of the Man's power over her were not available materials to the female poet, who tended to write of Love as the source of her suffering, and to view that victimization by Love as an almost inevitable fate. Or, like Marianne Moore and Elizabeth Bishop, she kept sexuality at a measured and chiseled distance in her poems.

One answer to Jane Harrison's question has to be that historically men and women have played very different parts in each others' lives. Where woman has been a luxury for man, and has served as the painter's model and the poet's muse, but also as comforter, nurse, cook, bearer of his seed, secretarial assistant,

141

and copyist of manuscripts, man has played a quite different role for the female artist. Henry James repeats an incident which the writer Prosper Mérimée described, of how, while he was living with George Sand,

> he once opened his eyes, in the raw winter dawn, to see his companion, in a dressing-gown, on her knees before the domestic hearth, a candlestick beside her and a red *madras* round her head, making bravely, with her own hands the fire that was to enable her to sit down betimes to urgent pen and paper. The story represents him as having felt that the spectacle chilled his ardor and tried his taste; her appearance was unfortunate, her occupation an inconsequence, and her industry a reproof—the result of all which was a lively irritation and an early rupture.[3]

The specter of this kind of male judgment, along with the mis-naming and thwarting of her needs by a culture controlled by males, has created problems for the woman writer: problems of contact with herself, problems of language and style, problems of energy and survival.

In rereading Virginia Woolf's *A Room of One's Own* (1929) for the first time in some years, I was astonished at the sense of effort, of pains taken, of dogged tentativeness, in the tone of that essay. And I recognized that tone. I had heard it often enough, in myself and in other women. It is the tone of a woman almost in touch with her anger, who is determined not to appear angry, who is *willing* herself to be calm, detached, and even charming in a roomful of men where things have been said which are attacks on her very integrity. Virginia Woolf is addressing an audience of women, but she is acutely conscious—as she always was—of being overheard by men: by Morgan and Lytton and Maynard Keynes and for that matter by her father, Leslie Stephen.[4] She drew the language out into an exacerbated thread in her determination to have her own sensibility yet protect it from those masculine presences. Only at rare moments in that essay do you hear the passion in her voice; she was trying to sound as cool as Jane Austen, as Olympian as Shakespeare, because that is the way the men of the culture thought a writer should sound.

No male writer has written primarily or even largely for

women, or with the sense of women's criticism as a consideration when he chooses his materials, his theme, his language. But
to a lesser or greater extent, every woman writer has written for
men even when, like Virginia Woolf, she was supposed to be
addressing women. If we have come to the point when this balance might begin to change, when women can stop being
haunted, not only by "convention and propriety" but by inter-
nalized fears of being and saying themselves, then it is an extraordinary moment for the woman writer—and reader.

I have hesitated to do what I am going to do now, which is
to use myself as an illustration. For one thing, it's a lot easier
and less dangerous to talk about other women writers. But there
is something else. Like Virginia Woolf, I am aware of the women
who are not with us here because they are washing the dishes
and looking after the children. Nearly fifty years after she spoke,
that fact remains largely unchanged. And I am thinking also of
women whom she left out of the picture altogether—women who
are washing other people's dishes and caring for other people's
children, not to mention women who went on the streets last
night in order to feed their children. We seem to be special
women here, we have liked to think of ourselves as special, and
we have known that men would tolerate, even romanticize us as
special, as long as our words and actions didn't threaten their
privilege of tolerating or rejecting us and our work according
to *their* ideas of what a special woman ought to be. An important insight of the radical women's movement has been how
divisive and how ultimately destructive is this myth of the special woman, who is also the token woman. Every one of us here
in this room has had great luck—we are teachers, writers, academicians; our own gifts could not have been enough, for we
all know women whose gifts are buried or aborted. Our struggles can have meaning and our privileges—however precarious
under patriarchy—can be justified only if they can help to change
the lives of women whose gifts—and whose very being—continue to be thwarted and silenced.

My own luck was being born white and middle-class into a
house full of books, with a father who encouraged me to read
and write. So for about twenty years I wrote for a particular man,
who criticized and praised me and made me feel I was indeed
"special." The obverse side of this, of course, was that I tried

143

for a long time to please him, or rather, not to displease him. And then of course there were other men—writers, teachers— the Man, who was not a terror or a dream but a literary master and a master in other ways less easy to acknowledge. And there were all those poems about women, written by men: it seemed to be a given that men wrote poems and women frequently inhabited them. These women were almost always beautiful, but threatened with the loss of beauty, the loss of youth—the fate worse than death. Or, they were beautiful and died young, like Lucy and Lenore. Or, the woman was like Maud Gonne, cruel and disastrously mistaken, and the poem reproached her because she had refused to become a luxury for the poet.

A lot is being said today about the influence that the myths and images of women have on all of us who are products of culture. I think it has been a peculiar confusion to the girl or woman who tries to write because she is peculiarly susceptible to language. She goes to poetry or fiction looking for *her* way of being in the world, since she too has been putting words and images together; she is looking eagerly for guides, maps, possibilities; and over and over in the "words' masculine persuasive force" of literature she comes up against something that negates everything she is about: she meets the image of Woman in books written by men. She finds a terror and a dream, she finds a beautiful pale face, she finds La Belle Dame Sans Merci, she finds Juliet or Tess or Salomé, but precisely what she does not find is that absorbed, drudging, puzzled, sometimes inspired creature, herself, who sits at a desk trying to put words together.

So what does she do? What did I do? I read the older women poets with their peculiar keenness and ambivalence: Sappho, Christina Rossetti, Emily Dickinson, Elinor Wylie, Edna Millay, H. D. I discovered that the woman poet most admired at the time (by men) was Marianne Moore, who was maidenly, elegant, intellectual, discreet. But even in reading these women I was looking in them for the same things I had found in the poetry of men, because I wanted women poets to be the equals of men, and to be equal was still confused with sounding the same.

I know that my style was formed first by male poets: by the men I was reading as an undergraduate—Frost, Dylan Thomas, Donne, Auden, MacNiece, Stevens, Yeats. What I chiefly learned from them was craft.[5] But poems are like dreams: in them you put what you don't know you know. Looking back at poems I wrote before I was twenty-one, I'm startled because beneath the conscious craft are glimpses of the split I even then experienced between the girl who wrote poems, who defined herself in writing poems, and the girl who was to define herself by her relationships with men. "Aunt Jennifer's Tigers" (1951), written while I was a student, looks with deliberate detachment at this split.[6]

> Aunt Jennifer's tigers stride across a screen,
> Bright topaz denizens of a world of green.
> They do not fear the men beneath the tree;
> They pace in sleek chivalric certainty.
>
> Aunt Jennifer's fingers fluttering through her wool
> Find even the ivory needle hard to pull.
> The massive weight of Uncle's wedding band
> Sits heavily upon Aunt Jennifer's hand.
>
> When Aunt is dead, her terrified hands will lie
> Still ringed with ordeals she was mastered by.
> The tigers in the panel that she made
> Will go on striding, proud and unafraid.

In writing this poem, composed and apparently cool as it is, I thought I was creating a portrait of an imaginary woman. But this woman suffers from the opposition of her imagination, worked out in tapestry, and her life-style, "ringed with ordeals she was mastered by." It was important to me that Aunt Jennifer was a person as distinct from myself as possible—distanced by the formalism of the poem, by its objective, observant tone—even by putting the woman in a different generation.

In those years formalism was part of the strategy—like asbestos gloves, it allowed me to handle materials I couldn't pick up barehanded. A later strategy was to use the persona of a man, as I did in "The Loser" (1958):

> *A man thinks of the woman he once loved: first, after her wedding, and then nearly a decade later.*

145

I

I kissed you, bride and lost, and went
home from that bourgeois sacrament,
your cheek still tasting cold upon
my lips that gave you benison
with all the swagger that they knew—
as losers somehow learn to do.

Your wedding made my eyes ache; soon
the world would be worse off for one
more golden apple dropped to ground
without the least protesting sound,
and you would windfall lie, and we
forget your shimmer on the tree.

Beauty is always wasted: if
not Mignon's song sung to the deaf,
at all events to the unmoved.
A face like yours cannot be loved
long or seriously enough.
Almost, we seem to hold it off.

II

Well, you are tougher than I thought.
Now when the wash with ice hangs taut
this morning of St. Valentine,
I see you strip the squeaking line,
your body weighed against the load,
and all my groans can do no good.

Because you are still beautiful,
though squared and stiffened by the pull
of what nine windy years have done.
You have three daughters, lost a son.
I see all your intelligence
flung into that unwearied stance.

My envy is of no avail.
I turn my head and wish him well
who chafed your beauty into use
and lives forever in a house
lit by the friction of your mind.
You stagger in against the wind.

I finished college, published my first book by a fluke, as it seemed to me, and broke off a love affair. I took a job, lived alone, went on writing, fell in love. I was young, full of energy, and the book seemed to mean that others agreed I was a poet. Because I was also determined to prove that as a woman poet I could also have what was then defined as a "full" woman's life, I plunged in my early twenties into marriage and had three children before I was thirty. There was nothing overt in the environment to warn me: these were the fifties, and in reaction to the earlier wave of feminism, middle-class women were making careers of domestic perfection, working to send their husbands through professional schools, then retiring to raise large families. People were moving out to the suburbs, technology was going to be the answer to everything, even sex; the family was in its glory. Life was extremely private; women were isolated from each other by the loyalties of marriage. I have a sense that women didn't talk to each other much in the fifties—not about their secret emptinesses, their frustrations. I went on trying to write; my second book and first child appeared in the same month. But by the time that book came out I was already dissatisfied with those poems, which seemed to me mere exercises for poems I hadn't written. The book was praised, however, for its "gracefulness"; I had a marriage and a child. If there were doubts, if there were periods of null depression or active despairing, these could only mean that I was ungrateful, insatiable, perhaps a monster.

About the time my third child was born, I felt that I had either to consider myself a failed woman and a failed poet, or to try to find some synthesis by which to understand what was happening to me. What frightened me most was the sense of drift, of being pulled along on a current which called itself my destiny, but in which I seemed to be losing touch with whoever I had been, with the girl who had experienced her own will and energy almost ecstatically at times, walking around a city or riding a train at night or typing in a student room. In a poem about my grandmother I wrote (of myself): "A young girl, thought sleeping, is certified dead" ("Halfway"). I was writing very little, partly from fatigue, that female fatigue of suppressed anger and loss of contact with my own being; partly from the discontinuity of female life with its attention to small chores, errands, work that others constantly undo, small children's constant needs. What

I did write was unconvincing to me; my anger and frustration were hard to acknowledge in or out of poems because in fact I cared a great deal about my husband and my children. Trying to look back and understand that time I have tried to analyze the real nature of the conflict. Most, if not all, human lives are full of fantasy—passive day-dreaming which need not be acted on. But to write poetry or fiction, or even to think well, is not to fantasize, or to put fantasies on paper. For a poem to coalesce, for a character or an action to take shape, there has to be an imaginative transformation of reality which is in no way passive. And a certain freedom of the mind is needed—freedom to press on, to enter the currents of your thought like a glider pilot, knowing that your motion can be sustained, that the buoyancy of your attention will not be suddenly snatched away. Moreover, if the imagination is to transcend and transform experience it has to question, to challenge, to conceive of alternatives, perhaps to the very life you are living at that moment. You have to be free to play around with the notion that day might be night, love might be hate; nothing can be too sacred for the imagination to turn into its opposite or to call experimentally by another name. For writing is re-naming. Now, to be maternally with small children all day in the old way, to be with a man in the old way of marriage, requires a holding-back, a putting-aside of that imaginative activity, and demands instead a kind of conservatism. I want to make it clear that I am *not* saying that in order to write well, or think well, it is necessary to become unavailable to others, or to become a devouring ego. This has been the myth of the masculine artist and thinker; and I do not accept it. But to be a female human being trying to fulfill traditional female functions in a traditional way *is* in direct conflict with the subversive function of the imagination. The word traditional is important here. There must be ways, and we will be finding out more and more about them, in which the energy of creation and the energy of relation can be united. But in those years I always felt the conflict as a failure of love in myself. I had thought I was choosing a full life: the life available to most men, in which sexuality, work, and parenthood could coexist. But I felt, at twenty-nine, guilt toward the people closest to me, and guilty toward my own being.

I wanted, then, more than anything, the one thing of which

there was never enough: time to think, time to write. The fifties and early sixties were years of rapid revelations: the sit-ins and marches in the South, the Bay of Pigs, the early antiwar movement, raised large questions—questions for which the masculine world of the academy around me seemed to have expert and fluent answers. But I needed to think for myself—about pacifism and dissent and violence, about poetry and society, and about my own relationship to all these things. For about ten years I was reading in fierce snatches, scribbling in notebooks, writing poetry in fragments; I was looking desperately for clues, because if there were no clues then I thought I might be insane. I wrote in a notebook about this time:

> Paralyzed by the sense that there exists a mesh of relationships—e.g., between my anger at the children, my sensual life, pacifism, sex (I mean sex in its broadest significance, not merely sexual desire)—an interconnectedness which, if I could see it, make it valid, would give me back myself, make it possible to function lucidly and passionately. Yet I grope in and out among these dark webs.

I think I began at this point to feel that politics was not something "out there" but something "in here" and of the essence of my condition.

In the late fifties I was able to write, for the first time, directly about experiencing myself as a woman. The poem was jotted in fragments during children's naps, brief hours in a library, or at 3:00 A.M. after rising with a wakeful child. I despaired of doing any continuous work at this time. Yet I began to feel that my fragments and scraps had a common consciousness and a common theme, one which I would have been very unwilling to put on paper at an earlier time because I had been taught that poetry should be "universal," which meant, of course, nonfemale. Until then I had tried very much *not* to identify myself as a female poet. Over two years I wrote a ten-part poem called "Snapshots of a Daughter-in-Law" (1958–1960), in a longer looser mode than I'd ever trusted myself with before. It was an extraordinary relief to write that poem. It strikes me now as too literary, too dependent on allusion; I hadn't found the courage yet to do without authorities, or even to use the pronoun "I"—

the woman in the poem is always "she." One section of it, No. 2, concerns a woman who thinks she is going mad; she is haunted by voices telling her to resist and rebel, voices which she can hear but not obey.

2.
Banging the coffee-pot into the sink
she hears the angels chiding, and looks out
past the raked gardens to the sloppy sky.
Only a week since They said: *Have no patience.*

The next time it was: *Be insatiable.*
Then: *Save yourself; others you cannot save.*
Sometimes she's let the tapstream scald her arm,
a match burn to her thumbnail,

or held her hand above the kettle's snout
right in the woolly steam. They are probably angels,
since nothing hurts her anymore, except
each morning's grit blowing into her eyes.

The poem "Orion," written five years later, is a poem of re-connection with a part of myself I had felt I was losing—the active principle, the energetic imagination, the "half-brother" whom I projected, as I had for many years, into the constellation Orion. It's no accident that the words "cold and egotistical" appear in this poem, and are applied to myself.

Far back when I went zig-zagging
through tamarack pastures
you were my genius, you
my cast-iron Viking, my helmed
lion-heart king in prison.
Years later now you're young

my fierce half-brother, staring
down from that simplified west
your breast open, your belt dragged down
by an oldfashioned thing, a sword
the last bravado you won't give over
though it weighs you down as you stride

and the stars in it are dim
and maybe have stopped burning.
But you burn, and I know it;
as I throw back my head to take you in
and old transfusion happens again:
divine astronomy is nothing to it.

Indoors I bruise and blunder,
break faith, leave ill enough
alone, a dead child born in the dark.
Night cracks up over the chimney,
pieces of time, frozen geodes
come showering down in the grate.

A man reaches behind my eyes
and finds them empty
a woman's head turns away
from my head in the mirror
children are dying my death
and eating crumbs of my life.

Pity is not your forte.
Calmly you ache up there
pinned aloft in your crow's nest,
my speechless pirate!
You take it all for granted
and when I look you back

it's with a starlike eye
shooting its cold and egotistical spear
where it can do least damage.
Breathe deep! No hurt, no pardon
out here in the cold with you
you with your back to the wall.

The choice still seemed to be between "love"—womanly, maternal love, altruistic love—a love defined and ruled by the weight of an entire culture; and egotism—a force directed by men into creation, achievement, ambition, often at the expense of others, but justifiably so. For weren't they men, and wasn't that their destiny as womanly, selfless love was ours? We know now that the alternatives are false ones—that the word "love" is itself in need of re-vision.

ADRIENNE RICH

There is a companion poem to "Orion," written three years later, in which at last the woman in the poem and the woman writing the poem become the same person. It is called "Planetarium," and it was written after a visit to a real planetarium, where I read an account of the work of Caroline Herschel, the astronomer, who worked with her brother William, but whose name remained obscure, as his did not.

Thinking of Caroline Herschel, 1750–1848, astronomer, sister of William; and others

A woman in the shape of a monster
a monster in the shape of a woman
the skies are full of them

a woman   "in the snow
among the Clocks and instruments
or measuring the ground with poles"

in her 98 years to discover
8 comets

she whom the moon ruled
like us
levitating into the night sky
riding the polished lenses

Galaxies of women, there
doing penance for impetuousness
ribs chilled
in those spaces   of the mind

An eye,
      "virile, precise and absolutely certain"
      from the mad webs of Uranisborg
                              encountering the NOVA

every impulse of light exploding
from the core
as life flies out of us
      Tycho whispering at last
      "Let me not seem to have lived in vain"

What we see, we see
and seeing is changing

the light that shrivels a mountain
and leaves a man alive

Heartbeat of the pulsar
heart sweating through my body

The radio impulse
pouring in from Taurus

     I am bombarded yet   I stand

I have been standing all my life in the
direct path of a battery of signals
the most accurately transmitted most
untranslateable language in the universe
I am a galactic cloud so deep   so invo-
luted that a light wave could take 15
years to travel through me   And has
taken   I am an instrument in the shape
of a woman trying to translate pulsations
into images   for the relief of the body
and the reconstruction of the mind.

In closing I want to tell you about a dream I had last summer. I dreamed I was asked to read my poetry at a mass women's meeting, but when I began to read, what came out were the lyrics of a blues song. I share this dream with you because it seemed to me to say something about the problems and the future of the woman writer, and probably of women in general. The awakening of consciousness is not like the crossing of a frontier—one step and you are in another country. Much of woman's poetry has been of the nature of the blues song: a cry of pain, of victimization, or a lyric of seduction.[7] And today, much poetry by women—and prose for that matter—is charged with anger. I think we need to go through that anger, and we will betray our own reality if we try, as Virginia Woolf was trying, for an objectivity, a detachment, that would make us sound more like Jane Austen or Shakespeare. We know more than Jane Austen or Shakespeare knew: more than Jane Austen because our lives are more complex, more than Shakespeare because we know more about the lives of women—Jane Austen and Virginia Woolf included.

Both the victimization and the anger experienced by women are real, and have real sources, everywhere in the environment, built into society, language, the structures of thought. They will go on being tapped and explored by poets, among others. We can neither deny them, nor will we rest there. A new generation of women poets is already working out of the psychic energy released when women begin to move out towards what the feminist philosopher Mary Daly has described as the "new space" on the boundaries of patriarchy.[8] Women are speaking to and of women in these poems, out of a newly released courage to name, to love each other, to share risk and grief and celebration.

To the eye of a feminist, the work of Western male poets now writing reveals a deep, fatalistic pessimism as to the possibilities of change, whether societal or personal, along with a familiar and threadbare use of women (and nature) as redemptive on the one hand, threatening on the other; and a new tide of phallocentric sadism and overt woman-hating which matches the sexual brutality of recent films. "Political" poetry by men remains stranded amid the struggles for power among male groups; in condemning U.S. imperialism or the Chilean junta the poet can claim to speak for the oppressed while remaining, as male, part of a system of sexual oppression. The enemy is always outside the self, the struggle somewhere else. The mood of isolation, self-pity, and self-imitation that pervades "nonpolitical" poetry suggests that a profound change in masculine consciousness will have to precede any new male poetic—or other—inspiration. The creative energy of patriarchy is fast running out; what remains is its self-generating energy for destruction. As women, we have our work cut out for us.

NOTES

1. G. B. Shaw, *The Quintessence of Ibsenism* (New York, Hill & Wang, 1922), p. 139.
2. J. G. Stewart, *Jane Ellen Harrison: A Portrait from Letters* (London, Merlin, 1959), p. 140.
3. Henry James, "Notes on Novelists," in *Selected Literary Criticism of Henry James*, Morris Shapiro, ed. (London, Heinemann, 1963), pp. 157–58.
4. A. R., 1978: This intuition of mine was corroborated when, early in 1978, I read the correspondence between Woolf and Dame Ethel Smyth (Henry W. and Albert A. Berg Collection, The New York Public Library, Astor, Lenox and Tilden Foundations); in a letter dated June 8, 1933, Woolf speaks of having kept her own personality out of *A Room of One's Own* lest she not be taken seriously: ". . . how personal,

so will they say, rubbing their hands with glee, women always are; *I even hear them as I write.*" (Italics mine.)

5. A. R., 1978: Yet I spent months, at sixteen, memorizing and writing imitations of Millay's sonnets; and in notebooks of that period I find what are obviously attempts to imitate Dickinson's metrics and verbal compression. I knew H. D. only through anthologized lyrics; her epic poetry was not then available to me.

6. A. R, 1978: Texts of poetry quoted herein can be found in A. R., *Poems Selected and New: 1950–1974* (New York, Norton, 1975).

7. A. R., 1978: When I dreamed that dream, was I wholly ignorant of the tradition of Bessie Smith and other women's blues lyrics which transcended victimization to sing of resistance and independence?

8. Mary Daly, *Beyond God the Father: Towards a Philosophy of Women's Liberation* (Boston, Beacon, 1973).

Poetry and the National Conscience

HOWARD NEMEROV

The word *and* is a very good word. It is one of the words that children learn earliest, but its usefulness increases as they grow. One of the best things about *and* is that it is so inconspicuous it can sneak in almost anywhere unnoticed, like a secret agent. Like a secret agent, too, *and* is extremely likely to belong to both sides at once. This property of *and* makes it supremely apt to appear in the titles of discourses, especially learned ones: on the shelf across from me at the time of writing I can see several such: Crowds and Power, Myth and Cosmos, The Raw and the Cooked, Art and Illusion, Permanence and Change . . . I myself am writing a book the chapters of which are about poetry *and* such a variety of other things that I think to call it *Poetry And—*.

What makes *and* so good for titles is its power of putting things together while keeping them apart. It says there is some relation, but is utterly noncommittal about specifying; it is like a marriage service with automatic divorce written into the contract.

An unsuspected fringe benefit to *and* is its power of conferring existence on whatever things stand to either side of it. If one says This *and* That, his hearers are prepared to accept the solidity of both as understood, and to concentrate on the relation between them. Yet I am in some doubts about the useful reality of both the hypostatical entities of our title. Is there, all simply, *Poetry?* Does there exist somewhere, like a Platonic archetype of a rectal thermometer kept in the Smithsonian, *The,* or even *A, National Conscience*? I think not, and will try to say why. But I note first that the passing reference to Plato probably came into my thoughts because Plato actually seems to believe, in a famous place in *The Republic*, that both poetry, or music, and something like a national conscience, or a national morale at any rate, really existed. So strongly did he believe in the relation between them that he banished the poets from the nation, fearing that their libertine and effeminate individualism might impair the soldiers' will to fight (you will remember that in the ideal state a third of the population is army).

There is of course a sense, useful in casual chat, in which both poetry and the national conscience do exist. It is only when you try to specify what they are that you run into trouble. For people who speak English, Poetry will turn out to be the works written by a traditionally sanctioned succession of people named Chaucer and Shakespeare and Milton and so on, with Homer and Virgil and Dante muttering away in the background. The national conscience might be a touch harder to specify, but we probably incline to locate it in what we call *the media* (possibly as inept a term as ever was), and particularly in that section of it, located on the eastern seaboard, that a former governor of Maryland recently said such mean things about. Or you might say that the national conscience was located in the mouth of the former governor of Maryland, rising in righteous indignation against the coalition of the N.A.M., the networks, the *New York Times*, the academic intellectuals, the other intellectuals, the Mafia, the black people, the poor whites, and for all I know the Junior League, who are destroying the country. Someone is always destroying the country.

And whenever we talk about anything big enough and multifarious enough to be invisible when we try to look at it, we are talking mythology. That is not necessarily a bad thing; though I know a teacher who after ten years of explaining to his pupils "When I say Mythology, I don't mean a damn lie" said to me late at night, "You know, Howard, when I say Mythology I mean a damn lie." Not necessarily a bad thing, but necessarily a necessary thing; we simply don't have non-mythological ways of talking.

There is a deeper and more implicit national conscience, though unhappily it is also mythological. If I kick my cat on the

157

front lawn in full view of the neighbors, I shall be reported to the S.P.C.A., and everyone except myself and possibly the cat will feel a touch more righteous; there are things, you see, that simply are not done. The fact, however, that humane societies routinely protect the stray animals entrusted to their care by killing them does not enter the question. In the same way, we are shocked, if we happen to think about it, at societies in which animal sacrifice is an accepted and necessary part of life, and we rather think such horrible things must have happened "in the olden times," as we children used to say. That our own society, for our health and security, tortures and sacrifices animals in numbers exponentially greater than Egypt could have managed in thirty generations, simply never enters in evidence, it doesn't come in the category of conscience but in the category of science. It comes not near our national conscience, which is extremely—and, I should add, necessarily—selective. The great human slogan has always been "After all, we've got to live," and if a shrewd voice murmurs from the shades that he doesn't see the necessity, we shall praise him and honor him and bestow great wealth upon him, but we shall also, just as he did himself, go on trying. And I fear that the national conscience may have to be defined as Mencken defined the individual one: The still small voice that tells you someone is watching.

Now as to poetry. Poets have often behaved, and do now often behave, as though they were, if not a national conscience, at least some kind of capital C Conscience, looking upon the doings of others as surely accursed and bound to lead to eternal perdition in the end. Some poets have made quite a good living at it, for prophecy is powerful magic that can be worked by anyone having sufficient *hubris,* or *chutzpah.* It's almost too easy. Prophets always predict disaster, and disaster unfailingly happens; far as I remember the only exception was Jonah, who succeeded in convincing the people of Nineveh to repent, and therefore failed as a prophet; the city was not destroyed. Jonah was furious, too, and that failure is almost undoubtedly the reason that his book is so much shorter than, say, the book of Isaiah, all three of him.

What fails to be observed in all this is that the world does not respond to these eloquent chidings by getting better; and in view of the continuing state of the world it would be simple

prudence for poets to dissociate themselves from the con-
science-keeping job entirely and at once, before somebody no-
tices what a complete and utter failure they've been at it.

There has been available for many years now a nice, genteel
way in which the poets could be national consciences comfortably, without saying mean things and without getting anybody
mad. What we were doing, with our heavenly witch hazel, was
"purifying the language of the tribe" (Rimbaud, popularized in
English by T. S. Eliot). The argument went on to say that as
soon as the language of the tribe had been purified enough,
people would be ever so much nicer to one another. I used to
sort of believe something of the kind myself, but was finally
compelled to admit that we were no better at being this sort of
conscience than at being the finger-shaking kind that said *naughty
naughty, you mustn't.* Just look at the shape the language of the
tribe is in now! The poets might as profitably have put in their
time underwater, washing the fish.

All this perhaps will seem sort of unfeeling. I remind you
that I am addressing the question of poetry and the national
conscience, and trying to do it in a professional way. As a person, as a citizen, I am aware that things are not well with us,
and my response to the situation, which is not part of the question here, is made as a person and as a citizen, not as a poet. In
the same way, when I did my time in various air forces, several
years spent in an improbable state of boredom, confusion and
terror all at the same time, I did so as a person and as a citizen,
not as a poet.

Before going on to my conclusion, I interject two obituary
remarks anent the poet and the national conscience.

> He was an advocate of universal peace, that condition
> wherein the rich might lie down on top of the poor with
> safety as well as pleasure.
> Epitaph on a poet: He appealed to man's higher nature,
> and nobody bought his books.

To wind up, I should try to say in a few words what I think
poetry actually is able to do for us sojourners in this vale of tears,
and why we value it, and why it is proper for us to value it. Poetry, I believe, is neither a sacrament nor a con game. But to

159

say so is to acknowledge the precarious, poised between nature of poetry, and its constant temptation, so often yielded to by the poets, to stray over into sacrament or into con game. Sacred books are written by poets, though also, it appears, by genealogists, priests, merchants and certified public accountants. And the look, the feel, almost the mind of a religion are potently though subtly altered by the becoming almost canonical of its greatest poetry; as *The Comedy* altered Roman Catholicism, so *Paradise Lost* and later on *The Prelude* altered Anglicanism. On the con game side, we have always with us the versifying parsons and riming salesmen of the word so attentively characterized by Macaulay: "venal and licentious scribblers, with just sufficient talent to clothe the thoughts of a pandar in the style of a bellman." He meant the writers most favored in Milton's time, but from no time have they been absent.

At the height of its powers, poetry is—or must we now say poetry was?—a magical means of conferring immunity for a time from the fear of pain and the fear of misery and the fear of death. Poetry accomplished this humane object by homeopathic means; the poets sing of almost nothing but human suffering, cruelty, fear, death, and loss of every kind, and they do this, or did this, in the richest and loveliest and most pleasure-bearing language they could find, so that suffering and loss came to their hearers under their aspects of power, heroism, nobility, courage and courtesy and love—and, of course, illusion. The poise of poetry was to sustain that illusion delicately between the highest truth revealed to the believer and the crummy nature of everyday life, which was and is what Hobbes called it: solitary, poor, nasty, brutish, and short.*

As most great magicks do, poetry operated successfully in this manner only under a certain prohibition, which was that the reality of newspapers must never be allowed to break through except for purposes clearly understood to be satirical and low; this prohibition, I think, must have been behind the unwritten and largely forgotten law of decorum. Of course, when the language and reality of newspapers does in fact replace serious poetry there are always excellent reasons for its doing so; the poetry

---

*Hobbes meant life in the state of nature. But his epithets seem to have become proverbial precisely because writers kept quoting them in application to life in society in their own times.

that sustained the sense of civilization has probably formalized and hardened too far from what people say and think and feel to be how things are. Something like that seems to have happened around 1800 in England, and again around the time of the First World War. And yet, as if by miracle, great poets again arose to find or make a living language, a sweet and lofty style. May it happen again, even out of so unlikely a source as the language of newspapers. Probably, indeed, it has happened again, but we were too busy reading the papers to have noticed.

On the Edge of Darkness: What Is Political Poetry?*

DENISE LEVERTOV

Destiny
will be changed one morning
when, at the edge of darkness,
they stand up.
. . . About them
it was said
they have nothing to lose but their chains.

NAZIM HIKMET

A good deal of poetry one can call *political* in some way has appeared in this country and elsewhere in recent years. When I asked a young poet who has written some such poems what he would want to hear about in a lecture on poetry and politics, he replied that he'd like some assurance that there was a tradition for political poems, the poetry of social criticism, and that it was not a rootless phenomenon. So I shall begin by trying to trace some precedents.

When we look for a tradition for the political, or polemical poem, we may find ourselves turning first to the epic, since Ezra Pound called the epic "a poem containing history." An unsatisfactory definition, for it leaves out the element of narrative, the presence of a hero protagonist (or a heroine, as in the Vietnamese national epic) whose adventures we follow through a course of historical events. Besides, there are hero tales which are in-

---

*Presented as a lecture at Boston University, 1975.

deed epics but are clearly cosmological, theological, rather than historical; which are epics of the inner, psychological, life of humanity, not of outer events. Valéry's assertion that "An epic is a poem that can be told. When one tells it, one has a bilingual text" is a nice aphorism on paraphrase, but even more unsatisfactory as a definition of epic than Pound's. One can "tell" the story sung in a ballad. One can "tell" the story line of many of Hardy's poems. One can even "tell," for instance, the story line of a George Herbert poem such as "The Collar" ("I struck the board and cried, No more!")—but this doesn't make any of them epics. In any case it is obvious that the presence of history—or of politics, as we call our immediate social environment when it is critically examined, whether favorably or unfavorably—such presence as an intrinsic factor doesn't make a poem into an epic, though the same factor may inform some epics. A sonnet, a ballad, a satiric epistle, an isolated quatrain or couplet may be as pivoted on historical consciousness, and as charged, or more so, with partisan conviction, as any accredited epic. Shelley's "I met Murder on the way/He wore a mask like Castlereigh," is a small model of the political poem which never fails to give me a *frisson*—to make my hair stand on end or the top of my head seem to rise, according to the well known tests of Housman and Emily Dickinson.

If we concede, then, that historical or socio-political motifs have appeared in poetic modes of many kinds, and cannot be identified with any mode in particular, we come straightway to the more essential question: Can partisan, polemical content, in whatever poetic form it appears, be good poetry? This seems to me strictly a modern question, having its roots in the Romantic period but not really troubling anyone until the late nineteenth century. The Romantic period accelerated the isolation of the poet from the community. Perhaps we may say that this isolation had begun, slowly, long before—perhaps from the time of the first printing presses and the consequent decline in the oral, communal experience of poetry and the growth of a literate élite. But the Romantic period intensified this isolation by seeing the artist as endowed with a special sort of temperament which was not only operative during *the making* of works of art, not only when the poet donned the Bardic mantle, and was actually writing, but which made him at all times supersensitive. Shake-

speare had written of "the poet's eye in a fine frenzy rolling"—
but let's recall the lines that follow:

The poet's eye, in a fine frenzy rolling,
Doth glance from heaven to earth, from earth to heaven;
And as imagination bodies forth
The forms of things unknown, the poet's pen
Turns them to shapes, and gives to airy nothing
A local habitation and a name.

The description is of a working poet, not of the poetic temperament. I don't know where the "supersensitive" image origi-
nated—partially no doubt in the cultivation by poets and artists
of a Bohemian style of life out of disgust and boredom with
bourgeois alternatives—but in any case, poets, or artists in general, did accept this image of themselves and fostered it. It was
an easy ego-trip. The public, predictably, began to think of them
as undependable fellows, at best whimsical and capricious, at
worst, dangerous madmen, and in any case not responsible citizens. The madness of the poet, as seen by the bourgeois, is not
the divine madness of the shaman poets of ancient or primitive
societies, but a quotidian foolishness and tendency to exagger-
ate, not worthy to be taken seriously. Thus a good measure of
effectiveness was taken away from the poet by what had *seemed*
an elevation of his role: that is, by the attribution to him of more
refined sensibilities and profounder passions than those of other
people. (My own belief, as I've testified elsewhere, is that a poet
is only a poet when engaged in making poems, and has no
rightful claim to *feeling* more than others, but only to being able
to *articulate* feeling through the medium of language.) Moreover, nineteenth-century bourgeois consciousness, as a concom-
itant of its understandable disrespect for the Romantic version
of The Poet, proceeded to denature or defuse certain chosen
poets (not without the collusion of the poets themselves) by en-
shrining them in temples of respectability—I'm thinking of the
adulation of Tennyson and of what his laureateship did to his
gifts; or of the vaporous earnestness (what a combination!) of
"Browning Societies." Much the same thing happened a little later
on to, of all people, Walt Whitman, who for a time was regarded as a sort of Kahil Gibran-like "philosopher." The question, Can a political poem be poetry? seems to me a wholly

modern one. The Romantic image of the poet was above all one which emphasized his individuality—his difference from other people rather than the ways in which he resembled them; and this led to the elevation of the lyric mode as the type or exemplar of poetry, because it was the most *personal* mode. Dramatic, satiric, and epic poetry had had precedence through centuries of Western history; and these modes offer obvious opportunities for the expression of ideas, convictions, and even mere opinions. Even before the lyric—both as a mode and as an element in other modes—came to be more and more highly valued (while its true nature was often misunderstood, e.g., "Gems from Thomas Moore," "Gems from Shakespeare," "The Sir Walter Scott Birthday Book" etc.), the novel had swiftly developed and had taken over many of the subjects previously accommodated by nonlyric poetry. Thus there developed a distrust of the political when it did turn up in verse, since poetry and lyric form became almost synonymous to many people—and still are, as anyone who has taught poetry workshops knows. How often does a student ever attempt a nonlyric mode unless assigned to do so?

However, writers who accepted the lyric as the available mode and whose bent was for poetry, not for prose, nevertheless had a variety of things to say; so that the lyric in the twentieth century, like prose fiction, has become a repository for content previously dealt with in dramatic, epic, narrative, or satiric modes. At this time, in America at any rate, there is no category of content not attempted in what appears, in structure, to be lyric verse. But whereas critics and the public are not dismayed when autobiography, psychological explorations, or at the other extreme, trivia, appear in lyric semblance, yet the political is often looked at askance and subjected to a more stringent examination. The question, *Is it really poetry, or is it just versified ideas?* must indeed be asked; but it should by rights be asked equally of all those poems which present content of all kinds *not* anciently considered the province of the lyric, and not only of political content. And if a degree of intimacy is a condition of lyric expression, surely—at times when events make feelings run high—that intimacy between writer and political belief does exist, and is as intense as other emotions.

Here it seems time to respond to the initial enquiry, Has the political poem a tradition? My answer would be, Yes, and that tradition includes "Piers Plowman," Sir Walter Raleigh's "The Lie," certain of Milton's sonnets and of Wordsworth's, most of Blake and of Wilfred Owen, to skip at random from name to name that instantly come to mind, confining myself arbitrarily to English poets. If I begin to look at other literatures I at once include Dante, Quevedo, Heine; while in our own century we have such poets as Neruda, Ritsos, Brecht, etc. as well as innumerable lesser-known ones or ones who write in languages that are infrequently translated into English. I am not attempting to *catalogue* even the major poets who have written political poems, and certainly not the minor ones. Nor do I want to digress into a discussion of the political stance of individual poets, except perhaps to note that most political poetry, if not actually revolutionary, takes its stand on the side of liberty and not of maintaining the status quo. Even poets whose avowed politics we may justifiably consider reactionary, such as Yeats, Pound, or Jeffers, see in their authoritarian allegiances virtues most of us would certainly not associate with the right wing. The same may be said about Neruda's poems of a certain period when he supposed Stalin to possess humane qualities we are sure he did not have. Political poems typically celebrate freedom and honor even when the poet suffers illusion about where these are to be found. There are poems that, crying out against injustice, call for bloody vengeance against tyrants; but poets who knowingly praise tyranny itself are rare indeed. (D'Annunzio is the only example I can recall.)

So, the poem of political content— even of politically *hortatory* content—does unquestionably have a long and illustrious history. What characterizes its contemporary manifestations? Most, indeed I'd almost say all, of the current poetry on political themes is lyrical in presentation though not necessarily in tone. By lyrical in presentation I mean it consists typically of short, or fairly short, poems written without personae: nakedly, candidly, speaking in the poet's unmediated character, often with actual syntactic incorporation of the first person singular, or sometimes the first person plural; but in any case written from a personal rather than a fictive, and a subjective rather than objective, standpoint. The musicality characteristic of its origins has become, as the lyric has expanded its range of content, something of a Cheshire cat's smile—it appears, disappears, reappears. However, this seems to be just as true where other kinds of content are concerned as it is in political poems. The kinds of political content we see in present-day American poetry are several, though one can say they represent a coalition of issues, united by a common desire for social change, and by an intense recognition of the urgency of struggle for survival itself in a world threatened as never before. Thus, we see bodies of poetry dealing with specific aspects of this struggle—poems about racism and the Black, Native American, Latino and other minorities; Feminist poems; Gay liberation poems; poems from the antiwar, antiarms-race, antinuclear movement and from the environmentalist branch of it; but not infrequently, poems in one such category are written by poets who also contribute to one or more of the other categories. A striking characteristic of contemporary political poetry is that, more than in the past, it is written by people who are active participants in the causes they write about, and not simply observers. It's a reciprocal phenomenon: people who are already poets in any case become involved in some aspect or aspects of these interrelated struggles, and it follows naturally that they write poems concerned with the causes they believe in; these in turn inspire others, both to participation and to the writing of poems. Whether these poems are good or not depends on the gifts of the poet, not on the subject matter. But what is interesting historically is the greater interplay between these poets' actions and their writing.

For many of us who are thus involved, it is possible that our sense of political urgency is at times an almost hectic stimulus. Certainly it is true that when one participates, for instance, in a vigil to commemorate the dead of Hiroshima and Nagasaki, or attends a teach-in about the nuclear superdanger we all ignore most of the time, then one's conscious awareness of these issues is intensified; and if one is led by a resulting commitment to the attempt to combat what threatens us, and thus to the experience of comradeship in actions involving some risk, such as civil disobedience, then one is living a stirring emotional life which—if one is given to writing poetry—is almost bound to result in poems directly related to these experiences, and to the beliefs one shares with companions who often present a humbling example of modesty, persistence, and courage.

> "Peace" was our password
> that stung from lip to lip . . .
>
> I shall not forget the light
> of recognition in your eyes
>
> your name is New Beginning
> I love you, New Beginning,

wrote the late Paul Goodman after one of the big demonstrations in Washington during the Viet Nam war, in a poem that typically does not isolate the personal from the social.

One kind of political poem demonstrates active empathy—the projection of a nonparticipant into the experience of others very different from himself; for example in Heine's famous poem about the Silesian weavers, one seems indeed to hear not Heine's voice but that of the weavers themselves. Yet at the same time how intimately it expresses his own bitterness. But more typical of contemporary poetry are the poems being written about prisons by prisoners; about racial or sexual injustices by people who suffer them and engage in struggle against them; about the horrors of war, not only by soldiers (which is nothing new) but also by activists against war, and about pollution of natural resources by people who in their daily lives work at organic farming, at conservation, or at litigation in behalf of the preservation of the environment; or who join in antinuclear and other protest actions and civil disobedience. It seems as if the sense of urgency, indeed of desperation, that permeates our lives, has the effect, if it does not paralyze us, of intensifying and diversifying our activities; it is not enough to write *or* act, we feel we must do both. And this means that there's less distance between event and poem, less time for reflection, more immediacy. These are neutral factors in themselves—they may be used to advantage or disadvantage.

The world-famous Turkish poet Nazim Hikmet, who spent more than seventeen years of his life in jail as a political prisoner, wrote a number of powerful poems in his confinement, poems which notably combine the context of oppression with the unquenchable love of life that characterized him.[1] A young Mexican-American, Jimmy Santiago Baca, whose first book[2] was also written in jail, presents another example of a poetry of di-

rect personal experience which is both political and lyrical. Such
poems are not didactic in an obvious way, not hortatory; they
don't tell one what to do. (Though Hikmet does give advice.)
But Bertholt Brecht, whose name can't fail to come to mind if
one is looking for a tradition in engaged poetry, had no com-
punction about being didactic. These three writers provide an
instructive range of possible approaches: Brecht's poems are dry,
crisp, they give one curt warnings, they are marching orders.
Hikmet is relaxed, expansive, generous—his confidence not only
in himself but in humanity is unshaken by a life that would have
embittered or crushed most people. Jimmy Santiago Baca, at
twenty-five, exhorts not others but himself; full of a rich, sensuous, romantic talent, his poems let us participate in a process
of personal growth and developing consciousness, not without
bitterness and rage but not dominated by those emotions. All
seem to me to *be* political poems despite their differences.

"I'd like to know if political poems have brought about any
changes," said my friend who wanted reassurance that there was
a tradition behind him. I don't think one can accurately measure the historical effectiveness of a poem; but one does know,
of course, that books influence individuals; and individuals, although they are part of large economic and social processes, influence history. Every mass is after all made up of millions of
individuals. Many forces combine to push now one individual,
now another, into prominence at certain crucial moments. The
flash of a poem onto the mind's screen, a novel imaginatively
entered and lived in at an open time in that person's life, certainly can be among those forces. A famous example of the historical impact of literature is that of Turgenev reading *Uncle
Tom's Cabin* and, at least partially because he was moved by it
(and with all its flaws it *is* moving), creating *A Sportsman's Notebook,* which in turn was at least one of the factors that impelled
the relatively liberal Tsar Alexander to free the serfs. Ford Ma-
dox Ford has a little fantasy on this theme. First he notes that,

> It is to be remembered that Alexander ordered the eman-
> cipation of the serfs three days after he had finished read-
> ing *A Sportsman's Sketches.* . . .

and then he goes on to imagine,

169

the humane Tsar lying down on a couch. . . . I don't know
why I imagine him lying down . . . perhaps because humane people when they want to enjoy themselves over a
good read in a book always lie down . . . the humane Tsar,
then, lying down with the *Sportsman's Sketches* held up to
his eyes began to read what Turgenev had observed when
shooting partridges over dogs . . . with the ineffable
scapegrace serf Yermolai at his heels. . . . And suddenly
the Tsar was going through the endless forests and over
the endless moors. He had the smell of the pines and
heather in his nostrils, the sunbaked Russian earth beneath his feet. . . . Yermolai did not have the second gun
as ready as he should; Yermolai had not even loaded the
second gun; Yermolai, the serf, had lagged behind; serf
Yermolai had disappeared altogether; he had found a wild
bees' nest in a hollow tree; he was luxuriously supping
honey ignoring the beestings. . . . And suddenly the Tsar
himself was Yermolai. . . . He was a serf who might be
thrashed, loaded with chains, banished to a hopeless district a thousand miles away, put to working in the salt
mines. . . . The Tsar was supping the heather-scented
brown honey in the hot sun. . . . He saw his Owner approaching. His Owner was fortunately a softy. Still it was
disagreeable to have the Owner cold to him. . . . And
quickly the Tsar sent his eyes over the country, through
the trees in search of a hut. If he saw a hut he would remember the story of its idiotic owners. He would tell the
idiotic story to the Owner and in listening to it the Owner
would become engrossed in the despairing ruin of those
idiotic creatures and would forget to be displeased and the
Tsar would have two undeserved pork chops and the remains of a bottle of champagne that night in the wood-
lodge.

And so the Tsar would become a woodcutter in danger of being banished for cutting the wrong trees, and a
small landowner being ruined by his own ignorance and
the shiftlessness of his serfs . . . and a house-serf dressed
as a footman with plush breeches to whom his Owner was
saying with freezing politeness: "Brother, I regret it. But
you have again forgotten to chill the Beaujolais. You must
prepare yourself to receive fifty lashes. . . ." And the Tsar
would be Turgenev shuddering over the Owner's magnif-
icently appointed table whilst outside the footman was re-

ceiving the fifty lashes. . . . And Alexander II would become the old, fat old maid, knitting whilst her companion read Pushkin to her, and crying over romantic passages and refusing to sell Anna Nicolaevna to Mr. Schubin, the neighbouring noble landowner who had fallen incomprehensibly in love with Anna Nicolaevna. . . . And the Autocrat of All the Russias would find himself being the serf-girl Anna Nicolaevna, banished into the dreadful Kursk district because the incomparable noble landowner Mr. Schubin had fallen in love with her. . . . And the great bearded Autocrat with the hairy chest would be twisting his fingers in his apron and crying . . . crying . . . crying. . . . And saying, "Is it possible that God and the Tsar permit such things to be?"

And so, on the third day, the Tsar stretches out his hand for his pen . . . and just those things would never be any more. . . . There would be other bad things, but not just those because the world had crept half a hair's breadth nearer to civilization. . . .

. . . You may imagine how Turgenev's eyes stood out of his head on the day when he met Mrs. Harriet Beecher Stowe . . . who for her part had never been below the Mason and Dixon line . . . and who was introduced to him as being the heroine that had made the chains to fall from the limbs of the slaves of a continent. . . . He said that she seemed to him to be a modest and sensible person. . . . Perhaps the reader will think out for himself all that that amazing meeting signified.

Still another aspect of the tradition of political poetry is the way in which, just as songs do, it can express and heighten a shared emotion, intensifying morale rather than making converts. "To have embodied hope for many people, even for one minute," said Neruda, "is something unforgettable and profoundly touching for any poet." The response to contemporary engaged poems, I have found, is frequently from readers who find their own experience confirmed in them, and from others who discover in such poems something that culminates a process of thought and feeling already under way, and propels them into some form of action.

I've been talking all this while about poetry that is political; that's all very well, but the question of whether it is poetic remains unanswered. Now we must enquire of our inner Sphinx, What does "poetic" *mean*? To which, of course, our Sphinx will disdain a direct response—yet perhaps a faint smile, a flutter of its eyelashes, a brief passage of Sphinx tongue over Sphinx lips, may indicate that the *senses* are implicated. The Sphinx tail may lash a little—a sure sign that the *aesthetic faculty* is involved.

We are to ask, then, of the political poem (which in our time means relatively brief, and therefore ostensibly lyric, poems that deal nevertheless with social observations and even opinions, such as the lyric used not typically to deal with) that it affect our senses and engage our aesthetic response just as much as one with whose content—spring, love, death, a rainbow—we can have no argument. Children of the twentieth century that we are, the old topics may indeed only exacerbate our *angst,* and we are long used to a wider and gloomier range. Yet we are still inheritors of the Romantic emphasis on the individual and upon individual epiphanies. And in habitually equating the poetic with the lyrical perhaps we are, after all, correct; but we have come to identify the short poem with the lyric *even when it lacks lyricism,* and consequently, often fail to recognize the lyric *spirit* if it appears in company with the didactic. Thus a totally unlyrical poem passes muster, even though it is flat and banal, merely because it is short and deals with a noncontroversial personal experience; whereas the passionate partisanship of a political poem may block the reader from responding to its sensuous and emotive power simply because expectation does not link these elements with political convictions. That is one reaction. More dangerous to poetry is the contrasting assumption by partisan poets and their constituencies that the subject matter carries so strong an emotive charge in itself that it is unnecessary to remember poetry's roots in song, magic, and the high craft that makes itself felt as exhilarating beauty even when the content voices rage or utters a grim warning. The results of this assumption give rise to much understandable distrust and prejudice.

No matter how much validity and courage the poet's opinions have, no matter that he or she may have died for them or gone into bitter exile on their account, "unless" (wrote William Carlos Williams), "unless all this is already in his writing—in the materials and structure of it—he might better have been a cowhand. . . . Everything else is secondary, but for the artist *that,*

which has made the greatest art one and permanent, that continual reassertion of structure, is first. . . . The altered structure of the inevitable revolution must be *in* the poem, in it. Made
of it. It must shine in the structural body of it. . . . Then, indeed, propaganda can be thoroughly welcomed . . . for by that
it has been transmuted into the materials of art. It has no life
unless to live or die judged by an artist's standards. But if, by
imposing . . . a depleted, restrictive and unrealized form, the
propagandist thinks he can make what he has to say convincing
by merely filling in that wooden structure with some ideas he
wants to put over—he turns up not only as no artist but a
weak fool."[3]

Political poetry, said Neruda, is never what young poets
should begin with. "Political poetry" (he added) "is more deeply
emotional than any other except love poetry. You must have
traversed the whole of poetry before you become a political
poet."[4] Clearly, then, political poetry does not obey special laws
but must be subject to those which govern *every* kind of poetry.
Paul Valéry was speaking of poetry's essential nature when he
said, "Poetry must extend over the whole being; it stimulates the
muscular organization by its rhythms, it frees or unleashes the
verbal faculties, ennobling their whole action; it regulates our
depths, for poetry aims to arouse . . . the unity or harmony of
the living person, an extraordinary unity that shows itself when
a person is possessed by an intense feeling that leaves none of
his powers disengaged."[5]

What those of us whose lives are permeated by a sense of
unremitting political emergency, and who are at the same time
writers of poetry, most desire in our work, I think, is to attain
to such osmosis of the personal and the public, of assertion and
of song, that no one would be able to divide our poems into
categories. The didactic would be lyrical, the lyrical would
be didactic. That is, at any rate, my own probably unattain-
able goal. . . .

To sum up: (1) Politics is a subject many poets and poems,
including some of the greatest, have treated throughout European history. It is no more alien to the medium than any other
human concern. (2) The suspicion with which political or social
content is often regarded is a modern phenomenon and arises
from a narrow and mistaken idea of the poem as always a pri-

vate expression of emotion which the reader is permitted to overhear, and that therefore the hortatory or didactic is an unsuitable mode of address for poets. (3) The political poetry of contemporary America is more often written by active participants in political and social struggle than it was in the past. (4) Many writers of political poetry persist in supposing the emotive power of their subject alone is sufficient to make their poems poetic. This accounts for a lot of semidoggerel. But the fact of their direct involvement in the situations about which they write may sometimes be an advantage if they are also really poets, imparting a concreteness to their passion and an authenticity to their metaphors. (5) Poetry can indirectly have an effect upon the course of events by awakening pity, terror, compassion and the conscience of leaders; and by strengthening the morale of persons working for a common cause. (6) For political poetry, as for any other kind, the *sine qua non* is that it elicit "the poetic emotion"—that which Valéry describes as a condition "in which . . . responses are exchanges between all [the reader's] sensitive and rhythmic powers." "The poet's profession," Valéry claims, "is to find by good fortune and to seek with industry the production of those special forms of language" which set up "this harmonious exchange between impression and expression."[6] And political verses attain to that exchange—that is, to the condition of poetry—by the same means as any other kind: good faith, passionate conviction and, in equal measure, the precise operations of the creative imagination which sifts and sorts, leaps and pounces upon, strokes and shoves into a design the adored *words* that are the treasure of a faculty in love with its medium, even upon what Hikmet called the very "edge of darkness."

NOTES

1. See *Things I Didn't Know I Loved: Selected Poems of Nazim Hikmet* translated by Randy Blasing and Mutlu Konuk (New York, Persea Books, 1975).
2. *Immigrants in Our Own Land* by Jimmy Santiago Baca (Louisiana State University Press, 1979).
3. "Against the Weather" (1939), in *The Selected Essays of William Carlos Williams* (New York, New Directions, 1969).
4. *Seven Voices,* interview with Rita Guibert (New York, Alfred A. Knopf, 1972).
5. In Paul Valéry, *The Art of Poetry* (New York, Houghton Mifflin, 1939).
6. In Valéry, *The Art of Poetry.*

The Revolutionary Tradition in Afro-American Literature

AMIRI BARAKA

In speaking about the general ghettoized condition of Afro-American literature within the framework of the so-called American literature, Bruce Franklin, a professor at Newark Rutgers University, had this to say in the *Minnesota Review:* "If we wish to continue to use the term 'American literature,' we must either admit that we mean white American literature or construe it to include the literature of several peoples, including the Afro-American nation. The latter course leads to a fundamental redefinition of American literature, its history, and the criteria appropriate to each and every American literary work. For the viewpoint of oppressed people can then no longer be excluded from the criticism and teaching of American literature."

Franklin went on to say, "The most distinctive feature of United States history is Afro-American slavery and its consequences. This truth is at the heart of our political, economic and social experience as a nation-state. It is also at the heart of our *cultural* experience, and therefore the slave narrative, like Afro-American culture in general, is not peripheral but central to American culture."

These words are so important because Franklin sums up not only the fact that what is called American literature is basically the literature of certain white men; he also points out the importance to American culture and life itself of Afro-American life and culture. But if we look at the standard history of American literature, Franklin points to *The Literary History of the U.S.* by Spiller, Thorp, Johnson, Canby, Ludwig and Gibson, a college standard, revised in its fourth edition in 1974. We find in its 1555 pages of small print four black writers—Chesnutt, Dunbar, Hughes and Wright—and in the section of literature produced by the South during the Civil War, they devote three chapters, and discuss such literary giants as Hugh Legare, William Wirt and George Fitzhugh, author of *Cannibals All, or Slaves Without Masters.* There is no mention of the slave narrative or slave poetry. There is no mention even of William Wells Brown, the nineteenth-century black novelist and playwright. They do not even mention Frederick Douglass!

So we must face the essential national chauvinism of what is taught as American literature. It should be obvious that it, like all other aspects of American life, represents the choice of a white elite, and what's more, even deemphasizes some aspects and confuses American literature, the white part of it, so that in many instances the anthologies and survey courses that we learn literature from are the choices of or have been influenced to a great extent by some of the most reactionary elements in this society. We have been raised up in literature too often on right-wing anthologies, and right-wing critics, pushing conservative and reactionary literature, playing down the progressive and revolutionary forces and excluding almost outright the oppressed nationalities and minorities and women.

It was the rebellions of the sixties, explosions in 110 U.S. cities, that created the few black studies and Afro-American studies departments that exist today. At the same time, these uprisings created the agonizingly small space that Afro-American literature takes up in the canon of academic and commercial written culture. A few authors got walk-on roles, to paraphrase Franklin again.

So first we must see the basic distortion that is given to all American literary history and to the official reflection of U.S. life and culture. This distortion occurs because the literary establishment and the academic establishment, far from being independent, represent in the main, the ideas and world view of the rulers of this country. These ideas, and the institutions from which they are mashed on us, constitute merely the superstructure of this society, a superstructure that reflects the economic foundations upon which they are built, the material base for U.S. life and culture, monopoly capitalism. So that in the main what is taught and pushed as great literature or great art, philosophy, &c, is mainly ideas and concepts that can help maintain the status quo, which includes not only the exploitation of the majority by a capitalist elite but also national oppression, racism, the oppression of women, and the extension of U.S. imperialism all over the world!

Afro-American literature as it has come into view fragmented by chauvinism and distorted by the same reactionary forces that have distorted American literature itself has indeed been laid out in the same confusing and oblique fashion. A method intended to hide more than it reveals, a method that wants to show that at best Afro-American literature is a mediocre and conservative reflection of the mediocre and conservative portrait that is given of all American literature.

In Afro-American literature, for instance, we have been taught that its beginnings rest with the writings of people like Phillis Wheatley and Jupiter Hammon. Ms. Wheatley, writing in the eighteenth century, is simply an imitation of Alexander Pope. First, it was against the law for black slaves to learn to read or write. So Ms. Wheatley's writings could only come under the "Gee whiz, it's alive" category of Dr. Frankenstein checking out his new monster! Also Wheatley's literature abounds with sentiments like " 'Twas mercy brought me from my pagan land," evincing gratitude at slavery—that the European slave trade had actually helped the Africans by exposing them to the great European culture. Which be the monster remarking how wise, how omniscient, be her creator!

Hammon is, if possible, even worse. In his stiff doggerel are such great ideas as Slavery was good for us Africans because it taught us humility, so when we get to heaven we'll know how to act around God. Pretty far out! (Both were privileged Northern house servants reflecting both their privilege and their removal and isolation from the masses of African/Afro-American slaves.)

But these two are pushed as Afro-American literature simply as a method of showing off trained whatnots demonstrating the glory of the trainer. But this is not the beginnings of Afro-American literature.

The black people of this country were brought here in slav-

ery chains on the fast clipper ships of rising European capitalism. It is impossible to separate the rise of capitalism, the
industrial revolution, the emergence of England and later
America as world powers from the trade in Africans. And from
the Africans' initial presence as commodities initiating world trade
through the triangular trade route of slaves to the New World,
cotton, rum, indigo, to England and manufactured goods to
Africa for the African feudal ruling classes who had sold the
other Africans into slavery, Black life has contributed to and
animated the Anglo-American life and culture. But a formal artifacted presence (as art) cd be easily denied slaves. The African
culture was banned by the slave masters as *subversive.* Christianity was used first as a measure of civilization (i.e., if you weren't
a Christian you weren't civilized—the papal bull states it is cool
to enslave non-Christians) but later it was used as a pacifier and
bringer of social control (its present function). The development of a *specifically* Afro-American culture must wait for the
emergence of the Afro-American people, the particular nationality composed of Africans reorganized by the fact and processes of slavery into an American people of African descent.

The most practical artifacts of that culture are the tools and
environment of day-to-day living. In these practical pursuits are
found the earliest Afro-American art—artifacted reflections of
the life of that people. The music, because it is most abstract
and could not therefore be so severely limited and checked by
slave culture, must have been the earliest of the "nonpractical"
arts to engage, (tho a work song is to help one work!) the work
song, chants, hollers, the spirituals, eventually the blues.

Afro-American literature rises as a reflection of the self-
consciousness and self-expression of the Afro-American people, but to be an Afro-American literature, truly, it must reflect
in the main the ideological and sociocultural portrait of that
people! The Wheatleys & Hammons reflect the ideology of
Charlie McCarthy in relationship to Edgar Bergen (is that before anybody's time?). The celebration of servitude is not the
ideological reflection of the Afro-American masses, but of their
tormentors.

In the slave narratives—the works of Frederick Douglass,
Henry Bibb, Moses Roper, Linda Brent, W. Wells Brown, the
Krafts, Henry "Box" Brown, Solomon Nothrup, James Pen-

nington and others—are found the beginnings of a genuine Afro-American literature—the stirring narratives of slave America, the exploits and heroism of resistance and escape, the ongoing struggle and determination of that people to be free. Beside this body of strong, dramatic, incisive, democratic literature, where is the literature of the slavemasters and—mistresses? Find it and compare it with the slave narratives and say which has a clearer, more honest and ultimately more artistically powerful perception of American Reality! (Yes, where are the William Gilmore Simmses, John Pendleton Kennedys, Augustus B. Longstreets and George Washington Harrises touted as the outstanding writers of the white slave South? Their literature is unreadable, even though overt racists like Allen Tate and the Southern Agrarians prated about it as a "gracious culture despite its defects," those defects consisting in the main of millions of black slaves, whose life expectancy by the beginning of the nineteenth century in the deep South, at maturity (18), was seven years). One of the main arguments for black slavery, Bruce Franklin points out in *The Victim as Criminal and Artist,* was that the blacks could do the manual labor "for which they were best suited," "leaving their owners free to create a fine, elegant and lasting culture" (p. 28). But check it out, at best such artistic efforts as represent this so-called lasting culture are embarrassing satires, the efforts of the Southern Agrarians to represent them as something else notwithstanding.

The slave narratives are portraits of a people in motion and they came into being created by the economic, social and political life of the U.S. The early part of the nineteenth century was marked by an intensification of slavery, the taking away of the limited civil rights of the free blacks as well. This was because slavery did not die out as was predicted towards the end of the eighteenth century. With the discovery of the cotton gin, to the feudalistic or patriarchal slavery imposed on blacks was now added capitalist exploitation. Karl Marx points out in *Capital* that once cotton became an international commodity, no longer used only in U.S. domestic markets, U.S. blacks were not only tied for life to domestic slavery but now had added to their inhuman burden the horrors of having to produce *surplus value* as a kind of slave and proletariat in combination. The seven-year life expectancy resulted "downriver" in the Black Belt cotton region because the slavemasters discovered that working slaves to death and then replacing them was more profitable than letting them live to grow old, less productive but still eating, wearing clothes and taking up space!

This period of intense repression is when Afro-American literature emerges. It is also the period when the resistance of the Afro-American people intensifies. It is now that Gabriel Prosser, Denmark Vesey, Nat Turner lead their uprisings and rebellions and Harriet Tubman the Underground Railway.

At the approach of the Civil War, there is also another strong movement in Afro-American literature, the pre-Civil War revolutionary black nationalists: David Walker, the activists—Henry Highland Garnett, Charles Lenox Redmond, C. L. Langston, as well as William Wells Brown, an escaped slave who became the first black playwright and novelist. It is a literature sparked by protest, an antislavery literature, a fighting oral literature that even when it was written was meant to be proclaimed from the lecterns and pulpits of the North and circulated secretly to inspire the black slaves in the South. These were black abolitionists, damning slavery in no uncertain terms, proclaiming death to slavery and calling for rebellion from the slaves. This was not the upperclass white abolitionists, morally outraged but politically liberal. These were black revolutionists, some, like Langston, even calling for black people to seize the land they toiled upon because it was only that land that provided a practical basis for the survival and development of the Afro-American people!

Usually in discussing Afro-American literature, the Wheatleys and Hammons are combined with perhaps Douglass and maybe Brown's *Clotel*. The other slave narratives and the pre-Civil War black revolutionary nationalists are largely ignored or their importance diminished. Charles Chesnutt, who lamented that "quality" black folks had to be lumped together with the ignorant black masses, is pushed as a kind of father of black literature. Next, Paul Laurence Dunbar and James Weldon Johnson are raised to the top rank, but an analysis of the content of these men's works is made vague or onesided, so that we are not aware perhaps that for all the positive elements of Dunbar's work, his use of dialect is positive insofar as it is the language of the black masses, but negative in the way that Dunbar frequently uses it in the context of parties, eating and other "coonery." Most of Dunbar's "serious" poetry is not in dialect.

Dunbar was deeply conservative and his short story "The Patience of Gideon" shows a young slave, Gideon, who is put in charge of the plantation as the massa goes off to fight the Civil War. Gideon stays despite the masses of slaves running away as soon as Massa leaves. Even Gideon's wife-to-be pleads with him to leave, but he will not: he has made a promise to Massa, and so even his woman leaves him alone with his promise to the slavemaster.

J. W. Johnson's quandary was how to create a "high art" out of Afro-American materials, not completely understanding that high art is by definition slavemaster, bourgeois' art, and that what was and is needed by all artists—or at least by those artists who intend for their works to serve the exploited and oppressed majority in this country—is that they be artistically powerful and politically revolutionary!

Johnson's *Autobiography of an Ex-Colored Man* tells of that quandary in social terms, with his protagonist existing in a never-never land between black and white and finally deciding because he is shamed and humiliated and horrified by the lynching of a black man that he cannot be a member of a race so disgraced. He disappears among the whites, forsaking art for commerce, pursuing the white lady of his heart!

The real giant of this period, the transitional figure, the connector between the nineteenth-century Reconstruction and the new literary giants of the twentieth century and the Harlem Renaissance, is W.E.B. Du Bois. His *Souls of Black Folks*, which issued the intellectual challenge to the capitulationist philosophy of Booker T. Washington, is the intellectual and spiritual forerunner of the writings of the Renaissance. Du Bois's *Black Reconstruction* remains the most important work on the Reconstruction period done by an American. He was a social scientist and historian, as well as a novelist, poet and political activist. He founded black theatrical troupes like Krigwa Players, organized international conferences of black activism as leader of the Pan-Africanist movement, led social movements in the U.S. like the Niagara Movement and NAACP, was a fighting literary editor, and his works of historical and sociological analysis are among the greatest written by an American. He studied and wrote about all aspects of black life and its connection with Africa and the slave trade. He was a socialist by 1910, and at the end of his life, inspired by and inspiring the African independence movements, residing in Nkrumah's Ghana, he became a communist. It is not possible to understand the history of ideas in the U.S. without reading Du Bois. Not to know his work is not to have a whole picture of Afro-American literature, sociology, history and struggle and to have a distorted view of American life in general.

Langston Hughes' manifesto *The Negro Artist and the Racial Mountain* is not possible without Du Bois and his total rejection of American racial paternalism and cultural aggression. The Harlem Renaissance is simply the flowering of a twentieth-century Afro-American intelligentsia which reflects the motion of black people in America. They reflect a peasant people in motion out of the South headed toward the urban north to serve as cheap labor for the developing U.S. imperialism cut off from its European immigrants by the coming of World War I. The Harlem Renaissance is a literature of the new city dwellers who have left their rural past. It is a literature of revolt, it is anti-imperialist and fights the cultural aggression that imperialism visits upon its colonial and nationally oppressed conquests—first by reflecting and proclaiming the beauty and strengths of the oppressed people themselves. By showing the lives of the people themselves in all its rawness, deprivation and ugliness. By showing them to themselves. It is a revolutionary nationalist literature at its strongest, especially the works of Claude McKay and Langston Hughes. It reflects the entrance into the twentieth century of Afro-American people and the U.S. in general. It is the sensibility of the Afro-American Nation that developed after the destruction of the Reconstruction governments and of the Reconstruction period, the most democratic period in U.S. life, the sensibility that survived the dark repression of the 1880s and 1890s, when the Northern industrial capitalists, no longer needing blacks to stabilize the South while the Wall Street conquerors stripped the Southern plantation aristocrats of economic and political independence, sold blacks back into near-slavery with the Hayes-Tilden Compromise of 1876, and crushed black political life with the Ku Klux Klan lynchings, the black codes, segregation and outright fascism!

The Harlem Renaissance influenced black culture world-wide, but it also reflected the fact that all over the world oppressed nations and colonial peoples were intensifying their struggle against imperialism. In Haiti, where the U.S. invaded in 1915, there was the *Indigisme* movement; in Puerto Rico it was called *Negrisismo;* in Paris, Senghor, Cesaire and Damas called it *Negritude,* and cited McKay and Hughes as their chief influences!

One aspect of the Harlem Renaissance in the "Roaring Twenties" as part of "the Jazz Age" was the stirring anti-imperialism, another part (showing how the bourgeoisie tries to transform everything to its own use) was the cult of exoticism which the commercializers and often pathological bourgeois "patrons" of the *New Negro* made of this cultural outpouring. This was the period, Hughes sd, when "the Negro was in vogue."

But by the beginning of the thirties, after the crash of 1929, and the Great Depression, which was only one of the many cyclical recessions, the bust part of the boom-bust cycle pointing toward the eventual destruction of capitalism, the exotic part of the Renaissance was over. The philanthropists turned to other pursuits, and just as in the factories where blacks are the last hired and the first fired, the literary flowering as manifested by U.S. publishers came to an end!

In the Depression thirties the revolutionary ideas of the Russian Bolsheviks, of Marx, Engels, Lenin and Stalin, had enormous influence on U.S. intellectuals. It was apparent that capitalism could not solve the problems of the exploited majority let alone black people, that the U.S. bourgeoisie was unfit to rule society. Black writers also show this influence, mostly as it was transmitted by the *then* revolutionary Communist Party U.S.A. The works of Hughes and McKay especially show this influence, and even though Hughes later copped out before the inquisitors of the HUAC, a collection of his thirties writings, *Good Morning Revolution,* is must reading to get at his really powerful works.

Richard Wright was one of the most publicized and skilled black writers of the thirties and forties. His early works, *Uncle Tom's Children, Native Son* and *Black Boy,* including the long suppressed section of this book called *American Hunger,* are among the most powerful works written by any American writer of the period. Wright was even more than Hughes influenced by Marxist-Leninist ideology, though Wright's individualism and idealism finally sabotaged him. He joined the CPUSA when he got to Chicago. (He came in from the John Reed Club, an anti-imperialist writers' organization. And if one believes *American Hunger,* the careerist aspect of this move vis-à-vis getting his early works published via the communists, &c is not insubstantial.) Wright had just come from Memphis and remained a member of the CPUSA until 1944. It was at this point, ironically, that the CP, burdened by opportunist reactionary leadership, sold out the black liberation movement by liquidating the correct revolutionary slogans LIBERATION FOR THE BLACK NATION! SELF-DETERMINATION FOR THE AFRO-AMERICAN NATION IN THE BLACK BELT SOUTH! The CP even liquidated itself, temporarily becoming the Communist Political Association, "a nonparty movement following the ideals of Washington, Jefferson, Lincoln and Tom Paine." But Wright's individualism and petty-bourgeois vacillation had begun to isolate him from the party years before, tho the errors and opportunism of CP leadership must be pointed out.

Many of the left, anti-imperialist, revolutionary, Marxist and even pro-Soviet ideas that grew to such prominence in the thirties were sustained into the forties because the U.S. by then had joined a united front with the U.S.S.R. against fascism. But by the fifties U.S. world dominance (which was enhanced by the fact of its emerging unscathed from World War II) dictated that it launch a cold war against the Soviet Union to try to dominate a world market. World War II allowed the insurgent colonial peoples to grow even stronger as the imperialists fought each other and in 1949 the Chinese Communists declared the People's Republic of China. This occasioned an attempted blockade and isolation of China as well by the U.S. and resulted in the Korean police action. This was accompanied by intense ideological repression inside the U.S.A. itself as McCarthyism emerged. The modern capitalist inquisition to purge all left and Marxist and anti-imperialist influences from U.S. intellectual life!

Hughes copped out before HUAC, sd he wdn't do it again and told James Eastland that all U.S. citizens had equality. A tragedy! Wright fled the U.S. to France and became an existentialist. Another event with tragic overtones. W.E.B. Du Bois was indicted as an agent of a foreign power! Paul Robeson was persecuted and eventually driven to his death as Jackie Robinson testified against him at HUAC. Powerful writers like Theodore Ward were covered with mountains of obscurity.

With the defection of the CPUSA to reformism, culminated by its 1957 pronouncement that it was now seeking socialism via the ballot in a "peaceful transition to socialism," that the road to socialism was integration not revolution, the late forties and the fifties were marked by the reevaluation of Wright's works. Both James Baldwin and Ralph Ellison condemned in spurious fashion "protest literature," and the general tone put out by well-published "spokespersons for black people" was that it was time to transcend the "limitations" of race, that Afro-American writing shd disappear into the mainstream like Lost Boundaries. Baldwin, of course, later refutes his own arguments by becoming a civil rights spokesman and activist, and by the sixties, with *Blues for Mr. Charlie,* he had even begun to question the nonviolent, passive, pseudo-revolution put forward by the black bourgeoisie through its most articulate spokesman Dr. M. L. King.

Ralph Ellison's *Invisible Man* was the classic work of the fifties in restating & shifting the direction of Afro-American literature. The work puts down both nationalism and Marxism, and opts for *individualism.* This ideological content couched in the purrs of an obviously elegant technique was important to trying to steer Afro-American literature away from protest, away from the revolutionary concerns of the thirties and early forties, and this primarily is the reason this work and the author are so valued by the literary and academic establishments in this country. Both Ellison and Baldwin wrote essays dismissing or finding flaws in Wright's ultimate concern in his best work.

But the fifties civil rights movement was also superseded by the people's rapid intensification of the struggle in the sixties, and black literature like everything else was quick to show this. The emergence of Malcolm X to oppose the black bourgeois line of nonviolent passive resistance which duplicated the reformist anti-Marxists of the CPUSA in their "nonviolent transition to socialism." Where the black bourgeoisie had dominated the black liberation movement of the fifties with the aid of the CPUSA and the big capitalists themselves, in the sixties Malcolm X came forward articulating the political line of the black majority—Self-Determination, Self-Respect and Self-Defense—and struggled out in the open against the civil rights line of the black bourgeoisie, who could see black people beaten and spit on and bombed in churches and whose only retaliation wd be to kneel in the dust and pray.

Just as Malcolm's influence turned the entire civil rights movement around, from the student movement which was SNCC to the militance of Stokely Carmichael and Rap Brown, so the whole movement changed. Malcolm's line of self-defense was picked up in the South by people like Robert Williams in North Carolina, by Carmichael in Alabama with the *first* Black Panther Party, and by the young brothers and sisters in California who marched into the California legislature in 1967 to declare that black people had the right to armed self-defense . . . these were the Black Panthers led by Huey P. Newton and Bobby Seale. And by the end of the sixties even tho the bourgeoisie had assassinated Malcolm X, the movement had changed radically, the black bourgeoisie were no longer in control of the movement, and from civil rights we were talking next about self-defense and then after Rap Brown about rebellion itself.

All these moves were reflected by black literature, and they are fundamentally movements and thrusts by the people themselves, which the literature bears witness to and is a reflector of. The Black Arts Movement of the sixties basically wanted to reflect the rise of the militancy of the black masses as reflected by Malcolm X. Its political line at its most positive was that literature must be a weapon of revolutionary struggle, that it must serve the black revolution. And its writers, Askia Muhammad Toure, Larry Neal, Clarence Reed, Don Lee, Sonia Sanchez, Carolyn Rodgers, Welton Smith, Marvin X, &c its publications, its community black arts theaters, its manifestos and activism were meant as real manifestations of black culture/black art as weapons of liberation. On the negative side, the black arts movement without the guidance of a scientific revolutionary organization, a Marxist-Leninist communist party, was, like the BLM itself, left with spontaneity. It became embroiled in cultural nationalism, bourgeois nationalism, substituting the mistrust and hatred of white people for scientific analysis of the real enemies of black people, until by the middle seventies a dead end had been reached that could only be surmounted by a complete change of world view, ideology. It is my view that this is exactly what is going on today in many places in the country; that Afro-American literature is going thru the quantitative changes necessary to make its qualitative leap back into the revolutionary positivism of the thirties and the positive aspect of the black-arts sixties. For certainly the literature will always be a reflection of what the people themselves are, as well as a projection of what they struggle to become. The Afro-American nation and its people as an oppressed nationality spread out around the rest of the U.S. nation-state still face a revolutionary struggle. That nation is still oppressed by imperialism, and its liberation and self-determination can only be gained through revolution. The next wave of Afro-American literature, and of a genuine people's literature, will dramatically record this.

For the Sake of a People's Poetry: Walt Whitman and the Rest of Us

JUNE JORDAN

In America, the father is white: It is he who inaugurated the experiment of this republic. It is he who sailed his way into slave ownership. It is he who availed himself of my mother: the African woman whose function was miserably defined by his desirings, or his rage. It is he who continues to dominate the destiny of the Mississippi River, the Blue Ridge Mountains, and the life of my son. Understandably, then, I am curious about this man.

Most of the time my interest can be characterized as wary, at best. Other times, it is the interest a pedestrian feels for the fast-traveling truck about to smash into him. Or her. Again. And at other times it is the curiosity of a stranger trying to figure out the system of the language that excludes her name and all of the names of all of her people. It is this last that leads me to the poet Walt Whitman.

Trying to understand the system responsible for every boring, inaccessible, irrelevant, derivative, and pretentious poem that is glued to the marrow of required readings in American classrooms, or trying to understand the system responsible for the exclusion of every hilarious, amazing, visionary, pertinent, and unforgettable poet from N.E.A. grants and from national publications, I come back to Walt Whitman.

What in the hell happened to him? Wasn't he a white man? Wasn't he some kind of a father to American literature? Didn't he talk about this New World? Didn't he see it? Didn't he sing this New World, this America, on a New World, an American scale of his own visionary invention?

It so happens that Walt Whitman is the one white father who shares the systematic disadvantages of his heterogeneous offspring trapped inside a closet that is, in reality, as huge as the continental spread of North and South America. What Whitman envisioned we, the people and the poets of the New World, embody. He has been punished for the political meaning of his vision. We are being punished for the moral questions that our very lives provoke.

At home as a child I learned the poetry of the Bible and the poetry of Paul Laurence Dunbar. As a student, I diligently followed orthodox directions from *The Canterbury Tales* right through *The Waste Land* by that consummate Anglophile whose name I can never remember. And I kept waiting. It was, I thought, all right to deal with daffodils in the seventeenth century on an island as much like Manhattan as I resemble Queen Mary. But what about Dunbar? When was he coming up again? And where were the Black poets altogether? And who were the women poets I might reasonably emulate? And wasn't there, ever, a great poet who was crazy about Brooklyn or furious about war? And I kept waiting. And I kept writing my own poetry. And I kept reading apparently underground poetry: poetry kept strictly off campus. And I kept reading the poetry of so many gifted students when I became a teacher myself, and I kept listening to the wonderful poetry of the multiplying numbers of my friends who were and who are New World poets until I knew, for a fact, that there was and that there is an American, a New World, poetry that is as personal, as public, as irresistible, as quick, as necessary, as unprecedented, as representative, as exalted, as speakably commonplace, and as musical, as an emergency phone call.

But I didn't know about Walt Whitman. Yes: I had heard about this bohemian, this homosexual even, who wrote something about The Captain and The Lilacs, but nobody ever told me he was crucial to a native American literature. Not only was Whitman not required reading, in the sense that Wordsworth and Robert Herrick are required reading, he was, on the contrary, presented as a rather hairy buffoon suffering from a

189

childish proclivity for exercise and open air. Nevertheless, it is through the study of all the poems and all the ideas of this particular white father that I have reached a tactical, if not strategic, understanding of the racist, sexist, and anti-American predicament that condemns most New World writing to peripheral/small press/unpublished manuscript status.

Before these United States, the great poems of the world earned their luster through undeniable forms of spontaneous popularity: Generations of a people chose to memorize and then to further elaborate and then to impart these songs to the next generation. I am talking about people: African families and Greek families and the families of the Hebrew tribes and all that multitude to whom the Bhagavad-Gita is as daily as the sun. If these poems were not always religious, they were certainly moral in motive, or in accomplishment, or both. None of these great poems could be mistaken for the poetry of another country, another time; you do not find a single helicopter taking off or landing in any of the sonnets of Elizabethan England, nor do you run across Jamaican rice and peas in any of the psalms. Evidently, one criterion for great poetry used to be the requirements of cultural nationalism.

But with the advent of the 36-year-old poet Walt Whitman, the phenomenon of a people's poetry, or great poetry and its spontaneous popularity, could no longer be assumed. The physical immensity and the far-flung population of this New World decisively separated the poet from the suitable means to produce and to distribute his poetry. Now there would have to be intermediaries—critics and publishers—whose marketplace principles of scarcity would, logically, oppose them to populist traditions of art. In place of the democratic concepts, elitist Old World concepts would, logically, govern their policies; in the context of such considerations, an American literary establishment antithetical to the New World meanings of America took root. And this is one reason why the pre-eminently American white father of American poetry is practically unknown outside the realm of caricature and rumor in his own country.

As a matter of fact, if you hope to hear about Whitman, your best bet is to leave home: Ignore prevailing American criticism and, instead, ask anybody anywhere else in the world this question: As Shakespeare is to England, Dante to Italy, Tolstoi to Russia, Goethe to Germany, Agostinho Neto to Angola, Pablo

Neruda to Chile, Mao Tse-tung to China, and Ho Chi Minh to Vietnam, who is the great American writer, the distinctively American poet, the giant American "literatus"? Undoubtedly, the answer will be *Walt Whitman*. He is the poet who wrote:

A man's body at auction,
(For before the war I often go to the slave-mart and watch
   the sale,)
I help the auctioneer, the sloven does not half know his
   business.

Gentlemen look on this wonder,
Whatever the bids of the bidders they cannot be high enough
   for it

"I Sing the Body Electric"

I ask you today: Who in America would publish those lines? They are all wrong! In the first place, there is nothing obscure, nothing contrived, nothing an ordinary straphanger in the subway would be puzzled by. In the second place, the voice of those lines is intimate and direct at once: It is the voice of the poet who assumes that he speaks to an equal and that he need not fear that equality; on the contrary, the intimate distance between the poet and the reader is a distance that assumes there is everything important, between them, to be shared. And what is poetic about a line of words that runs as long as a regular, a spoken idea? You could more easily imagine an actual human being speaking such lines than you could imagine an artist composing them in a room carefully separated from other rooms of a house, carefully separated from other lives of a family: This can't be poetry. Besides, these lines apparently serve an expressly moral purpose! Then is this didactic/political writing? This cannot be good poetry. And, in fact, you will never see, for example, *The New Yorker* publishing a poem marked by such splendid deficiencies.

Consider the inevitable, the irresistible simplicity of that enormous moral idea:

Gentlemen look on this wonder,
Whatever the bids of the bidders they cannot be high enough
   for it . . .

This is not only one man, this the father of those who shall be
   fathers in their turns,
In him the start of populous states and rich republics,
Of him countless immortal lives with countless embodiments and
   enjoyments.

"I Sing the Body Electric"

This is not an idea generally broadcast in America. It is an idea
to violate the marketplace: The poet is trying to rescue a human being while even the poem cannot be saved from the in-
solence of marketplace evaluation!

Indeed Walt Whitman and the traceable descendants of
Whitman, those who follow his democratic faith into obviously
New World forms of experience and art, they suffer from the
same establishment rejection and contempt that forced this archetypal American genius to publish, distribute, and review his
own work—by himself. The descendants I have in mind include
those unmistakably contemporaneous young poets who base
themselves upon domesticities such as disco, Las Vegas, Mc-
Donald's, and forty-dollar running shoes. Also within the Whitman tradition, Black and Third World poets traceably transform,
and further, the egalitarian sensibility that isolates that one white
father from his more powerful compatriots. And I am thinking
of those feminist poets who are evidently intent upon speaking
with a maximal number and diversity of other American lives.
And I am thinking of such first-rank heroes of the New World
as Pablo Neruda and Agostinho Neto. Except for these last two,
New World poets are overwhelmingly forced to publish their own
works, or seek the commitment of a small press or else give it
up entirely. That is to say, the only peoples who can test or ver-
ify the meaning of America as a democratic state, as a pluralis-
tic culture, are the very peoples whose contribution to a national
vision and discovery meet with general ridicule and disregard.
A democratic state does not, after all, exist for the few, but for
the many. A democratic state is not proven by the welfare of
the strong but by the welfare of the weak. And unless that many,
that manifold constitution of diverse peoples can be seen as integral to the national art/the national consciousness, you might
as well mean only Czechoslovakia when you talk about the U.S.A.,
or only Ireland, or merely France, or exclusively white men.

The fate of Pablo Neruda differs from the other Whitman descendants because Neruda was born into a sovereign New World country where a majority of the citizens did not mistake themselves for Englishmen or long to find themselves struggling, at most, with cucumber sandwiches and tea. He was never European. His anguish was not aroused by three-piece suits and rolled umbrellas. When he cries, toward the conclusion of *The Heights of Macchu Picchu,* "Arise to birth with me, my brother," he plainly does not allude to Lord or Colonel Anybody At All. As he writes, earlier, in that amazing poem:

I came by another way, river by river, street after street,
city by city, one bed and another,
forcing the salt of my mask through a wilderness;
and there, in the shame of the ultimate hovels, lampless and
    fireless,
lacking bread or a stone or a stillness, alone in myself,
I whirled at my will, dying the death that was mine.

Of course Neruda has not escaped all of the untoward consequences common to Whitman descendants. American critics and translators never weary of asserting that Neruda is a quote great unquote poet despite the political commitment of his art and despite the artistic consequences of that commitment. Specifically, Neruda's self-conscious decision to write in a manner readily comprehensible to the masses of his countrymen and his self-conscious decision to specify outright the United Fruit Company when that was the instigating subject of his poem become unfortunate moments in an otherwise supposedly sublime, not to mention surrealist, deeply Old World and European but nonetheless Chilean case history. To assure the validity of this perspective, the usual American critic and translator presents you with a smattering of the unfortunate, ostensibly political poetry and, on the other hand, buries you under volumes of Neruda's early work that antedates the Spanish Civil War or, in other words, that antedates Neruda's serious conversion to a political world view.

This kind of artistically indefensible censorship would have you perceive chasmic and even irreconcilable qualitative differences between the poet who wrote:

> You, my antagonist, in that splintering dream
> like the bristling glass of gardens, like a menace
> of ruinous bells, volleys
> of blackening ivy at the perfume's center
> enemy of the great hipbones my skin has touched
> with a harrowing dew

> "The Woes and the Furies"

and the poet who wrote, some twenty years later, these lines from
the poem entitled "The Dictators":

> lament was perpetual and fell, like a plant and its pollen,
> forcing a lightless increase in the blinded, big leaves.
> And bludgeon by bludgeon, on the terrible waters,
> scale over scale in the bog,
> the snout filled with silence and slime
> and vendetta was born.

According to prevalent American criticism, that later poem by
Neruda represents a lesser achievement precisely because it can
be understood by more people, more easily, than the first. It is
also denigrated because it attacks a keystone of the Old World
namely dictatorship, or, in other words, power and privilege for
the few.

The peculiar North American vendetta against Walt Whitman, against the first son of this democratic union, should be
further fathomed: Neruda's eminence is now acknowledged on
international levels; his work profoundly affects many North
American poets who do not realize, because they have never been
shown, the North American/the Walt Whitman origins for so
much that is singular and worthy in the poetry of Neruda. You
will even find American critics who congratulate Neruda for
overcoming the "Whitmanese" content of his art! This perfi-
dious arrogance is as calculated as it is common. You cannot
persuade anyone seriously familiar with Neruda's life and art
that he could have found cause, at any point, to disagree with
the tenets, the analysis, and the authentic New World vision
presented by Walt Whitman in his essay "Democratic Vistas,"
which remains the most signal and persuasive manifesto of New
World thinking and belief in print.

Let me define my terms in brief: New World does not mean New England. New World means non-European; it means new, it means big, it means heterogeneous, it means unknown, it means free, it means an end to feudalism, caste, privilege, and the violence of power. It means *wild* in the sense that a tree growing away from the earth enacts a wild event. It means *dem-ocratic* in the sense that, as Whitman wrote:

I believe a leaf of grass is no less than the journey-work of the
  stars . . .
And a mouse is miracle enough to stagger sextillions of infi-
  dels.

"Song of Myself"

New World means, in Whitman's words, "I keep as delicate around the bowels as around the head and heart." New World means, again, to quote Whitman, "By God! I will accept nothing which all cannot have their counterpart of on the same terms." In "Democratic Vistas," Whitman declared,

> As the greatest lessons of Nature through the universe are
> perhaps the lessons of variety and freedom, the same pre-
> sent the greatest lessons also in New World politics and
> progress . . . Sole among nationalities, these States have
> assumed the task to put in forms of history, power and
> practicality, on areas of amplitude rivaling the operations
> of the physical kosmos, the moral political speculations of
> ages, long, long deferr'd, the democratic republican prin-
> ciple, and the theory of development and perfection by
> voluntary standards, and self-reliance.

Listen to this white man; he is so weird! Here he is calling aloud for an American, a democratic spirit, an American, a democratic idea that could morally constrain and coordinate the material body of U.S.A. affluence and piratical outreach, more than a hundred years ago. He wrote:

> The great poems, Shakespeare included, are poisonous to
> the idea of the pride and dignity of the common people,
> the lifeblood of democracy. The models of our literature,

195

as we get it from other lands, ultra marine, have had their
birth in courts, and bask'd and grown in castle sunshine;
all smells of princes' favors. . . . Do you call those genteel little creatures American poets? Do you term that perpetual, pistareen, paste-pot work, American art, American
drama, taste, verse? . . . We see the sons and daughters
of The New World, ignorant of its genius, not yet inau-
gurating the native, the universal, and the near, still im-
porting the distant, the partial, the dead.

Abhorring the "thin sentiment of parlors, parasols, piano-song,
tinkling rhymes," Whitman conjured up a poetry of America, a
poetry of democracy that would not "mean the smooth walks,
trimm'd hedges, poseys and nightingales of the English poets,
but the whole orb, with its geologic history, the Kosmos, carrying fire and snow that rolls through the illimitable areas, light
as a feather, though weighing billions of tons."

Well, what happened?

Whitman went ahead and wrote the poetry demanded by his
vision. He became, by thousands upon thousands of words, a
great American poet:

There was a child went forth every day,
And the first object he look'd upon, that object he became
And that object became part of him for the day or a certain part
    of the day.
Or for many years or stretching cycles of years.

The early lilacs became part of this child,
And grass and white and red morning-glories, and white and
    red clover, and the song of the phoeba-bird,

        "There Was a Child Went Forth"

And elsewhere he wrote:

It avails not, time nor place—distance avails not,
I am with you, you men and women of a generation, or ever so
    many generations hence,
Just as you feel when you look on the river and sky, so I felt,

196

Just as any of you is one of a living crowd, I was one of a crowd,
Just as you are refresh'd by the gladness of the river and the
bright flow, I was refresh'd,
Just as you stand and lean on the rail, yet hurry with the swift
   current, I stood yet was hurried,
Just as you look on the numberless masts of ships and the thick-
   stemm'd pipes of steamboats, I look'd . . .

"Crossing Brooklyn Ferry"

This great American poet of democracy as cosmos, this poet of
a continent as consciousness, this poet of the many people as
one people, this poet of a diction comprehensible to all, of a vision insisting on each, of a rhythm/a rhetorical momentum to
transport the reader from the Brooklyn ferry into the hills of
Alabama and back again, of line after line of bodily, concrete
detail that constitutes the mysterious, the cellular tissues of a
nation indivisible but dependent upon and astonishing in its diversity, this white father of a great poetry deprived of its spontaneous popularity/a great poetry hidden away from the ordinary
people it celebrates so well, he has been, again and again, cast
aside as an undisciplined poseur, a merely freak eruption of
prolix perversities.

Last year, the *New York Times Book Review* saw fit to import
a European self-appointed critic of American literature to address the question: Is there a great American poet? Since this
visitor was ignorant of the philosophy and the achievements of
Walt Whitman, the visitor, Denis Donoghue, comfortably excluded every possible descendant of Whitman from his erst-
while cerebrations: Only one woman was mentioned. (She,
needless to add, did not qualify.) No poets under fifty, and not
one Black or Third World poet, received even cursory assess-
ment. Not one poet of distinctively New World values, and their
formal embodiment, managed to dent the illiterate suavity of
Donoghue's public display.

This *New York Times* event perpetuates American habits of
beggarly, absurd deference to the Old World. And these habits
bespeak more than marketplace intrusions into cultural realms:
We erase ourselves through self-hatred, we lend our silence to
the American anti-American process whereby anything and

anyone special to this nation state becomes liable to condemnation because it is what it is, truly.

Against self-hatred there is Whitman and there are all of the New World poets who insistently devise legitimate varieties of cultural nationalism. There is Whitman and all of the poets whose lives have been baptized by witness to blood, by witness to cataclysmic, political confrontations from the Civil War through the Civil Rights Era, through the Women's Movement, and on and on through the conflicts between the hungry and the fat, the wasteful, the bullies.

In the poetry of The New World, you meet with a reverence for the material world that begins with a reverence for human life, an intellectual trust in sensuality as a means of knowledge and of unity, an easily deciphered system of reference, aspiration to a believable, collective voice and, consequently, emphatic preference for broadly accessible language and/or "spoken" use of language, a structure of forward energies that interconnects apparently discrete or even conflictual elements, saturation by quotidian data, and a deliberate balancing of perception with vision: a balancing of sensory report with moral exhortation.

All of the traceable descendants of Whitman have met with an establishment, an academic, reception disgracefully identical: Except for the New World poets who live and write beyond the boundaries of the U.S.A., the offspring of this one white father encounter everlasting marketplace disparagement as crude or optional or simplistic or, as Whitman himself wrote, "hankering, gross, mystical, nude."

I too am a descendant of Walt Whitman. And I am not by myself struggling to tell the truth about this history of so much land and so much blood, of so much that should be sacred and so much that has been desecrated and annihilated boastfully.

My brothers and my sisters of this New World, we remember that, as Whitman said,

I do not trouble my spirit to vindicate itself or be understood,
I see that the elementary laws never apologize.

"Song of Myself"

We do not apologize because we are not Emily Dickinson, Ezra Pound, T. S. Eliot, Wallace Stevens, Robert Lowell, or Elizabeth Bishop. If we are nothing to them, to those who love them, they are nothing to us! Or, as Whitman exclaimed: "I exist as I am, that is enough."

New World poetry moves into and beyond the light of the lives of Walt Whitman, Pablo Neruda, Agostinho Neto, Gabriela Mistral, Langston Hughes, Margaret Walker, and Edward Brathwaite.

I follow this movement with my own life. I am calm and I am smiling as we go. Is it not written somewhere very near to me:

A man's body at auction . . .
Gentlemen, look on this wonder,
Whatever the bids of the bidders they cannot be high enough
    for it

And didn't that weird white father predict this truth that is always growing:

I swear to you the architects shall appear without fail,
I swear to you they will understand you and justify you,
The greatest among them shall be he who best knows you,
    and encloses all and is faithful to all,
He and the rest shall not forget you, they shall perceive that
    you are not an iota less than they,
You shall be fully glorified in them.

"A Song of the Rolling Earth"

Walt Whitman and all of the New World poets coming after him, we, too, go on singing this America.

From *A Romantic Education*

PATRICIA HAMPL

Prague is one of the most beautiful cities in the world. It is strange that it has never really been a tourist city. Even in the days of the Viennese Empire and the Baedeker tours, it wasn't a standard part of the grand tour. It retained its provincial, essentially bourgeois, personality. In certain ways, the Prague of those days might be compared to Montreal today. It was a dual-language city—Czech, the language of the larger population of native people, was not the ruling-class language—and it had the cultural and political febrility of such crossroads cities.

The thirty years of Socialism have deepened the city's isolation, and the two languages are gone: the German population, which was 80 percent Jewish, was destroyed by the War. It is today even less of a tourist town, more intensely introverted. But it is a loved city, loved by its residents and by those who do visit it. A Western tourist feels quite alone in Prague; it is an exhilarating, surprising sensation after the sometimes deflating familiarity of London or Paris. Perhaps the city is even more loved now than it ever was, for it does not belong to Europe, and maybe never will again. It is part of Eastern Europe, that loneliest of geographical designations. It is a good city for walking; and walking is a good way to feel love.

Petru Popescu, the Rumanian writer, is perhaps typical of the Eastern European intellectuals who came to feel a special love for Prague. He wrote this brief memoir, which appeared in *The Index on Censorship* in 1976:

> For artists who grew up behind the Iron Curtain (a curtain that deserved its name in the strictest sense until the

early Sixties), Prague was a city of many personalities, an embodiment of many intellectual dreams. . . . It . . . had a rhythm of peaceful common sense, the bourgeois patriarchality of back gardens and trellis walls, tiled floors and uneven stairs, on which the dignified citizens stumbled up and down, through beer-mist, in a landscape so untouched by history that it became incredible, miraculous. The noble towers, the middle class drinking evenings, the proletarian outskirts combined in a vast social lesson, just like the Catholic Slavs brewed slowly, allowing in their midst energetic German streaks and melancholy Jewish islands. Heavy, peaceful heart of Europe, beating towards the ruthless North, the devious East, the Latin South. The most complete city of Europe, patinated by time and drowned in music, profound like a requiem and disarming like a miniature, was the harbor of our travels in the mind. We spent here our unlived lives, we visited untouchable shores and we enjoyed the most delicious and sad kind of freedom, the freedom of the past.

Alas, these lines have spelled themselves in the past tense already. Where is all this now? Still there, in the city's eternity, and yet buried under all the narrow streets with cobblestones wounded by tanks. Thirty years after Munich, another outbreak of opaque, cretinous hate. Not only the musical romance and the baroque landscape were crushed. Curiously, from under the Russian tanks, Prague revealed itself as a solidarity of workers, as an old school of social-democracy and human popular management, of teacherish left-wing ideals. Fragile and myopic like the consumptive revolutionaries of yore, the heretic Communist party of what was before the war Europe's most hardworking and sincere democracy produced a wing of dedicated visionaries who, pushed forward by the stream of an exasperated nation, agreed to give up their police power and to govern by trust alone. Killed in the bud, this last hope of a working-class state seems to confront the world with another moral Spain. Alas, this republic was not able to enlist the help of international brigades. Normalised by the objectivity and realism of guns and tanks, Prague slips back into the past, its eternal refuge, while the people of Prague continue their imaginary lives. And we, the witnesses of this assassination, in a world more and more prepared philosophically to accept the rape of conscience.

I intended to take some notes from Marxist texts. It seemed the next step in acquainting myself with Czech intellectual history. I felt a great resistance to this reading and, before I came to Prague again, I had only read the *Communist Manifesto* and Trotsky's *My Life*—which doesn't count anyway, according to a friend of mine who has read *everything*, because "it's just his autobiography." I realize now what my resistance has been.

For one thing, the real imprint of Socialism in Eastern Europe has not come from Marxism, but from orthodoxy: form, not content. This is a simplification. But we can see, from the lives of the poets and intellectuals who perished in Lenin's or Stalin's time, that they were not a counterrevolution; they didn't have some other political alternative in mind. Typically, those who perished were faithful ideologues themselves (for example, in Czechoslovakia, Rudolf Slansky, the secretary general of the Communist Party) or, in the case of poets, they were "cloud-dwellers." (Stalin is supposed to have attached to Pasternak's secret police file the directive, "Do not touch this cloud-dweller.")

Ideologues and the poets who perished so absurdly together had in common perhaps only a single thing: the work of language. One could say they met in their devotion to language: a religious impulse.

Ideology and the bureaucracy it spawns create "a new language." How happily, in fact, the word *new* is used in the whole canon of revolutionary politics: Socialism offers nothing less than the opportunity to create "a new man." Who, wishing the best for the world, could be against that?

It is a stunning idea, and combines brilliantly, in a single image, the familiar, reassuring shadow of Christianity and the heretofore frightening—but at last domesticated—spectre of faceless technological life. The Industrial Revolution *seemed* (to Blake, to Wordsworth, even as late as Lawrence and to ourselves in the West) to be the end of "man," the breakup of the individual-at-home-in-the-world. But no, don't worry, there is a way out: one need not be a "man"; it is possible to be "a new man." The phrase acknowledges terror, even as it defies it. To be a new man is to leap the barriers of history, perhaps even of biology, and (this is the part that matters), to feel no loss, no strangeness. No absurdity.

In our own country, the misuse of language has gone straight to absurdity, without benefit of ideology. The worst evidence of our crimes in Vietnam was not that Curtis LeMay said, we'll "bomb the North Vietnamese back to the stone ages." That is the ancient and entirely familiar cry of the warrior. Much worse was the infamous statement made by an Air Force pilot: "We had to destroy the village in order to save it." This statement is haunting because it is utterly rational and utterly crazy. Our grief is that this reasoning made perfect sense to our government.

Those caught in the web of ideology in the Soviet Union and Eastern Europe perished, perhaps, because in the end they could not manage the hair-splitting language of orthodoxy which was the only language they recognized. No one could say for certain what the new man was, but it and other such abstract but highly charged phrases had to be defined over and over. And one person's definition was the next person's evidence against him. The history of Communism in Eastern Europe is full of "confessions"—leading to prison terms and executions—for transgressions against the new language.

George Steiner, in his essay "Text and Context," discusses this. "Marxism-Leninism and the ideological idiom professed in communist societies are 'bookish' to the root. The scheme of origins, authority and continuum in force in the Marxist world derives its sense of identity and its daily practices of validation or exclusion from a canon of texts. It is the reading of these texts—exegetic, Talmudic, disputative to an almost pathological degree of semantic scruple and interpretative nicety—which constitutes the presiding dynamic in Marxist education and in the attempts, inherently ambiguous as are all attempts to 'move forward' from sacred texts, to make of Marxism an unfolding, predictive reality-principle."

Poets, on the other hand—I'm thinking particularly of Mandelstam—are devoted to language at least partly because of its history, its peculiar ability to be the unconscious storehouse of a people's culture, values, point of view. Poetry is the richest form of language because it is the most concentrated utterance. It is immediate *and* ancient. Its ancientness is implicit: language truly is, always has been, *handed down* from parent to child. When a child in one of Kenneth Koch's poetry-writing classes wrote "Rose, where did you get that red?," he spoke a precise, contemporary thought, and also attached himself, unconsciously, to a long tradition—of roses and of poets.

Philosophically, too, poetry is attached to ancient values be-

203

cause the materials of the emotions remain what they have always been. Even when Pound said, "Make it new," he could not deny the ancient: the *it* stands for all there is to make new.

Mandelstam is emblematic not because of his typically tragic death, but because of his wistfulness. He was wistful for poetry. He wanted, he said, to "pronounce for the first time the blessed word with no meaning . . . in the Soviet night." In another poem, written in 1930, he says

> I could have whistled through life like a starling,
> eating nut pies . . .
> but clearly there's no chance of that.

What he is saying, I think, is: let me out of the ideological mind and the insanity of abstracted language. Mandelstam is not a new man; he is an ancient.

Even in our country where poetry is not read, as we're always told, the poet symbolizes the personal voice, so individual, so far from the abstract rationalism of the ideologue, that the Western stereotype of the poet is that of the divine crazy, the romantic (the word is used imprecisely, dismissively, even by poets). But the stereotype betrays a longing. I've never told anyone I write poetry without, after an initial shyness, getting the same reaction: respect, fascination, wistfulness (they too write poetry, or used to, or wish they could, or know someone who "can put words on paper"). The wistfulness of the grocer in St. Paul who said to me, "Poetry. Now that's something. That's a life." Not "that's the life"—he didn't think I was a bum. He meant it was work of value: *a life*. His wistfulness was not so far from Mandelstam's, a longing for a culture that sustains the imagination.

I haven't taken the notes, haven't read the classic theoretical texts that I intended to. I sense they can't explain the reason our civilization has been sliced in two, into Europe and "the other Europe." "The gestures of the individuals," Muriel Rukeyser wrote in *The Life of Poetry*, "are not history; but they are the images of history." And that is what I must study. The things I want to "observe perpetually" expose themselves in every contemporary gesture, just as poetry has always known, as it busies itself with roses.

* * *

"Are you going to write a 'Letter from Prague'?" Jaromil asked me one day as we walked along together.

"I'll write something," I said.

"I've read a lot of these 'Letters from Prague,' " he said. "What does it mean? A person comes, stays a week; he walks around and then he writes an article and says, 'The people seem contented—or discontented. Fresh vegetables appear to be plentiful, but the lines in stores are long—or the lines are short, but the vegetables are wilted. The people are well dressed—or the women don't have any sense of style.' Whether we stand in line, vegetables, what we wear—that's it. What do you think?"

"I noticed, as I rode by on the tram this morning, that a vegetable stand seemed to have wilted vegetables, mostly just kohlrabi and radishes—but it's only May. And the well-dressed women seem to be West German tourists. And I've noticed lines."

"That's what I mean," he said, shaking his head.

"I was joking," I said.

"Yes," he said, but he didn't laugh. We walked along together in silence.

* * *

What *is* it possible to know? I mean, beyond the fact that there are or are not wilted vegetables, and that the women do or do not have nice clothes (is it possible to know even that?). This is the question that haunts modern times: *did you know?* Did you know about Auschwitz? ("Only a few people knew." "We didn't know.") Did you know about My Lai? Did you know about the CIA in Chile? Did we know? When did we find out?

There is, in this question, the lingering nerve of an ethical culture: if we know, then we are responsible. We still feel we must answer for our knowledge. But clearly, it is necessary, at times, for whole nations to be sure they do not know certain things. East Germany, for example, has worked out its relation to Second World War history in a way that acknowledges *and* denies reality: yes, the horrors of the camps existed, but the cause was Fascism, which has been boldly routed by Socialism. As a result, East Germany, unlike West Germany, does not pay reparations to Jewish survivors.

As for us, who knows what more, exactly, will emerge from the Vietnam years? Was America really surprised by My Lai? It strikes me that I, an ordinary citizen in the Midwest with no special information, was not surprised. Horrified—yes, I was sickened; I remember the pictures. But I wasn't surprised. The whole business stank to high heaven for years. Years before My Lai, *Life* magazine ran that full-color picture of a GI wearing a string of ears slung around his waist. That, I think, is when I knew—knew all a person needs to know. I knew then that it was worse than war; it was a perversion of the national self, as well as the destruction of another nation.

It was not necessary to be told much to come to the realization that I *knew*. Apparently, moral intelligence is subtle and wily; it finds the news. We do not need to be told that there are concentration camps dotting Central and Eastern Europe, and they are located here and here. We do not need the U.S. Army or the American press to give the "facts" about My Lai. Atrocities cannot be hidden. They appear first in language: *We had to destroy the village in order to save it.*

But in order "not to know," large groups of people, whole nations, have to find a way to blunt their intelligence. A way must be found not to know. The cost must be enormous. History is traduced, but perhaps it always is. Worse than that, people must deny over and over the intelligence of their senses. It is a denial of the most ancient poetic intelligence. It is a denial of reality. At its most extreme, it is madness.

We are haunted by history because we denied its reality when it was the present. It keeps coming back, as Kundera says. It will keep coming back until we get the story straight. "During the war," Muriel Rukeyser says in *The Life of Poetry*, "we felt the silence in the policy of the governments of English-speaking countries. That policy was to win the war first, and work out the meanings afterward. The result was, of course, that the meanings were lost. You cannot put these things off." And therefore, the hunger for meaning increases.

But to answer my question, at least for now: what is it possible to know? Apparently, just about everything we need to know. This fact must be acknowledged: we do know when something vile and gigantically evil is happening among us. We may not know the names: Auschwitz, Buchenwald, Terezin (the "artists' concentration camp" that wasn't far from Prague), My Lai. But we know. It is impossible to believe otherwise.

Still, I often feel *wrong* to be approaching this history as I am—I who have been untouched by this kind of suffering. I go cold at the thought that silence *is* the only response, as so many of the real witnesses have said. Why such timidity? It comes, I think, from the peculiar relation the "untouched," such as myself, must have to the Holocaust. It remains the central episode of our history, the horror against which all other atrocities are measured, even previous ones, and by which innocence is gauged. My relation to it is not one of personal or even national guilt (as, say, a young German might feel). Mine is the confusion, the search, of someone unmarked. *Nothing bad has ever happened to me.* Nothing impersonally cruel and ruinous—and that is an odd, protected history or nonhistory to have in this century. I can only proceed, assuming that to be untouched has some significance in the presence of the deeply touched life of this city.

Or perhaps I must be more emphatic: the value of my inquiry *is* that I am unmarked. I have no "story," no documentation of the camps, the tortures, the cruelties. I have not lived in the post-War world Milosz describes as "a hard school, where ignorance was punished not by bad marks but by death." Such a world (and it is a world where the War and the peace that followed must be seen as one thing) forced the intellectuals here "to think sociologically and historically." People like me are entirely different.

We are part of the evidence that all that raw material from survivors and witnesses has gone out of journalism, even out of the testament of history, and has plunged into the psychic life of all of us. The horrors and the sadness, the endless mourning, is floating there, careening in the imagination, looking for a place. Looking for some way to be transformed. Looking, in a word, for culture. As I am.

Standing by Words

WENDELL BERRY

"He said, and stood . . ."
Paradise Regained, IV, 561

Two epidemic illnesses of our time—upon both of which virtual industries of cures have been founded—are the disintegration of communities and the disintegration of persons. That these two are related (that private loneliness, for instance, will necessarily accompany public confusion) is clear enough. And I take for granted that most people have explored in themselves and their surroundings some of the intricacies of the practical causes and effects; most of us, for example, have understood that the results are usually bad when people act in social or moral isolation, and also when, because of such isolation, they fail to act.

What seems not so well understood, because not enough examined, is the relation between these disintegrations and the disintegration of language. My impression is that we have seen, for perhaps a hundred and fifty years, a gradual increase in language that is either meaningless or destructive of meaning. And I believe that this increasing unreliability of language parallels the increasing disintegration, over the same period, of persons and communities.

My concern is for the *accountability* of language—hence, of the users of language. To deal with this matter I will use a pair of economic concepts: *internal accounting*, which considers cost and benefits in reference only to the interest of the money-making enterprise itself; and *external accounting*, which considers the costs and benefits to the "larger community." By altering the application of these terms a little, any statement may be said to account well or poorly for what is going on inside the speaker, or outside him, or both.

It will be found, I believe, that the accounting will be poor—incomprehensible or unreliable—if it attempts to be purely internal or purely external. One of the primary obligations of language is to connect and balance the two kinds of accounting.

And so, in trying to understand the degeneracy of language, it is necessary to examine, not one kind of unaccountability, but two complementary kinds. There is language that is diminished by subjectivity, which ends in meaninglessness. But that kind of language rarely exists alone (or so I believe), but is accompanied, in a complex relationship of both cause and effect, by a language diminished by objectivity, or so-called "objectivity" (inordinate or irresponsible ambition), which ends in confusion.

My standpoint here is defined by the assumption that no statement is complete or comprehensible in itself, that in order for a statement to be complete and comprehensible three conditions are required:

1. It must designate its object precisely.
2. Its speaker must stand by it: must believe it, be accountable for it, be willing to act on it.
3. This relation of speaker, word, and object must be conventional; the community must know what it is.

These are still the common assumptions of private conversations. In our ordinary dealings with each other, we take for granted that we cannot understand what is said if we cannot assume the accountability of the speaker, the accuracy of his speech, and mutual agreement on the structures of language and the meanings of words. We assume, in short, that language is communal, and that its purpose is to tell the truth.

That these common assumptions are becoming increasingly uncommon, particularly in the discourse of specialists of various sorts, is readily evident to anyone looking for evidence. How far they have passed from favor among specialists of language, to use the handiest example, is probably implicit in the existence of such specialists; one could hardly become a language specialist (a "scientist" of language) so long as one adhered to the old assumptions.

209

But the influence of these specialists is, of course, not confined to the boundaries of their specialization. They write textbooks for people who are not specialists of language, but who are apt to become specialists of other kinds. The general drift of the purpose of at least some of these specialists, and its conformability to the purposes of specialists of other kinds, is readily suggested by a couple of recently published textbooks for freshman English.

One of these, *The Contemporary Writer*, by W. Ross Winterowd,[1] contains a chapter on language, the main purpose of which is to convince the student of the illegitimate tyranny of any kind of prescriptive grammar and of the absurdity of judging language "on the basis of extralinguistic considerations." This chapter proposes four rules that completely overturn all the old common assumptions:

1. "Languages apparently do not become better or worse in any sense. They simply change."
2. "Language is arbitrary."
3. "Rightness and wrongness are determined . . . by the purpose for which the language is being used, by the audience at which it is directed, and by the situation in which the use is taking place."
4. ". . . a grammar of a language is a description of that language, nothing more and nothing less."

And these rules have a pair of corollaries that Mr. Winterowd states plainly. One is that "you [the freshman student] have a more or less complete mastery of the English language . . ." The other is that art—specifically, here, the literary art—is "the highest expression of the human need to play, of the desire to escape from the world of reality into the world of fantasy."

The second of these texts, *Rhetoric: Discovery and Change*, by Richard E. Young, Alton L. Becker, and Kenneth L. Pike,[2] takes the standardless functionalism of Winterowd's understanding of language and applies it to the use of language. "The ethical dimension of the art of rhetoric," these authors say, is in "the attempt to reduce another's sense of threat in the effort to reach the goal of cooperation and mutual benefit . . ." They distinguish between evaluative writing and descriptive writing, preferring the latter because evaluative writing tends to cause people "to become defensive," whereas "a description . . . does not make judgments . . ." When, however, a writer "must make judgments, he can make them in a way that minimizes the reader's sense of threat." Among other things, "he can acknowledge the personal element in his judgment. . . . There is a subtle but important difference between saying 'I don't like it' and 'It's bad.' "

The authors equate evaluation functionally, at least—with dogmatism: "The problem with dogmatism is that, like evaluation, it forces the reader to take sides." And finally they recommend a variety of writing which they call "provisional" because it "focuses on the process of enquiry itself and acknowledges the tentative nature of conclusions. . . . Provisional writing implies that more than one reasonable conclusion is possible."

The first of these books attempts to make the study of language an "objective" science by eliminating from that study all extralinguistic values and the issue of quality. Mr. Winterowd asserts that "the language grows according to its own dynamics." He does not say, apparently because he does not believe, that its dynamics includes the influence of the best practice. There is no "best." Anyone who speaks English is a "master" of the language. And the writers once acknowledged as masters of English are removed from "the world of reality" to the "world of fantasy," where they lose their force within the dynamics of the growth of language. Their works are reduced to the feckless status of "experiences": "we are much more interested in the imaginative statement of the message . . . than we are in the message . . ." Mr. Winterowd's linguistic "science" thus views language as an organism that has evolved without reference to habitat. Its growth has been "arbitrary," without any principle of selectivity.

Against Mr. Winterowd's definition of literature, it will be instructive to place a definition by Gary Snyder, who says of poetry that it is "a tool, a net or trap to catch and present; a sharp edge; a medicine, or the little awl that unties knots."[3] It will be quickly observed that this sentence enormously complicates Mr. Winterowd's simplistic statement-message dichotomy. What Mr. Winterowd means by "message" is an "idea" written in the dullest possible prose. His book is glib, and glibness is an inescapable doom of language without standards. One of the great practical uses of the literary disciplines, of course, is to resist glibness—to slow language down and make it thoughtful. This accounts, particularly, for the influence of verse, in its formal aspect, within the dynamics of the growth of language: verse checks the merely impulsive flow of speech, subjects it to another pulse, to measure, to extralinguistic consideration; by inducing the hesitations of difficulty, it admits into language the influence of the Muse and of musing.

The three authors of the second book attempt to found an ethics of rhetoric on the idea expressed in one of Mr. Winterowd's rules: "Rightness and wrongness are determined" by purpose, audience, and situation. This idea apparently derives from, though it significantly reduces, the ancient artistic concern for propriety or decorum. A part of this concern was indeed the fittingness of the work to its occasion: that is, one would not write an elegy in the meter of a drinking song—though that is putting it too plainly, for the sense of occasion exercised an influence both broad and subtle on form, diction, syntax, small points of grammar and prosody—everything. But occasion, as I understand it, was invariably second in importance to the subject. It is only the modern specialist who departs from this. The specialist poet, for instance, degrades the subject to "subject matter" (raw material), so that the subject exists for the poem's sake, is *subjected* to the poem, in the same way as industrial specialists see trees or ore-bearing rocks as raw material subjected to their manufactured end products. Quantity thus begins to dominate the work of the specialist poet at its source. Like an industrialist, he is interested in the subjects of the world for the sake of what they can be made to produce. He mines his experience for subject matter. The first aim of the propriety of the old poets, by contrast, was to make the language true to its subject—to see that it told the truth. That is why they invoked the Muse. The truth the poet chose as his subject was perceived as *superior* to his powers—and, by clear implication, to his occasion and purpose. But the aim of truth-telling is not stated in either of these textbooks. The second, in fact, makes an "ethical" aim of avoiding the issue, for, as the authors say, coining a formidable truth: "Truth has become increasingly elusive and men are driven to embrace conflicting ideologies."

This sort of talk about language, it seems to me, is fundamentally impractical. It does not propose as an outcome any fidelity between words and speakers or words and things or words and acts. It leads instead to muteness and paralysis. So far as I can tell, it is unlikely that one can speak at all, in even the most casual conversation, without some informing sense of what would be best to say—that is, without some sort of *standard*. And I do not believe that it is possible to act on the basis of a "tentative" or "provisional" conclusion. We may know that we are forming a conclusion on the basis of provisional or insufficient knowledge—that is a part of what we understand as the tragedy of our condition. But we must act, nevertheless, on the basis of *final* conclusions, because we know that actions, occurring in time, are irrevocable. That is another part of our tragedy. People who make a conventional agreement that all conclusions are provisional—a convention almost invariably implied by academic uses of the word "objectivity"—characteristically talk but do not act. Or they do not act deliberately, though time and materiality carry them into action of a sort, willy-nilly.

And there are times, according to the only reliable ethics we have, when one is required to tell the truth, whatever the urgings of purposes, audiences, and situation. Ethics requires this because, in the terms of the practical realities of our lives, the truth is safer than falsehood. To ignore this is simply to put language at the service of purpose—*any* purpose. It is, in terms of the most urgent realities of our own time, to abet a dangerous confusion between public responsibility and public relations. Remote as these theories of language are from practical contexts, they are nevertheless serviceable to expedient practices.

In affirming that there is a necessary and indispensable connection between language and truth, and therefore between language and deeds, I have certain precedents in mind. I begin with the Christian idea of the Incarnate Word, the Word entering the world as flesh, and inevitably therefore as action—which leads logically enough to the insistence in the Epistle of James that faith without works is dead:

> For if any be a hearer of the word, and not a doer, he is
> like unto a man beholding his natural face in a glass:

213

For he beholdeth himself, and goeth his way, and
straightway forgetteth what manner of man he was.[4]

I also have in mind the Confucian insistence on sincerity
(precision) and on fidelity between speaker and word as essen-
tials of political health: "Honesty is the treasure of states." I have
returned to Ezra Pound's observation that Confucius "collected
The Odes to keep his followers from abstract discussion. That is,
The Odes give particular instances. They do not lead to exagger-
ations of dogma."[5]

And I have remembered from somewhere Thoreau's sentence: "Where would you look for standard English but to the
words of a standard man?"

The idea of standing by one's word, of words precisely desig-
nating things, of deeds faithful to words, is probably native to
our understanding. Indeed, it seems doubtful whether without
that idea we could understand anything.

But in order to discover what makes language that can be
understood, stood by, and acted on, it is necessary to return to
my borrowed concepts of internal and external accounting. And
it will be useful to add two further precedents.

In *Mind and Nature*, Gregory Bateson writes that " 'things'
[his quotation marks] can only enter the world of communication and meaning by their names, their qualities and their attributes (i.e., by reports of their internal and external relations and
interactions)."[6]

And Gary Snyder, in a remarkably practical or practicable
or practice-able definition of where he takes his stand, makes
the poet responsible for "possibilities opening both inward and
outward."[7]

There can be little doubt, I think, that any accounting that
is *purely* internal will be incomprehensible. If the connection between inward and outward is broken—if, for instance, the experience of a single human does not resonate within the common
experience of humanity—then language fails. In *The Family Re-
union*, Harry says: "I talk in general terms / Because the particular has no language."[8] But he speaks, too, in despair, having
no hope that his general terms can communicate the particular
burden of his experience. We readily identify this loneliness of

personal experience as "modern." Many poems of our century have this loneliness, this failure of speech, as a subject; many more exhibit it as a symptom.

But it begins at least as far back as Shelley, in such lines as these from "Stanzas Written in Dejection, Near Naples":

> Alas! I have nor hope nor health,
>   Nor peace within nor calm around,
> Nor that content surpassing wealth
>   The sage in meditation found,
>   And walked with inward glory crowned—
> Nor fame, nor power, nor love, nor leisure.
>   . . . .
> I could lie down like a tired child,
>   And weep away the life of care
>   Which I have borne and yet must bear,
> Till death like sleep might steal on me . . .

This too is an example of particular experience concealing itself in "general terms"—though here the failure, if it was suspected, is not acknowledged. The generality of the language does not objectify it, but seals it in its subjectivity. In reading this— as, I think, in reading a great many poems of our own time— we sooner or later realize that we are reading a "complaint" that we do not credit or understand. If we fail to realize this, it is because we have departed from the text of the poem, summoning particularities of our own experience in support of Shelley's general assertions. The fact remains that Shelley's poem doesn't tell us what he is complaining about; his lines fail to "create the object [here, the experience] which they contemplate."[9] This failure is implicitly conceded by the editors of *The Norton Anthology of English Literature*, who felt it necessary to provide the following footnote:

> Shelley's first wife, Harriet, had drowned herself; Clara, his baby daughter by Mary Shelley, had just died; and Shelley himself was plagued by ill health, pain, financial worries, and the sense that he had failed as a poet.[10]

But I think the poem itself calls attention to the failure by its easy descent into self-pity, finally asserting that "I am one / Whom

215

men love not . . ." Language that becomes too subjective lacks currency, to use another economic metaphor; it will not pass. Self-pity, like bragging, will not pass. The powers of language are used illegitimately, to impose, rather than to elicit, the desired response.

Shelley is not writing gibberish here. It is possible to imagine that someone who does not dislike this poem may see in it a certain beauty. But it is the sickly beauty of generalized emotionalism. For once precision is abandoned as a linguistic or literary virtue, vague generalization is one of two remaining possibilities, gibberish being the second.

It is true, in a sense, that "the particular has no language"—that at least in public writing, and in speech passing between strangers, there may be only degrees of generalization. But there are, I think, two kinds of precision that are particular and particularizing. There is, first, the precision in the speech of people who share the same knowledge of place and history and work. This is the precision of direct reference or designation. It sounds like this: "How about letting me borrow your tall jack?" Or: "The old hollow beech blew down last night." Or, beginning a story, "Do you remember that time . . . ?" I would call this community speech. Its words have the power of pointing to things visible either to eyesight or to memory. Where it is not too much corrupted by public or media speech, this community speech is wonderfully vital. Because it so often works designatively it *has* to be precise, and its precisions are formed by persistent testing against its objects.

This community speech, unconsciously taught and learned, in which words live in the presence of their objects, is the very root and foundation of language. It is the source, the unconscious inheritance that is carried, both with and without schooling, into consciousness—but never *all* the way, and so it remains rich, mysterious, and enlivening. Cut off from this source, language becomes a paltry work of conscious purpose, at the service and the mercy of expedient aims. Theories such as those underlying the two text books I have discussed seem to be attempts to detach language from its source in communal experience, by making it arbitrary in origin and provisional in use. And this may be a "realistic" way of "accepting" the degradation of community life. The task, I think, is hopeless, and it shows the extremes of futility that academic specialization can lead to. If one wishes to promote the life of language, one must promote the life of a community—a discipline many times more trying, difficult, and long than that of linguistics, but having at least the virtue of hopefulness. It escapes the despair always implicit in specializations: the cultivation of discrete parts without respect or responsibility for the whole.

The other sort of precision—the sort available to public speech or writing as well as to community speech—is a precision that comes of tension either between a statement and a prepared context or, within a single statement, between more or less conflicting feelings or ideas. Shelley's complaint is incomprehensible not just because it is set in "general terms," but because the generalities are too simple. One doesn't credit the emotion of the poem because it is too purely mournful. We are—conventionally, maybe, but also properly—unprepared to believe without overpowering evidence that things are *all* bad. Self-pity may deal in such absolutes of feeling, but we don't deal with other people in the manner of self-pity.

Another general complaint about mortality is given in Act V, Scene 2, of *King Lear,* when Edgar says to Gloucester: "Men must endure / Their going hence, even their coming hither." Out of context this statement is even more general than Shelley's. It is, unlike Shelley's, deeply moving because it is tensely poised within a narrative context that makes it precise. We know exactly, for instance, what is meant by that "must": a responsible performance is required until death. But the complaint is followed immediately by a statement of another kind, forcing the speech of the play back into its action: "Ripeness is all. Come on."

Almost the same thing is done in a single line of Robert Herrick, in the tension between the complaint of mortality and the jaunty metric:

Out of the world he must, who once comes in . . .

Here the very statement of inevitable death sings its acceptability. How would you divide, there, the "statement of the message" from "the message"?

And see how the tension between contradictory thoughts particularizes the feeling in these three lines by John Dryden:

> Old as I am, for ladies' love unfit,
> The pow'r of beauty I remember yet,
> Which once inflamed my soul, and still inspires my wit.

These last three examples receive our belief and sympathy because they satisfy our sense of the complexity, the cross-graining, of real experience. In them, an inward possibility is made to open outward. Internal accounting has made itself externally accountable.

Shelley's poem, on the other hand, exemplifies the solitude of inward experience that continues with us, both in and out of poetry. I don't pretend to understand all the causes and effects of this, but I will offer the opinion that one of its chief causes is a simplistic idea of "freedom," which also continues with us, and is also to be found in Shelley. At the end of Act III of *Prometheus Unbound*, we are given this vision of a liberated humanity:

> The loathsome mask has fallen, the man remains
> Sceptreless, free, uncircumscribed, but man
> Equal, unclassed, tribeless, and nationless,
> Exempt from awe, worship, degree, the king
> Over himself . . .

This passage, like the one from the "Stanzas Written in Dejection," is vague enough, and for the same reason; as the first hastened to emotional absolutes, this hastens to an absolute idea. It is less a vision of a free man than a vision of a definition of a free man. But Shelley apparently did not notice that this headlong scramble of adjectives, though it may produce one of the possible definitions of a free man, also defines a lonely man, unattached and displaced. This free man is described as loving, and love is an emotion highly esteemed by Shelley. But it is, like his misery, a "free" emotion, detached and absolute. In this same passage of *Prometheus Unbound*, he calls it "the nepenthe, love"— love forgetful, or inducing forgetfulness, of grief or pain.

Shelley thought himself, particularly in *Prometheus Unbound,* a follower of Milton—an assumption based on a misunderstanding of *Paradise Lost.* And so it is instructive in two ways to set beside Shelley's definition of freedom, this one by Milton:

> To be free is precisely the same thing as to be pious, wise, just, and temperate, careful of one's own, abstinent from what is another's, and thence, in fine, magnanimous and brave.[11]

And Milton's definition, like the lines previously quoted from Shakespeare, Herrick, and Dryden, derives its precision from tension: he defines freedom in terms of responsibilities. And it is only this tension that can suggest the possibility of *living* (for any length of time) in freedom—just as it is the tension between love and pain that suggests the possibility of carrying love into acts. Shelley's freedom defined in terms of freedom, gives us only this from a "Chorus of Spirits" in Act IV, Scene I, of *Prometheus Unbound:*

> Our task is done,
> We are free to dive, or soar, or run;
> Beyond and around,
> Or within the bound
> Which clips the world with darkness round.
>
> We'll pass the eyes
> Of the starry skies
> Into the hoar deep to colonize . . .

Which, as we will see, has more in common with the technological romanticism of Buckminster Fuller than with anything in Milton.

In supposed opposition to this remote subjectivity of internal accounting, our age has developed a stance or state of mind which it calls "objective," and which produces a kind of accounting supposed to be external—that is, free from personal biases and considerations. This objective mentality, within the safe confines of its various specialized disciplines, operates with great precision and confidence. It follows tested and trusted

219

procedures, and uses a professional language which an outsider must assume to be a very exact code. When this language is used by its accustomed speakers on their accustomed ground, even when one does not understand it, it clearly voices the implication of a control marvelously precise over objective reality. It is only when it is overheard in confrontation with failure that this implication falters, and the adequacy of this sort of language comes in doubt.

The transcribed conversations of the members of the Nuclear Regulatory Commission during the crisis of Three Mile Island[12] provide a valuable exhibit of the limitations of one of these objective languages. At one point, for example, the commissioners received a call from Roger Mattson, Nuclear Reactor Regulation chief of systems safety. He said, among other things, the following:

> That bubble will be 5,000 cubic feet. The available volume in the upper head and the candy canes, that's the hot legs, is on the order of 2,000 cubic feet total. I get 3,000 excess cubic feet of noncondensibles. I've got a horse race. . . . We have got every systems engineer we can find . . . thinking the problem: how the hell do we get the noncondensibles out of there, do we win the horse race or do we lose the horse race.

At another time the commissioners were working to "engineer a press release," of which "The focus . . . has to be reassuring . . ." Commissioner Ahearne apparently felt that it was a bit *too* reassuring, and he would like it to *suggest* the possibility of a bad outcome, apparently a meltdown. He says:

> I think it would be technically a lot better if you said— something about there's a possibility—it's small, but, it could lead to serious problems.

And, a few sentences later, Commissioner Kennedy tells him:

> Well I understand what you're saying. . . . You could put a little sentence in right there . . . to say, were this—in the unlikely event that this occurred, increased temperatures would result and possible further fuel damage.

What is remarkable, and frightening, about this language is its inability to admit what it is talking about. Because these specialists have routinely eliminated themselves, as such and as representative human beings, from consideration according to the prescribed "objectivity" of their discipline, they cannot bring themselves to acknowledge to each other, much less to the public, that their problem involves an extreme danger to a lot of people. Their subject, as bearers of a public trust, is this danger, and it can be nothing else. It is a technical problem least of all. And yet when their language approaches this subject, it either diminishes it, or dissolves into confusions of syntax or purpose. Mr. Mattson speaks clearly and coherently enough so long as numbers and the jargon of "candy canes" and "hot legs" are adequate to his purpose. But as soon as he tries to communicate his sense of the urgency of the problem, his language collapses into a kind of rant around the metaphor of "a horse race." And the two commissioners, struggling with their obligation to inform the public of the possibility of a disaster, find themselves virtually languageless—without the necessary words and with only the shambles of a syntax. They cannot say what they are talking about. And so their obligation to *inform* becomes a tongue-tied—and therefore surely futile—effort to *reassure*. Public responsibility becomes public relations, apparently, for want of a language adequately responsive to its subject.

So inept is the speech of these commissioners that we must deliberately remind ourselves that they are not stupid, and are probably not amoral. They are highly trained, intelligent, worried men, whose understanding of language is by now to a considerable extent a public one. They are atomic scientists whose criteria of language are identical to those of at least some linguistic scientists. They determine the correctness of their statement to the press exactly according to Mr. Winterowd's rule: by their purpose, audience, and situation. Their language is governed by the ethical aim prescribed by the three authors of *Rhetoric: Discovery and Change:* they wish above all to speak in such a way as to "reduce another's sense of threat." But the result was not "cooperation and mutual benefit"; it was incoherence and dishonesty, leading to public suspicion, distrust, and fear.

This is language diminished by inordinate ambition: the

taking of more power than can be responsibly or beneficiently held. It is perhaps a law of human nature that such ambition always produces a confusion of tongues:

> And they said, Go to, let us build us a city and a tower, whose top may reach unto heaven; and let us make us a name, lest we be scattered . . .
>
> . . . .
>
> And the Lord said . . . now nothing will be restrained from them, which they have imagined to do.
> Go to, let us go down, and there confound their language, that they may not understand one another's speech.[13]

The professed aim is to bring people together—usually for the implicit, though unstated, purpose of subjecting them to some public power or project. Why else would rulers seek to "unify" people? The idea is to cause them to speak the same language—meaning either that they will agree with the government or be quiet, as in communist and fascist states, or that they will politely ignore their disagreements or disagree "provisionally," as in American universities. But the result—though power may survive for a while in spite of it—is confusion and dispersal. Real language, real discourse are destroyed. People lose understanding of each other, are divided and scattered. Speech of whatever kind begins to resemble the speech of drunkenness or madness.

What this dialogue of the NRC commissioners causes one to suspect—and I believe the suspicion is confirmed by every other such exhibit I have seen—is that there is simply no such thing as an accounting that is *purely* external. The notion that external accounting can be accomplished by "objectivity" is an illusion. Apparently the only way to free the accounting of what is internal to people, or subjective, is to make it internal to (that is, subject to) some other entity or structure just as limiting, or more so—as the commissioners attempted to deal with a possible public catastrophe in terms either of nuclear technology or of public relations. The only thing really externalized by such accounting is a bad result that one does not wish to pay for.

And so external accounting, alone, is only another form of internal accounting. The only difference is that this "objective" accounting does pretty effectively rule out personal considerations *of a certain kind.* (It does *not* rule out the personal desire for wealth, power, or intellectual certainty.) Otherwise, the talk of the commissioners and the lines from "Stanzas Written in Dejection" are equally and similarly incomprehensible. The languages of both are obviously troubled, we recognize the words, and learn something about the occasions, but we cannot learn from the language itself exactly what the trouble is. The commissioners' language cannot define the problem of their public responsibility, and Shelley's does not develop what I suppose should be called the narrative context of his emotion, which therefore remains incommunicable.

Moreover, these two sorts of accounting, so long as they remain discrete, both work to keep the problem abstract, all in the mind. They are both, in different ways, internal to the mind. The real occasions of the problems are not admitted into consideration. In Shelley's poem, this may be caused by a despairing acceptance of loneliness. In the NRC deliberations it is caused, I think, by fear; the commissioners take refuge in the impersonality of technological procedures. They cannot bear to acknowledge considerations and feelings that might break the insulating spell of their "objective" dispassion.

Or, to put it another way, their language and their way of thought make it possible for them to think of the crisis only as a technical event or problem. Even a meltdown is fairly understandable and predictable within the terms of their expertise. What is unthinkable is the evacuation of a massively populated region. It is the disorder, confusion, and uncertainty of that exodus that they cannot face. The one is, in Mr. Mattson's phrase, "a failure mode that has never been studied." The other is forty years—or forty centuries—in the wilderness. In dealing with the unstudied failure mode, the commissioners' minds do not have to leave their meeting room. It is an *internal* problem. The other, the human, possibility, if they were really to deal with it, would send them shouting into the streets. Even worse, perhaps, from the point of view of their discipline, it would force them to face the absurdity of the idea of "emergency planning"—the idea, in other words, of a controlled catastrophe. They would have to admit, against all the claims of professional standing and job security, that the only way to control the danger of a nuclear power plant is not to build it. That is to say, if they had a language strong and fine enough to consider *all* the considerations, it would tend to force them out of the confines of "objective" thought and into action, out of solitude into community.

It is the *purity* of objective thought that finally seduces and destroys it. The same thing happens, it seems to me, to the subjective mind. For certain emotions, especially the extremely subjective ones of self-pity and self-love, isolation holds a strong enticement: it offers to keep them pure and neat, aloof from the disorderliness and the mundane obligations of the human common ground.

The only way, so far as I can see, to achieve an accounting that is verifiably and reliably external is to admit the internal, the personal, as an appropriate, necessary consideration. If the NRC commissioners, for example, had spoken a good common English, instead of the languages of their specialization and of public relations, then they might have spoken of their personal anxiety and bewilderment, and so brought into consideration what they had in common with the people whose health and lives they were responsible for. They might, in short, have sympathized openly with those people—and so have understood the probably unbearable burden of their public trusteeship.

To be bound within the confines of either the internal or the external way of accounting is to be diseased. To hold the two in balance is to validate both kinds, and to have health. I am not using these terms "disease" and "health" according to any clinical definitions, but am speaking simply from my own observation that when my awareness of how I feel overpowers my awareness of where I am and who is there with me, I am sick, dis-eased. This can be appropriately extended to say that if what I think obscures my sense of whereabouts and company, I am diseased. And the converse is also true: I am diseased if I become so aware of my surroundings that my own inward life is obscured, as if I should so fix upon the value of some mineral in the ground as to forget that the world is God's work and my home.

But still another example is necessary, and other terms.

In an article entitled "The Evolution and Future of American Animal Agriculture," G. W. Salisbury and R. G. Hart[14] consider the transformation of American agriculture "from an art form into a science." The difference, they say, is that the art of agriculture is concerned "only" with the "how . . . of farming," whereas the science is interested in the "whys."

As an example—or, as they say, a "reference index"—of this change, the authors use the modern history of milk production: the effort, from their point of view entirely successful, "to change the dairy cow from the family companion animal she became after domestication and through all man's subsequent history into an appropriate manufacturing unit of the twentieth century for the efficient transformation of unprocessed feed into food for man."

The authors produce "two observations" about this change, and these constitute their entire justification of it:

> First, the total cow population was reduced in the period 1944 through 1975 by 67 percent, but second, the yield per cow during the same period increased by 60 percent. In practical terms, the research that yielded such dramatic gains produced a savings for the American public as a whole of approximately 50 billion pounds of total digestible nitrogen per year in the production of a relatively constant level of milk.

The authors proceed to work this out in dollar values and to say that the quantity of saved dollars finally "gets to the point that people simply do not believe it." And later they say that, in making this change, "The major disciplines were genetics, reproduction, and nutrition."

This is obviously a prime example of internal accounting in the economic sense. The external account is not fully renderable; the context of the accounting is vast, some quantities are not known, and some of the costs are not quantifiable. However, there can be no question that the externalized costs are large. The net gain is not, as these authors imply, identical with the gross. And the industrialization of milk production is a part of a much larger enterprise that may finally produce a highly visible, if not entirely computable, net loss.

At least two further observations are necessary:

1. The period, 1944–1975, also saw a drastic decrease in the number of dairies, by reason of the very change cited by Salisbury and Hart. The smaller—invariably the smaller—dairies were forced out because of the comparative "inefficiency" of their "manufacturing units." Their failure was part

of a major population shift, which seriously disrupted the life both of the country communities and of the cities, broke down traditional community forms, and so on.

2. The industrialization of agriculture, of which the industrialization of milk production is a part, has caused serious problems that even agricultural specialists are beginning to recognize: soil erosion, soil compaction, chemical poisoning and pollution, energy shortages, several kinds of money troubles, obliteration of plant and animal species, disruption of soil biology.

Both the human and the agricultural/ecological costs are obviously great. Some of them have begun to force their way into the accounts, and are straining the economy. Others are, and are likely to remain, external to all ledgers.

The passages I have quoted from Professors Salisbury and Hart provide a very neat demonstration of the shift from a balanced internal-external accounting (the dairy cow as "family companion animal") to a so-called "objective" accounting (the dairy cow as "appropriate manufacturing unit of the twentieth century"), which is, in fact, internal to an extremely limited definition of agricultural progress.

The discarded language, oddly phrased though it is, comes close to a kind of accountability: the internal (family) and the external (cow) are joined by a moral connection (companionship). A proof of its accountability is that this statement can be the basis of moral behavior: "Be good to the cow, for she is our companion."

The preferred phrase—"appropriate manufacturing unit of the twentieth century"—has nothing of this accountability. One can say, of course: "Be good to the cow, for she is productive (or expensive)." But that could be said of a machine; it takes no account of the cow as a living, much less a fellow, creature. But the phrase is equally unaccountable as language. "Appropriate" to what? Though the authors write "appropriate . . . of the twentieth century," they may mean "appropriate . . . *to* the twentieth century." But are there no families and no needs for companionship with animals in the twentieth century? Or perhaps they mean "appropriate . . . for the efficient transformation of unprocessed feed into food for man." But the problem remains. Who is this "man"? Someone, perhaps, who needs no companionship with family or animals? We are constrained to suppose so, for "objectivity" has apparently eliminated "family" and "companion" as terms subject to personal bias—perhaps as "merely sentimental." By the terms of this "objective" accounting, then, "man" is a creature who needs to eat, and who is for some unspecified reason more important than a cow. But for a reader who considers himself a "man" by any broader definition, this language is virtually meaningless. Because the terms of personal bias (that is, the terms of *value*) have been eliminated, the terms of judgment ("appropriate" and "efficient") mean nothing. The authors' conditions would be just as well satisfied if the man produced the milk and the cow bought it, or if a machine produced it and a machine bought it.

Sense, and the possibility of sense, break down here because too much that clearly belongs in has been left out. Like the NRC commissioners, Salisbury and Hart have eliminated themselves as representative human beings, and they go on to eliminate the cow as a representative animal—all "interests" are thus removed from the computation. With apparently rigorous scrupulosity they pluck out the representative or symbolic terms in order to achieve a pristinely "objective" accounting of the performance of a "unit." And so we are astonished to discover, at the end of this process, that they have complacently allowed the dollar to stand as representative of *all* value. What announced itself as a statement about animal agriculture has become, by way of several obscure changes of subject, a crudely simplified statement about industrial economics. This is not, in any respectable sense, language, or thought, or even computation. Like the textbooks I have discussed, and like the dialogue of the NRC, it is a pretentious and dangerous deception, forgiveable only insofar as it may involve self-deception.

If we are to begin to make a reliable account of it, this recent history of milk production must be seen as occurring within a system of nested systems. This system might be suggested by a sketch of five concentric circles, with the innermost representing the individual human, the second representing the family, the third the community, the fourth agriculture, and the outermost and largest representing nature. So long as the smaller

227

systems are enclosed within the larger, and so long as all are connected by complex patterns of interdependency, as we know they are, then whatever affects one system will affect the others.

It seems that this system of systems is safe so long as each system is controlled by the next larger one. If at any point the hierarchy is reversed, the destruction of the entire system begins. This system of systems is perhaps an updated, ecological version of the Great Chain of Being. That is, it may bring us back to a hierarchical structure not too different from the one that underlies *Paradise Lost*—a theory of the form of Creation which is at the same time a moral form, and which is violated by the "disobedience" or *hubris* of attempting to rise and take power above one's proper place.

But the sketch I have made of the system of systems is much too crude, for the connections between systems, insofar as this is a human structure, are not "given" or unconscious or automatic, but involve disciplines. Persons are joined to families, families to communities, etc., by disciplines that must be deliberately made, remembered, taught, learned, and practiced.

The system of systems begins to disintegrate when the hierarchy is reversed because that begins the disintegration of the connecting disciplines. Disciplines, typically, degenerate into professions, professions into careers. The accounting of Salisbury and Hart is defective because it upsets the hierarchies and so, perhaps unwittingly, fails to consider all the necessary considerations. They do present their "reference index" as occurring within a system of systems—but a drastically abbreviated one, which involves a serious distortion. In a graph of this system, the innermost circle represents the dairyman, the second the dairy, the third agriculture, and the fourth—which contains the first three—represents economics. Two things are wrong with this. First, too much has been left out. Second, the outer circle is too much within the interest of the inner. The dairyman is not *necessarily* under the control of simple greed—but this structure supplies no hint of a reason why he should not be.

The system of systems, as I first described it, involves three different kinds of interests:

1. The ontogenetic. This is self-interest and is at the center.
2. The phylogenetic. This is the interest that we would call

"humanistic." It reaches through family and community and into agriculture. But it does not reach far enough into agriculture because, by its own terms, it cannot.

3. The ecogenetic. This is the interest of the whole "household" in which life is lived. (I don't know whether I invented this term or not. If I did, I apologize.)

These terms give us another way to characterize the flaw in the accounting of Salisbury and Hart. Their abbreviated system of systems fails either to assemble enough facts, to account fully for the meaning of the facts, or to provide any standard of judgment because the ontogenetic interest is both internal and external to it.

The system of systems, as I first sketched it, has this vulnerability: that the higher interests can be controlled or exploited by the lower simply by leaving things out—a procedure just as available to ignorance as to the highest cunning of "applied science." And given even the most generous motives, ignorance is always going to be involved.

There is no reliable standard for behavior anywhere within the system of systems except truth. Lesser standards produce destruction—as, for example, the standards of public relations make gibberish of language.

The trouble, obviously, is that we do not know much of the truth. In particular, we know very little ecogenetic truth.

And so yet another term has to be introduced. The system of systems has to be controlled from above and outside. There has to be a religious interest of some kind above the ecogenetic. It will be sufficient to my purpose here just to say that the system of systems is enclosed within mystery, in which some truth can be known, but never all truth.

Neither the known truth nor the mystery is internal to any system. And here, however paradoxical it may seem, we begin to see a possibility of reliable accounting and of responsible behavior. The appropriateness of words or deeds can be determined only in reference to the whole "household" in which they occur. But this whole, as such, cannot enter into the accounting. (If it could, then the only necessary language would be mathematics, and the only necessary discipline would be military.) It can only come in as mystery: a factor of X which stands not for

the unknown but the unknowable. This is an X that cannot be solved—which may be thought a disadvantage by some;
its advantage is that, once it has been let into the account, it
cannot easily be ignored. You cannot leave anything out of
mystery, because by definition everything is always in it.

The practical use of religion, then, is to keep the accounting
in as large a context as possible—to see, in fact, that the account
is never "closed." Religion forces the accountant to reckon with
mystery—the unsolvable X that keeps the debit and credit or
cost and benefit columns open so that no "profit" can ever be
safely declared. It forces the accounting outside of every enclo-
sure that it might be internal to. Practically, this X means that
all "answers" must be worked out within a limit of humility and
restraint, so that the initiative to act would always imply a knowing acceptance of accountability for the results. The establishment and maintenance of this limit seems to me the ultimate
empirical problem—the real "frontier" of science, or at least of
the definition of the possibility of a *moral* science. It would place
science under the rule of the old concern for propriety, correct
proportion, proper scale—from which, in modern times, even
the arts have been "liberated." That is, it would return to all work,
artistic or scientific, the possibility of an external standard of
quality. The quality of work or of a made thing would be determined by how conservingly it fitted into the system of systems. Judgment could then begin to articulate what is already
obvious: that some work preserves the household of life, and
some work destroys it. And thus a real liberation could take place:
life and work could go free of those "professional standards"
(and professional languages) that are invariably destructive of
quality, because they always work as sheep's clothing for various
kinds of ontogenetic motives. It is because of these professional
standards that the industries and governments, while *talking* of
the "betterment of the human condition," can *act* to enrich and
empower themselves.

The connections within the system of systems are *practical*
connections. The practicality consists in the realization that—
despite the blandishments of the various short-circuited "professional" languages—you cannot speak or act in your own best
interest without espousing and serving a higher interest. It is
not knowledge that enforces this realization, but the humbling

awareness of the insufficiency of knowledge, of mystery.

Applying then the standard of ecogenetic health to the work of Salisbury and Hart, we get a third way to describe its failure: it makes a principle of replacing the complex concern for quality ("how") with the drastically simplifying concern for quantity. Thus motive is entirely "liberated" from method: any way is good so long as it increases per unit production. But everything except production is diminished in the process, and Salisbury and Hart do not have a way of accounting for, hence no ability even to recognize, these diminishments. All that has been diminished could have been protected by a lively interest in the question of "how," which Salisbury and Hart—like the interests they are accounting for—ruled out at the beginning. They were nevertheless working under what I take to be a rule: When you subtract quality from quantity, the gross result is not a net gain.

And so a reliable account is personal at the beginning and religious at the end. This does not mean that a reliable account includes the whole system of systems, for no account can do that. It does mean that the account is made in precise reference to the system of systems—which is another way of saying that it is made in respect for it. Without this respect for the larger structures, the meaning shrinks into the confines of some smaller structure, and becomes special, partial, and destructive.

It is this sort of external accounting that deals with connections, and thus inevitably raises the issue of quality. Which, I take it, is always the same as the issue of propriety: How appropriate is the tool to the work, the work to the need, the need to other needs and the needs of others and to the health of the household or community of all creatures?

And this kind of accounting gives us the great structures of poetry—as in Homer, Dante, and Milton. It is these great structures, I think, that carry us into the sense of being, in Gary Snyder's phrase, "at one with each other."[15] They teach us to imagine the life that is divided from us by difference or enmity: as Homer imagined the "enemy" hero, Hector; as Dante, on his pilgrimage to Heaven, imagined the damned; as Milton, in his awed study of the meaning of obedience, epitomized sympathetically in his Satan the disobedient personality. And as, now, ecological insight proposes again a poetry with the power to imagine the

231

lives of animals and plants and streams and stones. And this imagining is eminently appropriate to the claims and privileges of the great household.

Unlike the problems of quantity, the problems of propriety are never "solved," but are ceaselessly challenging and interesting. This is the antidote to the romance of big technological solutions. Life would be interesting—there would be exciting work to do—even if there were no nuclear power plants or "agri-industries" or space adventures. The elaborations of elegance are at least as fascinating, and more various, more democratic, more healthy, more practical—though less glamorous—than the elaborations of power.

Without this ultimate reference to the system of systems, and this ultimate concern for quality, any rendering of account falls into the service of a kind of tyranny: it accompanies, and in one way or another invariably enables, the taking of power, from people first and last, but also from all other created things.

In this degenerative accounting, language is almost without the power of designation because it is used conscientiously to refer to nothing in particular. Attention rests upon percentages, categories, abstract functions. The reference drifts inevitably toward the merely provisional. It is not language that the user will likely be required to stand by or to act on, for it does not define any personal ground for standing or acting. Its only practical utility is to support with "expert opinion" a vast, impersonal technological action already begun. And it works directly against the conventionality, the community life, of language, for it holds in contempt, not only all particular grounds of the private fidelity and action, but the common ground of human experience, memory, and understanding from which language rises and on which meaning is shaped. It is a tyrannical language: tyrannese.

Do people come consciously to such language and to such implicit purpose? I hope not. I do not think so. It seems likely to me that, first, a certain kind of confusion must occur. It is a confusion about the human place in the universe, and it has been produced by diligent "educational" labors. This confusion is almost invariably founded on some romantic proposition about the "high destiny of man" or "unlimited human horizons." For an example I turn to R. Buckminster Fuller,[16] here defending the "cosmic realism" of space colonization:

> Conceptualizing realistically about humans as passengers on board 8,000-mile diameter Spaceship Earth traveling around the Sun at 60,000 miles an hour while flying formation with the Moon, which formation involves the 365 revolutions per each Sun circuit, and recalling that humans have always been born naked, helpless and ignorant though superbly equipped cerebrally, and endowed with hunger, thirst, curiosity and procreative instincts, it has been logical for humans to employ their minds' progressive discoveries of the cosmic principles governing all physical interattractions, interactions, reactions and intertransformings, and to use those principles in progressively organizing, to humanity's increasing advantage, the complex of cosmic principles interacting locally to produce their initial environment which most probably was that of a verdant south seas coral atoll—built by the coral on a volcano risen from ocean bottom ergo unoccupied by any animals, having only fish and birds as well as fruits, nuts and coconut milk.

That is a single sentence. I call attention not only to the vagueness and oversimplification of its generalities, but, more important, to the weakness of its grammar and the shapelessness and aimlessness of its syntax. The subject is an "it" of very tentative reference, buried in the middle of the sentence—an "it," moreover, that cannot possibly be the subject of the two complicated participial constructions that precede it. The sentence, then, begins with a dangling modifier half its length. On the other end, it peters out in a description of the biology of a coral atoll, the pertinence of which is never articulated. In general, the sentence is a labyrinth of syntactical confusions impossible to map. When we reflect that "sentence" means, literally, "a way of thinking" (Latin: *sententia*) and that it comes from the Latin *sentire*, to feel, we realize that the concepts of sentence and sentence structure are not merely grammatical or merely academic—not negligible in any sense. A sentence is both the opportunity and the limit of thought—what we have to think with, and what we have to think in. It is, moreover, a *feelable* thought,

233

a thought that impresses its sense not just on our understanding, but on our hearing, our sense of rhythm and proportion. It is a pattern of felt sense.

A sentence completely shapeless is therefore a loss of thought, an act of self-abandonment to incoherence. And indeed Mr. Fuller shows himself here a man who conceives a sentence, not as a pattern of thought apprehensible to sense, but merely as a clot of abstract concepts. In such a syntactical clot, words and concepts will necessarily tend to function abstractly rather than referentially. It is the statement of a man for whom words have replaced things, and who has therefore ceased to think particularly about any thing.

The idea buried in all those words is, so far as I can tell, a simple one: humans are born earth-bound, ignorant, and vulnerable, but intelligent; by their intelligence they lift themselves up from their primitive origin and move to fulfill their destiny. As we learn in later sentences, this destiny is universal in scope, limitless ("ever larger"), and humans are to approach it by larger and larger technology. The end is not stated, obviously, because it is not envisioned, because it is not envisionable. The idea, then, is that humans are extremely intelligent, and by the use of their technological genius they are on their way somewhere or other. It seems to me not unreasonable to suggest that the aimlessness, the limitlessness, of Mr. Fuller's idea produces the aimlessness and shapelessness of his sentence.

By contrast, consider another view of the human place in the universe, not a simple view or simply stated, but nevertheless comely, orderly, and clear:

> There wanted yet the Master work, the end
> Of all yet done; a Creature who not prone
> And Brute as other Creatures, but endu'd
> With Sanctity of Reason, might erect
> His Stature, and upright with Front serene
> Govern the rest, self-knowing, and from thence
> Magnanimous to correspond with Heav'n,
> But grateful to acknowledge whence his good
> Descends, thither with heart and voice and eyes
> Directed in Devotion, to adore
> And worship God Supreme . . .[17]

These lines of Milton immediately suggest what is wrong, first, with Mr. Fuller's sentence, and then with the examples of tyrannese that preceded it. They all assume that the human prerogative is unlimited, that we *must* do whatever we have the power to do. Specifically, what is lacking is the idea that humans have a place in Creation and that this place is limited by responsibility on the one hand and by humility on the other—or, in Milton's terms, by magnanimity and devotion. Without this precision of definition, this setting of bounds or ends to thought, we cannot mean, or say what we mean, or mean what we say; we cannot stand by our words because we cannot utter words that can be stood by; we cannot speak of our own actions as persons, or even as communities, but only of the actions of percentages, large organizations, concepts, historical trends, or the impersonal "forces" of destiny or evolution.

Or let us consider another pair of statements. The first, again from Buckminster Fuller, following the one just quoted, elaborates his theme of technological destiny:

> First the humans developed fish catching and carving tools, then rafts, dug-out canoes and paddles and then sailing outrigger canoes. Reaching the greater islands and the mainland they developed animal skin, grass and leaf-woven clothing and skin tents. They gradually entered safely into geographical areas where they would previously have perished. Slowly they learned to tame, then breed, cows, bullocks, water buffalo, horses and elephants. Next they developed oxen, then horsedrawn vehicles, then horseless vehicles, then ships of the sky. Then employing rocketry and packaging up the essential life-supporting environmental constituents of the biosphere they made sorties away from their mothership Earth and finally ferried over to their Sun orbiting-companion, the Moon.

The other is from William Faulkner's story, "The Bear."[18] Isaac McCaslin is speaking of his relinquishment of the ownership of land:

> . . . He created the earth, made it and looked at it and said it was all right, and then He made man. He made the

235

earth first and peopled it with dumb creatures, and then
He created man to be His overseer on the earth and to
hold suzerainty over the earth and the animals on it in His
name, not to hold for himself and his descendants inviol-
able title forever, generation after generation, to the ob-
longs and squares of the earth, but to hold the earth mutual
and intact in the communal anonymity of brotherhood, and
all the fee He asked was pity and humility and sufferance
and endurance and the sweat of his face for bread.

The only continuity recognized by Mr. Fuller is that of technological development, which is in fact not a continuity at all,
for, as he sees it, it does not proceed by building on the past
but by outmoding and replacing it. And if any other human
concern accompanied the development from canoe to space ship,
it is either not manifest to Mr. Fuller, or he does not think it
important enough to mention.

The passage from Faulkner, on the other hand, cannot be
understood except in terms of the historical and cultural continuity that produced it. It awakens our memory of Genesis and
Paradise Lost, as *Paradise Lost* awakens our memory of Genesis.
In each of these the human place in Creation is described as a
moral circumstance, and this circumstance is understood each
time, it seems to me, with a deeper sense of crisis, as history has
proved humanity more and more the exploiter and destroyer
of Creation rather than its devout suzerain or steward. Milton
knew of the conquests of Africa and the Americas, the brutality
of which had outraged the humane minds of Europe, providing occasion and incentive to raise again the question of the human place in Creation; and the devils of *Paradise Lost* are, among
other things, conquistadors. (They are also the most expedient
of politicians and technologists: ". . . by strength/They measure all . . .") Faulkner's Isaac McCaslin, a white Mississippian
of our own time, speaks not just with Milton's passion as a moral
witness, but with the anguish of a man who inherits directly the
guilt of the conqueror, the history of expropriation, despolia-
tion, and slavery.

It is of the greatest importance to see how steadfastly this
thrust of tradition, from Genesis to Milton to Faulkner, works
toward the definition of personal place and condition, respon-

sibility and action. And one feels the potency of this tradition to reach past the negativity of Isaac McCaslin's too simple relinquishment toward the definition of the atoning and renewing work that each person must do. Mr. Fuller's vision, by contrast, proposes that we have ahead of us only the next technological "breakthrough"—which, now that we have "progressed" to the scale of space ships, is not work for persons or communities, but for governments and corporations. What we have in these two statements is an open conflict between unlimited technology and traditional value. It is foolish to think that these two are compatible. Value and technology can meet only on the ground of restraint.

The technological determinists have tyrannical attitudes, and speak tyrannese, at least partly because their assumptions cannot produce a moral or a responsible definition of the human place in Creation. Because they assume that the human place is any place, they are necessarily confused about where they belong.

Where does this confusion come from? I think it comes from the specialization and abstraction of intellect, separating it from responsibility and humility, magnanimity and devotion, and thus giving it an importance that, in the order of things and in its own nature, it does not and cannot have. The specialized intellectual assumes, in other words, that intelligence is all in the mind. For illustration, I turn again to *Paradise Lost*, where Satan, fallen, boasts in "heroic" defiance that he has

> A mind not to be chang'd by Place or Time.
> The mind is its own place, and in itself
> Can make a Heav'n of Hell, a Hell of Heav'n,
> What matter where, if I be still the same . . .[19]

I do not know where one could find a better motto for the modernist or technological experiment, which assumes that we can fulfill a high human destiny any where, any way, so long as we can keep up the momentum of innovation; that the mind is "its own place" even within ecological degradation, pollution, poverty, hatred, and violence.

What we know, on the contrary, is that in any culture that could be called healthy or sane we find a much richer, larger

237

concept of intelligence. We find, first, some way of acknowledging in action the existence of "higher intelligence." And we find that the human mind, in such a culture, is invariably strongly *placed*, in reference to other minds in the community, in cultural memory and tradition, and in reference to earthly localities and landmarks. Intelligence survives both by internal coherence and external pattern; it is both inside and outside the mind. People are born both with and into intelligence. What is thought refers precisely to what is thought about. It is this outside intelligence that we are now ignoring and consequently destroying.

As industrial technology advances and enlarges, and in the process assumes greater social, economic, and political force, it carries people away from where they belong by history, culture, deeds, association, and affection. And it destroys the landmarks by which they might return. Often it destroys the nature or the character of the places they have left. The very possibility of a practical connection between thought and the world is thus destroyed. Culture is driven into the mind, where it cannot be preserved. Displaced memory, for instance, is hard to keep in mind, harder to hand down. The little that survives is attenuated—without practical force. That is why the Jews, in Babylon, wept when they remembered Zion. The mere memory of a place cannot preserve it, nor apart from the place itself can it long survive in the mind. "How shall we sing the Lord's song in a strange land?"

The enlargement of industrial technology is thus analogous to war. It continually requires the movement of knowledge and responsibility away from home. It thrives and burgeons upon the disintegration of homes, the subjugation of homelands. It requires that people cease to cooperate directly to fulfill local needs from local sources, and begin instead to deal with each other always across the rift that divides producer and consumer, and always competitively. The idea of the independence of individual farms, shops, communities, and households is anathema to industrial technologists. The rush to nuclear energy and the growth of the space colony idea are powered by the industrial will to cut off the possibility of a small-scale energy technology—which is to say the possibility of small-scale personal and community acts. The corporate producers and their

238

sycophants in the universities and the government will do virtually anything (or so they have obliged us to assume) to keep people from acquiring necessities in any way except by *buying* them.

Industrial technology and its aspirations enlarge along a line described by changes of verb tense: I need this tool; I will need this tool; I would need that tool. The conditional verb rests by nature upon *ifs*. The ifs of technological rationalization (*if* there were sufficient demand, money, knowledge, energy, power) act as wedges between history and futurity, inside and outside, value and desire, and ultimately between people and the earth and between one person and another.

By such shifts in the tenses of thought (as sometimes also by the substitution of the indefinite for the definite article) it is possible to impair or destroy the power of language to designate, to shift the focus of reference from what is outside the mind to what is inside it. And thus what already exists is devalued, subjugated, or destroyed for the sake of what *might* exist. The modern cult of planners and "futurologists" has thus achieved a startling resemblance to Swift's "academy of projectors":[20]

> In these colleges, the professors contrive new rules and methods of agriculture and building, and new instruments and tools for all trades and manufactures; whereby, as they undertake, one man shall do the work of ten: a palace may be built in a week, of materials so durable, as to last for ever without repairing. All the fruits of the earth shall come to maturity, at whatever season we think fit to chuse, and encrease an hundred fold more than they do at present; with innumerable other happy proposals. The only inconvenience is, that none of these projects are yet brought to perfection; and, in the mean time, the whole country lies miserably waste . . .

People who are willing to follow technology wherever it leads are necessarily willing to follow it away from home, off the earth, and outside the sphere of human definition, meaning, and responsibility. One has to suppose that this would be all right if they did it only for themselves and if they accepted the terms of their technological romanticism absolutely—that is, if they would depart absolutely from all that they propose to supersede, never to return. But past a certain scale, as C. S. Lewis wrote,[21] the person who makes a technological choice does not choose for himself alone, but for others; past a certain scale, he chooses for *all* others. Past a certain scale, if the break with the past is great enough, he chooses for the past, and if the effects are lasting enough he chooses for the future. He makes, then, a choice that can neither be chosen against nor unchosen. Past a certain scale, there is no dissent from a technological choice.

People speaking out of this technological willingness cannot speak precisely, for what they are talking about does not yet exist. They cannot mean what they say because their words are avowedly speculative. They cannot stand by their words because they are talking about, if not *in*, the future, where they are not standing and cannot stand until long after they have spoken. All the grand and perfect dreams of the technologists are happening in the future, but nobody is there.

What can turn us from this deserted future, back into the sphere of our being, the great dance that joins us to our home, to each other and to other creatures, to the dead and the unborn? I think it is love. I am perforce aware how baldly and embarrassingly that word now lies on the page—for we have learned at once to overuse it, abuse it, and hold it in suspicion. But I do not mean any kind of abstract love (adolescent, romantic, or "religious"), which is probably a contradiction in terms, but particular love for particular things, places, creatures, and people, requiring stands and acts, showing its successes or failures in practical or tangible effects. And it implies a responsibility just as particular, not grim or merely dutiful, but rising out of generosity. I think that this sort of love defines the effective range of human intelligence, the range within which its works can be dependably beneficient. Only the action that is moved by love for the good at hand has the hope of being responsible and generous. Desire for the future produces words that cannot be stood by. But love makes language exact, because one loves only what one knows. One cannot love the future or anything in it, for nothing is known there. And one cannot unselfishly make a future for someone else. The love for the future is self-love—love for the present self, projected and magnified into the future, and it is an irremediable loneliness.

Because love is not abstract, it does not lead to trends or percentages or general behavior. It leads, on the contrary, to the perception that there is no such thing as general behavior. There is no abstract action. Love proposes the work of settled households and communities, whose innovations come about in response to immediate needs and immediate conditions, as opposed to the work of governments and corporations, whose innovations are produced out of the implicitly limitless desire for future power or profit. This difference is the unacknowledged cultural break in Mr. Fuller's evolutionary series: oxen, horse-drawn vehicles, horseless vehicles, ships of the sky. Between horse-drawn vehicles and horseless vehicles human life disconnected itself from local sources; energy started to flow away from home. A biological limit was overrun, and with it the deepest human propriety.

Or, to shift the terms, love defines the difference between the "global village" which is a technological and a totalitarian ideal, directly suited to the purposes of centralized governments and corporations, and the Taoist village-as-globe, where the people live frugally and at peace, pleased with the good qualities of necessary things, so satisfied where they are that they live and die without visiting the next village, though they can hear its dogs bark and its roosters crow.[22]

We might conjecture and argue a long time about the meaning and even the habitability of such a village. But one thing, I think, is certain: it would not be a linguistic no man's land in which words and things, words and deeds, words and people failed to stand in reliable connection or fidelity to one another. People and other creatures would be known by their names and histories, not by their numbers or percentages. History would be handed down in songs and stories, not reduced to evolutionary or technological trends. Generalizations would exist, of course, but they would be distilled from experience, not "projected" from statistics. They would sound, says Lao Tzu,[23] this way:

> "Alert as a winter-farer on an icy stream,"
> "Wary as a man in ambush,"
> "Considerate as a welcome guest,"
> "Selfless as melting ice,"

241

"Green as an uncut tree,"
"Open as a valley . . ."

I come, in conclusion, to the difference between "projecting" the future and making a promise. The "projecting" of the "futurologists" *uses* the future as the safest possible context for whatever is desired; it binds one only to selfish interest. But making a promise binds one *to someone else's future*. If the promise is serious enough, one is brought to it by love, and in awe and fear. Fear, awe, and love bind us to no selfish aims, but to each other. And they enforce a speech more exact, more clarifying, and more binding than any speech that can be used to sell or advocate some "future." For when we promise in love and awe and fear there is a certain kind of mobility that we give up. We give up the romanticism of progress, that is always shifting its terms to fit its occasions. We are speaking where we stand, and we shall stand afterwards in the presence of what we have said.

NOTES

1. Harcourt Brace Jovanovich, 1975, pp. 291–303, 235.
2. Harcourt, Brace & World, 1970, pp. 8, 203–211.
3. "Poetry, Community, & Climax," *Field* 20, Spring 1979, p. 29.
4. 1:23 & 24.
5. *Confucius*, New Directions, 1951, pp. 89, 191.
6. E. P. Dutton, 1979, p. 61.
7. Ibid., p. 21.
8. T. S. Eliot, *The Complete Poems and Plays*, Harcourt, Brace and Company, 1952, p. 235.
9. T. S. Eliot, *Selected Essays*, Harcourt, Brace and Company, 1950, p. 269.
10. W. W. Norton & Company, Volume 2, 1962, pp. 418–419.
11. *Second Defense of the People of England, The Works of John Milton*, Vol. VIII, Columbia University Press, 1933, pp. 249–251.
12. I am indebted, for a useful sampling from these transcripts and a perceptive commentary on them, to Paul Trachtman, "Phenomena, comment, and notes," *Smithsonian*, July 1979, pp. 14–16.
13. *Genesis* 11:1–9.
14. *Perspectives in Biology and Medicine*, Spring 1979, pp. 394–409.
15. Ibid., p. 34.
16. *Space Colonies*, edited by Stewart Brand, Penguin, 1977, p. 55.
17. *Paradise Lost*, VII, pp. 505–515.
18. *Go Down, Moses*, The Modern Library, 1955, p. 257.
19. Ibid., pp. 253–256.
20. *Gulliver's Travels*, Everyman's Library, 1961, p. 189.
21. *The Abolition of Man*, Macmillan, 1975, pp. 70–71.
22. *Tao Te Ching*, LXXX.
23. Ibid., XV (Witter Bynner translation, Capricorn Books, 1962, p. 33).

El Salvador:
An Aide-Mémoire

CAROLYN FORCHÉ

I

The year Franco died, I spent several months on Mallorca translating the poetry of Claribel Alegría, a Salvadoran in voluntary exile. During those months the almond trees bloomed and lost flower, the olives and lemons ripened, and we hauled baskets of apricots from Claribel's small *finca*. There was bathing in the *cala*, fresh squid under the palm thatch, drunk Australian sailors to dance with at night. It was my first time in Europe and there was no better place at that time than Spain. I was there when Franco's anniversary passed for the first time in forty years without notice—and the lack of public celebration was a collective hush of relief. I traveled with Claribel's daughter, Maya Flakoll, for ten days through Andalusia by train, visiting poetry shrines. The *gitanos* had finally pounded a cross into the earth to mark the grave of Federico Garcia Lorca, not where it had been presumed to be all this time, not beneath an olive tree, but in a bowl of land rimmed by pines. We hiked the eleven kilometers through the Sierra Nevada foothills to La Fuente Grande and held a book of poems open over the silenced poet.

On Mallorca I lost interest in the *cala* sunbathing, the parties that carried into the morning, the staggering home winedrunk up the goat paths. I did not hike to the peak of the Teix with baskets of *entremesas* nor, despite well-intentioned urgings, could I surrender myself to the island's diversionary summer mystique.

I was busy with Claribel's poems, and with the horrific accounts of the survivors of repressive Latin American regimes. Claribel's home was frequented by these wounded: writers who had been tortured and imprisoned, who had lost husbands, wives, and closest friends. In the afternoon, more than once I joined Claribel in her silent vigil near the window until the mail came, her "difficult time of day," alone in a chair in the perfect light of thick-walled Mallorquín windows. These were her afternoons of despair, and they haunted me. In those hours I first learned of El Salvador, not from the springs of her nostalgia for "the fraternity of dipping a tortilla into a common pot of beans and meat," but from the source of its pervasive brutality. My understanding of Latin American realities was confined then to the romantic devotion to Vietnam-era revolutionary pieties, the sainthood of Ernesto Che rather than the debilitating effects of the cult of personality that arose in the collective memory of Guevara. I worked into the late hours on my poems and on translations, drinking "101" brandy and chain-smoking Un-X-Dos. When Cuban writer Mario Benedetti visited, I questioned him about what "an American" could do in the struggle against repression.

"As a *North*american, you might try working to influence a profound change in your country's foreign policy."

Over coffee in the mornings I studied reports from Amnesty International-London and learned of a plague on Latin exiles who had sought refuge in Spain following Franco's death: a right-wing death squad known as the "AAA"—Anti-Communista Apostólica, founded in Argentina and exported to assassinate influential exiles from the southern cone.

I returned to the United States and in the autumn of 1977 was invited to El Salvador by persons who knew Claribel. "How much do you know about Latin America?" I was asked. Then: "Good. At least you know that you know nothing." A young writer, politically unaffiliated, ideologically vague, I was to be blessed with the rarity of a moral and political education—what at times would seem an unbearable immersion, what eventually would become a focused obsession. It would change my life and work, propel me toward engagement, test my endurance and find it wanting, and prevent me from ever viewing myself or my country again through precisely the same fog of unwitting connivance.

I was sent for a briefing to Dr. Thomas P. Anderson, author of *Matanza,* the definitive scholarly history of Salvador's revolution of 1932, and to Ignacio Lozano, a California newspaper editor and former ambassador (under Gerald Ford) to El Salvador. It was suggested that I visit Salvador as a journalist, a role that would of necessity become real. In January 1978 I landed at Ilopango, the dingy center-city airport which is now Salvador's largest military base. Arriving before me were the members of a human rights investigation team headed by then Congressman John Drinan, S.J. (Democrat of Massachusetts). I had been told that a black Northamerican, Ronald James Richardson, had been killed while in the custody of the Salvadoran government and that a Northamerican organization known as the American Institute for Free Labor Development (AIFLD, an organ of the AFL-CIO and an intelligence front) was manipulating the Salvadoran agricultural workers. Investigation of the "Richardson Case" exposed me to the sub-rosa activities of the Salvadoran military, whose highest-ranking officers and government officials were engaged in cocaine smuggling, kidnapping, extortion, and terrorism; through studying AIFLD's work, I would learn of the spurious intentions of an organization destined to become the architect of the present agrarian reform. I was delivered the promised exposure to the stratified life of Salvador, and was welcomed to "Vietnam, circa 1959." The "Golden Triangle" had moved to the isthmus of the Americas, "rural pacification" was in embryo, the seeds of rebellion had taken root in destitution and hunger.

Later my companion and guide, "Ricardo," changed his description from "Vietnam" to "a Nazi forced labor camp." "It is not hyperbole," he said quietly. "You will come to see that." In those first twenty days I was taken to clinics and hospitals, to villages, farms, prisons, coffee mansions and processing plants, to cane mills and the elegant homes of American foreign service bureaucrats, nudged into the hillsides overlooking the capital, where I was offered cocktails and platters of ocean shrimp; it was not yet known what I would write of my impressions or where I would print them. Fortuitously, I had published nationally in my own country, and in Salvador "only poetry" did not carry the pejorative connotation I might have ascribed to it then. I knew nothing of political journalism but was willing to learn—it seemed, at the time, an acceptable way for a poet to make a living.

I lay on my belly in the *campo* and was handed a pair of field glasses. The lenses sharpened on a plastic tarp tacked to four maize stalks several hundred yards away, beneath which a woman sat on the ground. She was gazing through the plastic roof of her "house" and hugging three naked, emaciated children. There was an aqua plastic dog-food bowl at her feet.

"She's watching for the plane," my friend said. "We have to get out of here now or we're going to get it too." I trained the lenses on the woman's eye, gelled with disease and open to a swarm of gnats. We climbed back in the truck and rolled the windows up just as the duster plane swept back across the field, dumping a yellow cloud of pesticide over the woman and her children to protect the cotton crop around them.

At the time I was unaware of the pedagogical theories of Paulo Freire (*Pedagogy of the Oppressed*), but found myself learning in situ the politics of cultural immersion. It was by Ricardo's later admission "risky business," but it was thought important that a few Northamericans, particularly writers, be sensitized to Salvador prior to any military conflict. The lessons were simple and critical, the methods somewhat more difficult to detect. I was given a white lab jacket and, posing as a Northamerican physician, was asked to work in a rural hospital at the side of a Salvadoran doctor who was paid two hundred dollars a month by her government to care for one hundred thousand *campesinos*. She had no lab, no X ray, no whole blood, plasma, or antibiotics, no anesthetics or medicines, no autoclave for sterilizing surgical equipment. Her forceps were rusted, the walls of her operating room were studded with flies; beside her hospital, a coffee-processing plant's refuse heaps incubated the maggots, and she paid a *campesina* to swish the flies away with a newspaper while she delivered the newborn. She was forced to do caesarean sections at times without enough local anesthetic. Without supplies, she worked with only her hands and a cheap ophthalmoscope. In her clinic I held children in my arms who died hours later for want of a manual suction device to remove the fluid from their lungs. Their peculiar skin rashes spread to my hands, arms, and belly. I dug maggots from a child's open wound with a teaspoon. I contracted four strains of dysentery and was treated by stomach antiseptics, effective yet damaging enough to be banned by our own FDA. This doctor had worked in the *campo* for years, a lifetime of delivering the offspring of thirteen-year-old mothers who thought the navel marked the birth canal opening. She had worked long enough to feel that it was acceptable to ignore her own cervical cancer, and hard enough in Salvador to view her inevitable death as the least of her concerns.

I was taken to the homes of landowners, with their pools set like aquamarines in the clipped grass, to the afternoon games of canasta over quaint local *pupusas* and tea, where parrots hung by their feet among the bougainvillea and nearly everything was imported, if only from Miami or New Orleans. One evening I dined with a military officer who toasted America, private enterprise, Las Vegas, and the "fatherland," until his wife excused herself and in a drape of cigar smoke the events of "The Colonel" were told, almost a *poème trouvé*. I had only to pare down the memory and render it whole, unlined, and as precise as recollection would have it. I did not wish to endanger myself by the act of poeticizing such a necessary reportage. It became, when I wrote it, the second insistence of El Salvador to infiltrate what I so ridiculously preserved as my work's allegiance to Art. No more than in any earlier poems did I choose my subject.

The following day I was let into Ahuachapán prison (now an army *cuartel*). We had been driving back from a meeting with Salvadoran feminists when Ricardo swung the truck into a climb through a tube of dust toward the run-down fortification. I was thirsty, infested with intestinal parasites, fatigued from twenty days of ricocheting between extremes of poverty and wealth. I was horrified, impatient, suspicious of almost everyone, paralyzed by sympathy and revulsion. I kept thinking of the kindly, silver-haired American political officer who informed me that in Salvador, "there were always five versions of the truth." From this I was presumably to conclude that the truth could not therefore be known. Ricardo seemed by turns the Braggioni of Porter's "Flowering Judas" and a pedagogical genius of considerable vision and patience. As we walked toward the gate, he palmed the air to slow our pace.

"This is a criminal penitentiary. You will have thirty minutes inside. Realize, please, at all times where you are, and whatever you see here, understand that for political prisoners it is always much worse. O.K."

We shook hands with the chief guard and a few subordinates, clean-shaven youths armed with G-3s. There was first the stench: rotting blood, excrement, buckets of urine, and corn slop. A man in his thirties came toward us, dragging a swollen green leg, his pants ripped to the thigh to accommodate the swelling. He was introduced as "Miguel" and I as a "friend." The two men shook hands a long time, standing together in the filth, a firm knot of warmth between them. Miguel was asked to give me a "tour," and he agreed, first taking a coin from his pocket and slipping it into the guard station soda machine. He handed me an orange Nehi, urging me somewhat insistently to take it, and we began a slow walk into the first hall. The prison was a four-square with an open court in the center. There were bunk rooms where the cots were stacked three deep and some were hung with newsprint "for privacy." The men squatted on the ground or along the walls, some stirring small coal fires, others ducking under urine-soaked tents of newspaper. It was suppertime, and they were cooking their dry tortillas. I used the soda as a relief from the stench, like a hose of oxygen. There were maybe four hundred men packed into Ahuachapán, and it was an odd sight, an American woman, but there was no heckling.

"Did you hear the shots when we first pulled up?" Ricardo asked. "Those were warnings. A visitor—behave."

Miguel showed me through the workrooms and latrines, finishing his sentences with his eyes: a necessary skill under repressive regimes, highly developed in Salvador. With the guards' attention diverted, he gestured toward a black open doorway and suggested that I might wander through it, stay a few moments, and come back out "as if I had seen nothing."

I did as he asked, my eyes adjusting to the darkness of that shit-smeared room with its single chink of light in the concrete. There were wooden boxes stacked against one wall, each a meter by a meter, with barred openings the size of a book, and within them there was breathing, raspy and half conscious. It was a few moments before I realized that men were kept in those cages, their movement so cramped that they could neither sit, stand, nor lie down. I recall only magnified fragments of my few minutes in that room. I was rooted to the clay floor, unable to move either toward or away from the cages. I turned from the room toward Miguel, who pivoted on his crutch and with his eyes on the ground said in a low voice, *"La oscura,"* the dark place. "Sometimes a man is kept in there a year, and cannot move when he comes out."

We caught up with Ricardo, who leaned toward me and whispered, "Tie your sweater sleeves around your neck. You are covered with hives."

In the cab of the truck I braced my feet against the dashboard and through the half-cracked window shook hands with the young soldiers, smiling and nodding. A hundred meters from the prison I lifted Ricardo's spare shirt in my hands and vomited. We were late for yet another meeting, the sun had dropped behind the volcanoes, my eyes ached. When I was empty the dry heaves began, and after the sobbing a convulsive shudder. Miguel was serving his third consecutive sentence, this time for organizing a hunger strike against prison conditions. In that moment I saw him turn back to his supper, his crutch stamping circles of piss and mud beside him as he walked. I heard the screams of a woman giving birth by caesarean without anesthetic in Ana's hospital. I saw the flies fastened to the walls in the operating room, the gnats on the eyes of the starving woman, the reflection of flies on Ana's eyes in the hospital kitchen window. The shit, I imagined, was inside my nostrils and I would smell it the rest of my life, as it is for a man who in battle tastes a piece of flesh or gets the blood under his fingernails. The smell never comes out; it was something Ricardo explained once as he was falling asleep.

"Feel this," he said, maneuvering the truck down the hill road. "This is what oppression feels like. Now you have begun to learn something. When you get back to the States, what you do with this is up to you."

Between 1978 and 1981 I traveled between the United States and Salvador, writing reports on the war waiting to happen, drawing blueprints of prisons from memory, naming the dead. I filled soup bowls with cigarette butts, grocery boxes with files on American involvement in the rural labor movement, and each week I took a stool sample to the parasite clinic. A priest I knew was gangraped by soldiers; another was hauled off and beaten nearly to death. On one trip a woman friend and I were chased by the death squad for five minutes on the narrow back roads that circle the city; her evasive driving and considerable luck saved us. One night a year ago I was interviewing a defecting member of the Christian Democratic Party. As we started out of the drive to go back to my hotel, we encountered three plainclothesmen hunched over the roof of a taxicab, their machine guns pointed at our windshield. We escaped through a grove of avocado trees. The bodies of friends have turned up disemboweled and decapitated, their teeth punched into broken points, their faces sliced off with machetes. On the final trip to the airport we swerved to avoid a corpse, a man spread-eagled, his stomach hacked open, his entrails stretched from one side of the road to the other. We drove over them like a garden hose. My friend looked at me. *Just another dead man*, he said. And by then it had become true for me as well: the unthinkable, the sense of death within life before death.

II

"I see an injustice," wrote Czeslaw Milosz in *Native Realm;* "a Parisian does not have to bring his city out of nothingness every time he wants to describe it." So it was with Wilno, the Lithuanian/Polish/Byelorussian city of the poet's childhood, and so it has been with the task of writing about Salvador in the United States. The country called by Gabriela Mistral "the Tom Thumb of the Americas" would necessarily be described to Northamericans as "about the size of Massachusetts." As writers we could begin with its location on the Pacific south of Guatemala and west of Honduras and with Ariadne's thread of statistics: 4.5 million people, 400 per square kilometer (a country without silence or privacy), a population growth rate of 3.5 percent (such a population would double in two decades). But what does "90 percent malnutrition" mean? Or that "80 percent of the population has no running water, electricity, or sanitary services"? I watched women push feces aside with a stick, lower their pails to the water, and carry it home to wash their clothes, their spoons and plates, themselves, their infant children. The chief cause of death has been amoebic dysentery. One out of four children dies before the age of five; the average human life span is forty-six years. What does it mean when a man says, "It is better to die quickly fighting than slowly of starvation"? And that such a man suffers toward that decision in what is now being called "Northamerica's backyard"? How is the language used to draw battle lines, to identify the enemy? What are the current euphemisms for empire, public defense of private wealth, extermination of human beings? If the lethal weapon is the soldier, what is meant by "nonlethal military aid"? And what determined the shift to helicopter gunships, M-16s, M-79 grenade launchers? The State Department's white paper entitled "Communist Interference in El Salvador" argues that it is a "case of indirect armed aggression against a small Third World country by Communist powers acting through Cuba." James Petras in *The Nation* (March 28, 1981) has argued that the report's "evidence is flimsy, circumstantial or nonexistent; the reasoning and logic is slipshod and internally inconsistent; it assumes what needs to be proven; and finally, what facts are presented refute the very case the State Department is attempting to demonstrate." On the basis of this report, the popular press sounded an alarm over the "flow of arms." But from where have arms "flowed," and to whom and for what? In terms of language, we could begin by asking why Northamerican arms are weighed in dollar value and those reaching the opposition measured in tonnage. Or we could point out the nature of the international arms market, a complex global network in which it is possible to buy almost anything for the right price, no matter the country of origin or destination. The State Department conveniently ignores its own intelligence on arms flow to the civilian right, its own escalation of military assistance to the right-wing military, and even the discrepancies in its final analysis. But what does all this tell us about who is fighting whom for what? Americans have been told that there is a "fundamental difference" between "advisers" and military "trainers." Could it simply be that the euphemism for American military personnel must be changed so as not to serve as a mnemonic device for the longest war in our failing public memory? A year ago I asked the American military attaché in Salvador what would happen if one of these already proposed advisers returned to the U.S. in a flag-draped coffin. He did not argue semantics.

"That," he said, smiling, "would be up to the American press, wouldn't it?"

251

Most of that press had held with striking fidelity to the State Department text: a vulnerable and worthy "centrist" government besieged by left- and right-wing extremists, the former characterized by their unacceptable political ideology, the latter rendered nonideologically unacceptable, that is, only in their extremity. The familiar ring of this portrayal has not escaped U.S. apologists, who must explain why El Salvador is not "another Vietnam." Their argument hinges, it seems, on the rapidity with which the U.S. could assist the Salvadoran military in the task of "defeating the enemy." Tactically, this means sealing the country off, warning all other nations to "cease and desist" supplying arms, using violations of that warning as a pretext for blockades and interventions, but excepting ourselves in our continual armament of what we are calling the "government" of El Salvador. Ignoring the institutional self-interest of the Salvadoran army, we blame the presumably "civilian" right for the murder of thousands of *campesinos,* students, doctors, teachers, journalists, nuns, priests, and children. This requires that we ignore the deposed and retired military men who command the activities of the death squads with impunity, and that the security forces responsible for the killings are under the command of the army, which is under the command of the so-called centrist government and is in fact the government itself.

There are other differences between the conflicts of El Salvador and Vietnam. There is no People's Republic of China to the north to arm and ally itself with a people engaged in a protracted war. The guerrillas are not second-generation Vietminh, but young people who armed themselves after exhaustive and failed attempts at nonviolent resistance and peaceful change. The popular organizations they defend were formed in the early seventies by *campesinos* who became socially conscious through the efforts of grass-roots clergymen teaching the Medellín doctrines of social justice: the precursors of these organizations were prayer and Bible study groups, rural labor organizations and urban trade unions. As the military government grew increasingly repressive, the opposition widened to include all other political parties, the Catholic majority, the university and professional communities, and the small-business sector.

Critics of U.S. policy accurately recognize parallels between the two conflicts in terms of involvement, escalation, and justification. The latter demands a vigilant "euphemology" undertaken to protect language from distortions of military expedience and political convenience. Noam Chomsky has argued that "among the many symbols used to frighten and manipulate the populace of the democratic states, few have been more important than terror and terrorism. These terms have generally been confined to the use of violence by individual and marginal groups. Official violence, which is far more extensive in both scale and destructiveness, is placed in a different category altogether. This usage has nothing to do with justice, causal sequence, or numbers abused." He goes on to say that "the question of proper usage is settled not merely by the official or unofficial status of the perpetrators of violence but also by their political affiliations." State violence is excused as "reactive," and the "turmoil" or "conflict" is viewed ahistorically.

It is true that there have been voices of peaceful change and social reform in El Salvador—the so-called centrists—but the U.S. has never supported them. We backed one fraudulently elected military regime after another, giving them what they wanted and still want: a steady infusion of massive economic aid with which high-ranking officers can ensure their personal futures and the loyalty of their subordinates. In return we expect them to guarantee stability, which means holding power by whatever means necessary for the promotion of a favorable investment climate, even if it requires us to exterminate the population, as it has come to mean in Salvador. The military, who always admired "Generalissimo Franco," and are encouraged in their anti-Communist crusade, grow paranoid and genocidal. Soldiers tossed babies into the air near the Sumpul River last summer for target practice during the cattle-prod roundup and massacre of six hundred peasants. Whole families have been gunned down or hacked to pieces with machetes, including the elderly and the newborn. Now that the massacre and the struggle against it have become the occasion to "test American resolve," the Salvadoran military is all too aware of the security of its position and the impunity with which it may operate. Why would a peasant, aware of the odds, of the significance of American backing, continue to take up arms on the side of the opposition? How is it that such opposition endures, when daily men and women are doused with gasoline and burned alive in the streets as a lesson

253

to others; when even death is not enough, and the corpses are mutilated beyond recognition? The answer to that question in El Salvador answers the same for Vietnam.

III

We were waved past the military guard station and started down the highway, swinging into the oncoming lane to pass slow sugar cane trucks and army transports. Every few kilometers, patrols trekked the gravel roadside. It was a warm night, dry but close to the rainy season. Juan palmed the column shift, chain-smoked, and motioned with his hot-boxed cigarette in the direction of San Marcos. Bonfires lit by the opposition were chewing away at the dark hillside. As we neared San Salvador, passing through the slums of Candelaria, I saw that the roads were barricaded. More than once Juan attempted a shortcut, but upon spotting military checkpoints, changed his mind. To relieve the tension, he dug a handful of change from his pocket and showed me his collection of deutsche marks, Belgian francs, Swedish öre and kronor, holding each to the dashboard light and naming the journalist who had given it to him, the country, the paper. His prize was a coin from the Danish reporter whose cameras had been shot away as he crouched on a rooftop to photograph an army attack on protest marchers. That was a month before, on January 22, 1980, when some hundred lost their lives; it was the beginning of a savage year of extermination. Juan rose from his seat and slipped the worthless coins back into his pocket.

Later that spring, Rene Tamsen of WHUR radio, Washington, D.C., would be forced by a death squad into an unmarked car in downtown San Salvador. A Salvadoran photographer, Cesar Najarro, and his *Crónica del Pueblo* editor would be seized during a coffee break. When their mutilated bodies were discovered, it would be evident that they had been disemboweled before death. A Mexican photojournalist, Ignacio Rodriguez, would fall in August to a military bullet. After Christmas an American free-lancer, John Sullivan, would vanish from his downtown hotel room. Censorship of the press. In January 1981, Ian Mates would hit a land mine and that South African TV cameraman would bleed to death. In a year, no one would want the Salvador assignment. In a year, journalists would appear before cameras trembling and incredulous, unable to reconcile

their perceptions with those of Washington, and even established media would begin to reflect this dichotomy. Carter policy had been to downplay El Salvador in the press while providing
"quiet" aid to the repressive forces. Between 1978 and 1980, in-
vestigative articles sent to national magazines mysteriously disappeared from publication mailrooms, were oddly delayed in
reaching editors, or were rejected after lengthy deliberations,
most often because of El Salvador's "low news value." The
American interreligious network and human rights community
began to receive evidence of a conscious and concerted censorship effort in the United States. During interviews in 1978 with
members of the Salvadoran right-wing business community, I
was twice offered large sums of money to portray their government favorably in the American press. By early 1981, desk editors knew where El Salvador was and the playdown policy had
been replaced by the Reagan administration's propaganda effort. The right-wing military cooperated in El Salvador by serving death threats on prominent journalists, while torturing and
murdering others. American writers critical of U.S. policy were
described by the Department of State as "the witting and unwitting dupes" of Communist propagandists. Those who have
continued coverage of Salvador have found that the military
monitors the wire services and all telecommunications, that
pseudonyms often provide no security, that no one active in the
documentation of the war of extermination can afford to be
traceable in the country; effectiveness becomes self-limiting. It
became apparent that my education in El Salvador had prepared me to work only until March 16, 1980, when after several
close calls I was urged to leave the country. Monsignor Romero
met with me, asking that I return to the U.S. and "tell the
American people what is happening."

"Do you have any messages for [certain exiled friends]?"

"Yes. Tell them to come back."

"But wouldn't they be killed?"

"We are all going to be killed—you and me, all of us," he
said quietly. A week later he was shot while saying mass in the
chapel of a hospital for the incurable.

In those days I kept my work as a poet and journalist separate, of two distinct *mentalidades,* but I could not keep El Salvador from my poems because it had become so much a part of
my life. I was cautioned to avoid mixing art and politics, that

one damages the other, and it was some time before I realized that "political poetry" often means the poetry of protest, accused of polemical didacticism, and not the poetry which implicitly celebrates politically acceptable values. I suspect that underlying this discomfort is a naive assumption: that to locate a poem in an area associated with political trouble automatically renders it political.

All poetry is both pure and engaged, in the sense that it is made of language but it is also art. Any theory that takes one half of the social-aesthetic dynamic and accentuates it too much results in a breakdown. Stress of purity generates a feeble aestheticism which fails, in its beauty, to communicate. On the other hand, propagandistic hack work has no independent life as poetry. What matters is not whether a poem is political, but the quality of its engagement.

In *The Consciousness Industry*, Hans Magnus Enzensberger has argued the futility of locating the political aspect of poetry outside poetry itself, and that:

> Such obtuseness plays into the hands of the bourgeois esthetic which would like to deny poetry any social aspect. Too often the champions of inwardness and sensibility are reactionaries. They consider politics a special subject best left to professionals, and wish to detach it completely from all other human activity. They advise poetry to stick to such models as they have devised for it, in other words, to high aspirations and eternal values. The promised reward for this continence is timeless validity. Behind these high-sounding proclamations lurks a contempt for poetry no less profound than that of vulgar Marxism. For a political quarantine placed on poetry in the name of eternal values itself serves political ends.

All language, then, is political; vision is always ideologically charged; perceptions are shaped a priori by our assumptions and sensibility is formed by a consciousness at once social, historical, and aesthetic. There is no such thing as nonpolitical poetry. The time, however, to determine what those politics will be is not the moment of taking pen to paper, but during the whole of one's life. We are responsible for the quality of our vision, we have a say in the shaping of our sensibility. In the many thousand daily choices we make, we create ourselves and the voice with which we speak and work.

256

From our tradition we inherit a poetic, a sense of appropriate subjects, styles, forms, and levels of diction; that poetic might insist that we be attuned to the individual in isolation, to particular sensitivity in the face of "nature," to special ingenuity in inventing metaphor. It might encourage a self-regarding, inward-looking poetry. Since Romanticism, didactic poetry has been presumed dead and narrative poetry has had at best a half life. Demonstration is inimical to a poetry of lyric confession and self-examination, therefore didactic poetry is seen as crude and unpoetic. To suggest a return to the formal didactic mode of Virgil's *Georgics* or Lucretius's *De Rerum Natura* would be to deny history, but what has survived of that poetic is the belief that a poet's voice must be inwardly authentic and compelling of our attention; the poet's voice must have authority.

I have been told that a poet should be of his or her time. It is my feeling that the twentieth-century human condition demands a poetry of witness. This is not accomplished without certain difficulties; the inherited poetic limits the range of our work and determines the boundaries of what might be said. There is the problem of metaphor, which moved Neruda to write: "the blood of the children/flowed out onto the streets/like . . . like the blood of the children." There is the problem of poeticizing horror, which resembles the problem of the photographic image that might render starvation visually appealing. There are problems of reduction and oversimplification; of our need to see the world as complex beyond our comprehension, difficult beyond our capacities for solution. If I did not wish to make poetry of what I had seen, what is it I thought poetry was?

At some point the two *mentalidades* converged, and the impulse to witness confronted the prevailing poetic; at the same time it seemed clear that eulogy and censure were no longer possible and that Enzensberger is correct in stating: "The poem expresses in exemplary fashion that it is not at the disposal of politics. That is its political content." I decided to follow my impulse to write narratives of witness and confrontation, to disallow obscurity and conventions, which might prettify that which I wished to document. As for that wish, the poems will speak for themselves, obstinate as always. I wish also to thank my friends and *compañeros* in El Salvador for persuading me during a period of doubt that poetry could be enough.

257

The Commerce of the Creative Spirit

LEWIS HYDE

See how Thy beggar works in Thee
By art.
GEORGE HERBERT

At the corner drugstore my neighbors and I can now buy a line of romantic novels written with a formula developed through market research. An advertising agency polled a group of women readers. What age should the heroine be? (She should be between nineteen and twenty-seven.) Should the man she meets be married or single? (Recently widowed is best.) The hero and heroine are not allowed in bed together until they are married. Each novel is 192 pages long. Even the name of the series and the design of the cover have been tailored to the demands of the market. (The name Silhouette was preferred over Belladonna, Surrender, Tiffany, and Magnolia; gold curlicues were chosen to frame the cover.) Six new titles appear each month and 200,000 copies of each title are printed.

Why do we suspect that Silhouette Romances will not be enduring works of art? What is it about a work of art, even when it is bought and sold in the market, that makes us distinguish it from such pure commodities as these?

The following essay is a portion of a book-length meditation on these questions, or, to put it generally, on the problem of the creative artist born into a market economy. My central assumption is that a work of art is better described as a gift than as a commodity. The sense of this assertion is most readily apprehended, perhaps, if one thinks of the relationship between an artist and his or her audience. That art which matters to us—which moves the heart, or revives the soul, or delights the senses, or offers courage for living, however we choose to describe the experience—that work is received as a gift is received. Even if we have paid a fee at the door of the museum or concert hall, when we are touched by a work of art something comes to us which has nothing to do with the "price." True art is a gift which offers to pass through and transform the self. And when we come upon such work we feel gratitude—we are grateful that the artist lived, grateful that he labored in the service of his gifts.

The particular form that my elaboration of these ideas has taken may best be introduced through a description of how I came to my topic in the first place. For some years now I myself have tried to make my way as a poet, a translator, and a sort of "scholar without institution." Inevitably the money question comes up; these are notoriously nonremunerative labors, and the landlord is not interested in your book of translations the day the rent falls due. A necessary corollary seems to follow the proposition that a work of art is a gift: there is nothing in the labor of art itself that will automatically make it pay. Quite the opposite in fact. Every modern artist who has chosen to labor with a gift must sooner or later wonder how he or she is to survive in a society dominated by market exchange. And if the fruits of a gift are gifts themselves, how is the artist to nourish himself, spiritually as well as materially, in an age whose values are market values and whose commerce consists almost exclusively in the purchase and sale of commodities?

Every culture offers its citizens an image of what it is to be a man or woman of substance. There have been times and places in which a person came into his social being through the dispersal of his gifts, the "big man" or "big woman" being that one through whom the most gifts flowed. The mythology of a market society reverses the picture: getting rather than giving is the mark of a substantial person, and the hero is "self-possessed," "self-made." So long as these assumptions rule, a disquieting sense of triviality, of worthlessness even, will nag the man or woman who labors in the service of a gift and whose "products" are not adequately described as commodities. Where we reckon our substance by our acquisitions, the gifts of the gifted man are powerless to make him substantial.

259

Moreover, as the morality tales of tribal peoples make clear, a gift which cannot be given away ceases to be a gift. The spirit of a gift is kept alive by its constant donation. If this is the case, then the gifts of the inner world must be accepted as gifts in the outer world if they are to retain their vitality. Where gifts have no public currency, therefore, where the gift as a form of property is neither recognized nor honored, our inner gifts will find themselves excluded from the very commerce which is their nourishment. Or, to say the same thing from a different angle, where commerce is exclusively a traffic in merchandise, the gifted cannot enter into the give-and-take which assures the livelihood of their spirit.

These two lines of thought—the idea of art as a gift and the problem of the market—did not converge for me until I began to read through the work that has been done in anthropology on gifts as a kind of property and gift exchange as a kind of commerce. Many tribal groups circulate a large portion of their material wealth as gifts. Tribesmen are typically enjoined against buying and selling food, for example; even though there may be a strong sense of "mine and thine," food is always given as a gift and the transaction is governed by the ethics of gift exchange, not those of barter or cash purchase. Not surprisingly, people live differently who treat a portion of their wealth as a gift. To begin with, unlike the sale of a commodity, the giving of a gift tends to establish a relationship between the parties involved.* Furthermore, when gifts circulate within a group, their commerce leaves a series of inter-connected relationships in its wake, and a kind of decentralized cohesiveness emerges. There are five or six related observations of this kind that can be made about a commerce of gifts, and in reading through the anthropological literature I began to realize that a description of gift exchange might offer me the language, the way of speaking, through which I could address the situation of creative artists.

I have attempted elsewhere to establish that language (see *CoEvolution Quarterly*, Fall 1982; *Kenyon Review*, Fall 1981). In the present essay I hope to show why it is proper and fitting to apply the language of gift exchange to the life of art.

---

*It is this element of relationship which leads me to speak of gift exchange as an "erotic" commerce, opposing *eros* (the principle of attraction, union, involvement which binds together) to *logos* (reason and logic in general, the principle of differentiation in particular). A market economy is an emanation of *logos*.

I

Let us begin at the beginning, with the question of the sources of an artist's work.

An essential portion of any artist's labor is not creation so much as invocation. Part of the work cannot be made, it must be received, and we cannot have this gift except, perhaps, by supplication, by courting, by creating within ourselves that "begging bowl" to which the gift is drawn. The fourteenth century Christian mystic, Meister Eckhart once wrote: "It were a very grave defect in God if, finding thee so empty and so bare, he wrought no excellent work in thee nor primed thee with glorious gifts." It is the artist's hope that we may say the same of the creative spirit. In an autobiographical essay Czeslaw Milosz speaks of his "inner certainty" as a young writer "that a shining point exists where all lines intersect. . . . This certainty also involved my relationship to that point," he tells us. "I felt very strongly that nothing depended on my will, that everything I might accomplish in life would not be won by my own efforts but given as a gift."

Not all artists use these very words, but there are few artists who have not had this sense that some element of their work comes to them from a source they do not control.

Harold Pinter in a letter to the director of his play *The Birthday Party:*

> The thing germinated and bred itself. It proceeded according to its own logic. What did I do? I followed the indications, I kept a sharp eye on the clues I found myself dropping. The writing arranged itself with no trouble into dramatic terms. The characters sounded in my ears—it was apparent to me what one would say and what would be the other's response, at any given point. It was apparent to me what they would not, could not, ever, say, whatever one might wish. . . .
>
> When the thing was well cooked I began to form certain conclusions. The point is, however, that by that time the play was now its own world. It was determined by its own engendering image.

Theodore Roethke in a lecture:

> I was in that particular hell of the poet: a longish dry period. It was 1952, I was 44, and I thought I was done. I was living alone in a biggish house in Edmonds, Washington. I had been reading—and re-reading—not Yeats, but Raleigh and Sir John Davies. I had been teaching the five-beat line for weeks—I knew quite a bit about it, but write it myself?—*no:* so I felt myself a fraud.
>
> Suddenly, in the early evening, the poem "The Dance" started, and finished itself in a very short time—say thirty minutes, maybe in the greater part of an hour, it was all done. I felt, I *knew*, I had hit it. I walked around and wept; and I knelt down—I always do after I've written what I know is a good piece. But at the same time I had, as God is my witness, the actual sense of a Presence—as if Yeats himself were *in* that room. The experience was in a way terrifying, for it lasted at least half an hour. That house, I repeat, was charged with a psychic presence: the very walls seemed to shimmer. I wept for joy. . . . He, they—the poets dead—were with me.

Such moments of unwilled reception are not all there is to the creation of a work of art, of course. Notice Roethke: "I had been teaching the five-beat line for weeks." Or Pinter: "I kept a sharp eye." All artists work to acquire and perfect the tools of their craft, and all art involves evaluation, clarification, and revision. But these are secondary tasks. They cannot begin (sometimes they must not begin) until the *materia*, the body of the work, is on the page or on the canvas. A circulation of ceremonial or ritual gifts among tribal peoples is commonly accompanied by an ethic which forbids the participants to speak of the value of their gifts; such silence has its equivalent in the creative spirit. Premature evaluation cuts off the flow. The imagination does not barter its "engendering images." When we begin a work we have no choice but to accept what has come to us, hoping that, as in fairy tales, the cinders some forest spirit saw fit to bestow may turn to gold when we have carried them back to the hearth. Allen Ginsberg has been our consistent spokesman for that phase of the work in which the artist lays evaluation aside so that the gift may come forward:

> The parts that embarrass you the most are usually the most interesting poetically, are usually the most naked of all, the

rawest, the goofiest, the strangest and most eccentric and at the same time, most representative, most universal. . . . That was something I learned from Kerouac, which was that spontaneous writing could be embarrassing. . . . The cure for that is to write things down which you will not publish and which you won't show people. To write secretly . . . so you can actually be free to say anything you want. . . .

It means abandoning being a poet, abandoning your careerism, abandoning even the idea of writing any poetry, really abandoning, giving up as hopeless—abandoning the possibility of really expressing yourself to the nations of the world. Abandoning the idea of being a prophet with honor and dignity, and abandoning the glory of poetry and just settling down in the muck of your own mind. . . . You really have to make a resolution just to write for yourself . . . , in the sense of not writing to impress yourself, but just writing what your self is saying.

Having accepted what has been given to him—either in the sense of inspiration or in the sense of talent—the artist often feels compelled, feels the *desire,* to make the work and offer it to an audience. In both the material and the spiritual world, there is a law: the gift must stay in motion. "Publish or perish" is an internal demand of the creative spirit, one that we learn from the gift itself, not from any school or church. In her *Journal of a Solitude* May Sarton writes: "There is only one real deprivation, I decided this morning, and that is not to be able to give one's gift to those one loves most. . . . The gift turned inward, unable to be given, becomes a heavy burden, even sometimes a kind of poison. It is as though the flow of life were backed up."

So long as the gift is not withheld, the creative spirit will remain a stranger to the economics of scarcity. It is one of the mysteries of this form of commerce that a gift is not used up in use. To have painted a painting does not empty the vessel out of which the paintings come. On the contrary it is the talent which is not in use that is lost or atrophies, and to bestow one of our creations is the surest invocation to the next. There is an instructive series of gifts in *The Homeric Hymn to Hermes.* Hermes invents the first musical instrument, the lyre, and gives it to his brother, Apollo, whereupon he immediately invents a second musical instrument, the pipes. The implication is that giving the first creation away makes the second one possible. Bestowal creates that empty place into which new energy may flow. The alternative is petrifaction, writer's block, "the flow of life backed up."

To whom does the artist address the work? In 1924 Marcel Mauss, a French sociologist, wrote a now famous "Essay on the Gift," in which he suggests that every gift "strives to bring to its original clan and homeland some equivalent to take its place." And though it might be hard to say with any certainty where we will find the "homeland" of an inner gift, artists in every age have offered us myths to suggest where we should look. Some take their gifts to be bestowals of the gods or, more often perhaps, of a personal deity, a guardian angel, *genius,* or muse—a spirit who gives the artist the initial substance of his art and to whom, in return, he dedicates the fruit of his labor. Such, for example, was Whitman's myth. The initial stirrings of his work he took to be bestowals of his soul (or of a young boy, sometimes—or both), and his responsive act was to "make the work" (this being the motto that sat on Whitman's desk) and speak it back to the soul, the boy.

Ezra Pound's creative life was animated by a myth in which "tradition" appears as both the source and ultimate repository of his gifts. Pound's first master, Yeats, articulated the sensibility: "I . . . made a new religion, almost an infallible church of poetic tradition, of a fardel of stories, and of personages, and of emotions, inseparable from their first expression, passed on from generation to generation by poets and painters. . . . I wished for a world, where I could discover this tradition perpetually, and not in pictures and in poems only, but in tiles round the chimney-piece and in the hangings that kept out the draft." For Pound, I think, what gifts we have come ultimately from the gods, but a "live tradition" is the storehouse in which the wealth of that endowment is preserved. Pound speaks certain names over and over again—Homer, Confucius, Dante, Cavalcanti—the lineage of gifted souls whose works had informed his own. To the end of his days he dedicated a portion of his labor to the renewal of their spirits.

To offer but one more of these myths of closing the circle, of artists directing their work back toward its sources, the Chilean poet Pablo Neruda took the beginnings of his art to lie not with spirits or with the past, but with something human, current, and almost anonymous. His gifts sprang, he felt, from brotherhood, from "the people," and he quite consciously offered his art in recognition of the debt: "I have attempted to give something resiny, earthlike, and fragrant in exchange for human brotherhood." He counted as "the laurel crown for my poetry" not his Nobel Prize but a time when "from the depths of the Lota coal mine, a man came up out of the tunnel into the full sunlight on the fiery nitrate field, as if rising out of hell, his face disfigured by his terrible work, his eyes inflamed by the dust, and stretching his rough hand out to me . . . , he said: 'I have known you for a long time, my brother.'" To find an unknown worker who had heard his poems was sign enough that his gift had managed to bear some equivalent back to its original clan and homeland.

When I first read through the literature on the ceremonial gifts of tribal peoples, and when I read all the fairy tales I could find in which gifts are exchanged, I noticed a curious thing: people seem to feel that gifts increase in worth as long as they are kept in circulation. There are a number of reasons for this, two of which I shall touch on here. First, gift exchange can be an erotic or synthetic commerce, drawing community out of the mass. Where an exchange of gifts succeeds in transforming otherwise disparate people into a group, the gifts themselves will seem to "increase," for in social life the whole—the community—really is greater than the sum of its parts.

Second, many gift institutions have to do with true, organic growth, and in these cases the gifts "increase" because they are actually alive. First fruits rituals make a good example. An offering of first fruits is a return gift that recognizes the fact that natural abundance is itself a gift (from nature or the gods). "All that opens the womb is mine," says the Lord in the Old Testament, "all your male cattle, the firstlings of cow and sheep. . . ." In recognition, the Jews therefore returned the firstborn to the Lord, sacrificing them at the altar.

Such rituals are almost universal among tribal peoples. Among Indian tribes on the North Pacific coast, to take just one more example, the skeletons of salmon caught during the annual salmon runs were given back to the sea "so that" the fish might remain plentiful year after year. Again, the connection is made between treating a thing as a gift and its continued abundance or fertility. (For an expanded discussion of "increase," see *CoEvolution Quarterly*, Fall 1982. On gifts and social cohesion, see *Working Papers*, March–April 1983.)

I read first fruits rituals as just-so stories of the creative spirit: just as treating nature's bounty as a gift assures the fertility of nature, so to treat the products of the imagination as gifts assures the fertility of the imagination. What we receive from nature or from the imagination comes to us from beyond our sphere of influence, and the lesson of such aboriginal rituals seems to be that the continued fertility of these things depends on their remaining "beyond us," on their not being drawn into the smaller ego. First fruits rituals protect the spirit of the gift by making evident the true structure of our relationship to the sources of our wealth. The salmon are not subject to the will of the Indians; the imagination is not subject to the will of the artist. To accept the fruits of these things as gifts is to acknowledge that we are not their owners or masters, we are if anything their servants, their ministers.

To say the same thing in a slightly different fashion, first fruits rituals make a simple injunction in regard to fertility: do not exploit the essence. The bones of the salmon and the fat of the lamb are directed back toward their homeland, and by that return the beneficiaries of these gifts avoid what we normally mean by exploitation. The return gift is, then, the fertilizer that assures the fertility of the source.

The fruit of the creative spirit is the work of art itself, and if there is a first fruits ritual for artists it must either be the willing "waste" of art (in which one is happy to labor all day with no hope of production, nothing to sell, nothing to show off, just fish thrown back into the sea as soon as they are caught) or else, when there is a product, it must be this thing we have already seen, the dedication of the work back toward its origins. Black Elk, the Oglala Sioux holy man, dedicated his book, *Black Elk Speaks*, as follows: "What is good in this book is given back to the six grandfathers and to the great men of my people." Such is the dedication implicit in the work of any person who feels his creativity to have been informed by a tradition. It is the artistic equivalent of what Maori tribesmen in New Zealand call "nourishing *hau*," nourishing the spirit of the gift. For an artist, "feeding *hau*" is as much a matter of attitude or intent as it is of any specific action; the attitude is, at base, the kind of humility which prevents the artist from drawing the essence of his creation into the personal ego (in what other line of work does the worker say, "I knelt down—I always do after I've written what I know is a good piece"?). In *The Real Work*, Gary Snyder speaks of coming into such an attitude, and of its consequences:

> I finished off the trail crew season and went on a long mountain meditation walk for ten days across some wilderness. During that process—thinking about things and my life—I just dropped poetry. I don't want to sound precious, but in some sense I did drop it. Then I started writing poems that were better. From that time forward I always looked on the poems I wrote as gifts that were not essential to my life; if I never wrote another one, it wouldn't be a great tragedy. Ever since, every poem I've written has been like a surprise. . . .
>
> You get a good poem and you don't know where it came from. "Did I say that?" And so all you feel is: you feel humility and you feel gratitude. And you'd feel a little uncomfortable, I think, if you capitalized too much on that without admitting at some point that you got it from the Muse, or whoever, wherever, or however.

When we are in the frame of mind which nourishes *hau* we identify with the spirit of the gift, not with its particular embodiments, and whoever has identified with the spirit will seek to keep the gift in motion. Therefore the sign of this identity is generosity, gratefulness, or the act of gratitude;

> Thou that hast giv'n so much to me,
> Give one thing more, a gratefull heart;
> See how Thy beggar works in Thee
> By art:
>
> He makes thy gifts occasion more,
> And sayes, if he in this be crost,
> All Thou hast given him heretofore
> Is lost.

> George Herbert, from
> "Gratefulnesse" (1633)

We nourish the spirit by disbursing our gifts, not by capitalizing upon them (not capitalizing "too much," says Synder—there seems to be a little leeway). The artist who is nourishing *hau* is not self-aggrandizing, self-assertive, or self-conscious, he is, rather, self-squandering, self-abnegating, self-forgetful—all the marks of the creative temperament the bourgeoisie find so amusing. "Art is a virtue of the practical intellect," writes Flannery O'Connor, "and the practice of any virtue demands a certain asceticism and a very definite leaving-behind of the niggardly part of the ego. The writer has to judge himself with a stranger's eye and a stranger's severity. . . . No art is sunk in the self, but rather, in art the self becomes self-forgetful in order to meet the demands of the thing seen and the thing being made." Rainer Maria Rilke uses similar terms in an early essay describing the attributes of art as a way of life:

> Not any self-control or self-limitation for the sake of specific ends, but rather a carefree letting go of oneself; not caution, but rather a wise blindness; not working to acquire silent, slowly increasing possessions, but rather a continuous squandering of all perishable values.

I want to return now to the question of the increase of gifts in relation to works of the imagination, using as a point of departure another remark of Flannery O'Connor's. Describing her sense of how the fiction writer works, O'Connor once wrote: "The eye sees what it has been given to see by concrete circumstances, and the imagination reproduces what, by some related gift, it is able to make live."

When we say that "the whole is greater than the sum of its parts" we are usually speaking of things that "come alive" when their elements are integrated into one another. We describe such things by way of organic metaphors because living organisms are the prime example. There is a difference in kind between a viable organism and its constituent parts, and when the parts become the whole we experience the difference as an increase, as "the whole is greater." And because a circulation of gifts has a cohesive or synthetic power it is almost as a matter of definition that we say such increase is a gift (or is the fruit of a gift). Gifts are the agents of that organic cohesion we perceive as liveliness.

This is one of the things we mean to say, it seems to me, when we speak of a person of strong imagination as being "gifted." In *Biographia Literaria,* Coleridge describes the imagination as "essentially vital" and takes as its hallmark its ability "to shape into one," an ability he named "the esemplastic power." The imagination has the power to assemble the elements of our experience into coherent, lively wholes: it has a gift.

An artist who wishes to exercise the esemplastic power of the imagination must submit himself to a "gifted state," one in which he is able to discern the connections inherent in his materials and "give the increase," bring the work to life. The artist who succeeds in this endeavor "realizes" his gift. That is, he makes it real, makes it a thing: its spirit is embodied in the work.

Once an inner gift has been realized it may be passed along, communicated to the audience. And sometimes this embodied gift—the work—can reproduce the gifted state in the audience that receives it. Let us say that the "suspension of disbelief" by which we become receptive to a work of the imagination is in fact "belief," a momentary faith by virtue of which the spirit of the artists' gift may enter and act upon our being. Sometimes then, sometimes—if we are awake, if the artist really was gifted— the work will induce a moment of grace, a communion, a period during which we too know the hidden coherence of our being and feel the fullness of our lives. Any such art is itself a gift, a cordial to the soul.

If we pause now to contrast the esemplastic cognition of imagination to the analytic cognition of *logos*-thought we will be in a position to see one of the connections between the creative spirit and the bond that a gift establishes. Two brief folk tales will help set up the contrast. There is a group of tales which portray for us the particular kind of thought which destroys a gift. In a tale from Lithuania, for example, riches that the fairies have given to mortals turn to paper as soon as they are measured or counted. The motif is the reverse, really, of another common fairy tale transformation: worthless goods—coals, ashes, wood shavings—turning into gold when they are received as gifts. If the increase of gifts is in the erotic bond, then the increase is lost when exchange is treated as a commodity transaction (when, in this case, it is drawn into the part of the mind which reckons value and quantity).

A second example will expand the point. A brief entry in a mid-nineteenth century collection of English fairy tales tells of a Devonshire man to whom the fairies had given an inexhaustible barrel of ale. Year after year the liquor ran freely. Then one day the man's maid, curious to know the cause of this extraordinary power, removed the cork from the bung hole and looked into the cask. It was full of cobwebs; when the spigot next was turned the ale had ceased to flow.

The moral is this: The gift is lost in self-consciousness. To count, measure, reckon value, or seek the cause of a thing, is to step outside the circle, to cease being "all of a piece" with the flow of gifts and become, instead, one part of the whole reflecting upon another part. We participate in the esemplastic power of a gift by way of a particular kind of unconsciousness, then: unanalytic, undialectical consciousness.

To offer a last illustration that is closer to the concerns of artists, most of us have had the experience of becoming suddenly tongue-tied before an audience or before someone whom we perceive to be judging us. In order to sing in front of other people, for example, the singer cannot step back and observe his own voice, he can't, that is, fall into that otherwise useful frame of mind which perceives the singer and the audience as separate things, the one listening to the other. Instead he must enter that illusion (an illusion which becomes a reality if the singer is gifted) that he and the audience are one and the same thing. A friend of mine had a strange experience when she took her first piano lessons. During an early session, to the surprise of both her teacher and herself, she suddenly began to play. "I didn't know how to play the piano," she says, "but I could play it." The teacher was so excited she left the room to find someone else to witness the miracle. As the two of them came back into the practice room, however, my friend's ability left her as suddenly as it had appeared. Again, the moral seems to be that the gift is lost in self-consciousness. (Thus O'Connor: "In art the self becomes self-forgetful.") As soon as the musician senses that someone else is watching her, she begins to watch herself. Rather than using her gift, she is reflecting upon it. Cobwebs.

Any circulation of gifts draws its participants into a wider self, and the commerce of art is no exception. The creative spirit moves in a "body" or "ego" larger than that of any single person. Works of art are drawn from, and their bestowal nourishes, those parts of our being which are not entirely personal, parts which derive from nature, from the group and the race, from history and tradition, and from the spiritual world. The Greeks have two words for "life," *bios* and *zoë*. *Bios* is limited life, characterized life, life that dies; *zoë* is the life which endures, the thread which runs through *bios*-life and is not broken when the particular is lost. In the realized gifts of the gifted we may taste that *zoë*-life which shall not perish even though each of us, and each generation, shall perish.

Such is the context within which to cite Joseph Conrad's description of the artist. The artist, Conrad tells us, must descend within himself to find the terms of his appeal:

> His appeal is made to our less obvious capacities: to that part of our nature which, because of the warlike conditions of existence, is necessarily kept out of sight within the more resisting and hard qualities—like the vulnerable body within a steel armor. . . . The artist appeals . . . to that in us which is a gift and not an acquisition—and, therefore, more permanently enduring. He speaks to our capacity for delight and wonder, to the sense of mystery surrounding our lives; to our sense of pity, and beauty, and pain; to the latent feeling of fellowship with all creation—to the subtle but invincible conviction of solidarity that knits together the loneliness of innumerable hearts, to the solidarity . . . which binds together all humanity— the dead to the living and the living to the unborn. . . .

Once we realize that the thread of *zoë*-life runs beyond the physical body, beyond the individual self, it becomes harder to differentiate the various levels—biological, social, spiritual—of our being. There is a larger self, a species-essence, which is a general possession of the race. And the symbolizations—all true gifts, but of course I mean especially works of art, paintings, songs, the tiles round the chimney-piece—these symbolizations which express and carry the "facts" of *zoë*-life constitute the speech by which that larger self articulates and renews its spirit. By Whitman's aesthetic, the artist's work is a word "en-masse," an expression of Conrad's "subtle but invincible conviction of

271

solidarity." The work of art is a copula: a bond, a band, a link by which the several are knit into one. Men and women who dedicate their lives to the realization of their gifts tend the office of that communion by which we are joined to one another, to our times, to our generation, and to the race. Just as the artist's imagination "has a gift" which brings the work to life, so in the realized gifts of the gifted the spirit of the group "has a gift." These creations are not "merely" symbolic, they do not "stand for" the larger self; they are its necessary embodiment, a language without which it would have no life at all.

In introducing these two Greek terms I said the zoë-life is the unbroken thread, the spirit that survives the destruction of its vessels. But here we must add that zoë-life may be lost as well, through the wholesale destruction of its vehicles. The spirit of a community or collective can be wiped out, tradition can be destroyed. We tend to think of genocide as the physical destruction of a race or group, but the term may be aptly expanded to include the obliteration of the *genius* of a group, the killing of its creative spirit through the destruction, debasement, or silencing of its art (I am thinking, for example, of Milan Kundera's analysis of the "organized forgetting" which has been imposed upon the nations of Eastern Europe). Those parts of our being which extend beyond the individual ego cannot survive unless they can be constantly articulated. And there are individuals—all of us, I would say, but men and women of spiritual and artistic temperament in particular—who cannot survive, either, unless the symbols of zoë-life circulate among us as a commonwealth.

To offer a single example that strikes both the collective and individual levels of this issue, in her autobiography the writer and actress Maya Angelou recalls her graduation from an all-black junior high school. The assembled students and teachers had fallen silent, momentarily shamed by a casually racist speech from a white administrator, when one of Angelou's classmates began to sing a song they all knew as "the Negro national anthem," its words written by a black man, its music by a black woman. "Oh, Black known and unknown poets," Angelou writes, "how often have your auctioned pains sustained us . . . ? If we were a people much given to revealing secrets, we might raise monuments and sacrifice to the memories of our poets, but slavery cured us of that weakness. It may be enough, however, to have it said that we survive in exact relationship to the dedication of our poets (including preachers, musicians and blues singers)." The elders who passed the Sacred Pipe of the Sioux to Black Elk warned him that "if the people have no center they will perish." Just as a circulation of ceremonial gifts among tribal peoples preserves the vitality of the tribe, so the art of any peoples, if it is a true emanation of their spirit, will stand surety for the lives of the citizenry.

II

It has been the implication of much of this essay that there is an irreconcilable conflict between gift exchange and the market and that, as a consequence, the artist in the modern world must suffer a constant tension between the gift sphere to which his work pertains and the market society which is his context. Such, at any rate, were my assumptions when I began to write my book, five years ago. I not only placed creative life wholly within the gift economy but I assumed that the artist of enduring gifts would be he who managed to defend himself against all temptations to commercialize his calling.

My position has changed somewhat. I still believe that the primary commerce of art is a gift exchange, that unless the work is the realization of the artist's gift and unless we, the audience, can feel the gift it carries, there is no art; I still believe that a gift can be destroyed by the marketplace; but I no longer feel the poles of this dichotomy to be so strongly opposed. There can be some communication between gift and commodity, gift exchange and the market. And it is this communication we must seek if, like most tribal peoples, we are a community which must deal with strangers, or if we are artists in a market society. It is pointless simply to attack the market. We can, sometimes, change the scope of its influence, but we cannot change its nature. The market is an emanation of *logos,* and *logos* is as much a part of the human spirit as *eros* is; we cannot do away with it. We must therefore accept that, within certain limits, what has come to us as a gift may be sold in the marketplace, just as what has been earned in the marketplace may be given as a gift. Within certain limits, gift wealth may be rationalized and market wealth may be eroticized. The problem is to find the limits.

I posed a dilemma at the beginning of this essay: how, if art is essentially a gift, is the artist to survive in a society dominated by the market? Modern artists have resolved this dilemma in several different ways, each of which, it seems to me, has two essential features. First, the artist allows himself to step outside the gift economy which is the primary commerce of his art and make some peace with the market. Like the Jew of the Old Testament who has a law of the altar at home and a law of the gate for dealing with strangers, the artist who wishes neither to lose his gift nor starve his belly reserves a protected gift-sphere in which the work is created but, once the work is made, he allows himself some contact with the market. And then—the necessary second phase—if he is successful in the marketplace, he converts market wealth into gift wealth: he contributes his earnings to the support of his art.

To be more specific, there are three primary ways in which modern artists have resolved the problem of their livelihood: they have taken second jobs, they have found patrons to support them, or they have managed to place the work itself on the market and pay the rent with fees and royalties. The underlying structure that is common to all of these—a double economy and the conversion of market wealth to gift wealth—may be easiest to see in the case of the artist who has taken a secondary job, some work more or less unrelated to his art: night watchman, merchant seaman, Berlitz teacher, doctor or insurance executive. . . . The second job frees his art from the burden of financial responsibility so that when he is creating the work he may turn from questions of market value and labor in that protected gift-sphere of which I spoke. He earns a wage in the marketplace and gives it to his art.

The case of patronage (or nowadays, grants) is a little more subtle. The artist who takes a second job becomes, in a sense, his own patron: he decides his work is worthy of support, just as the patron does, but then he himself must go out and raise the cash. The artist who manages to attract an actual patron may seem to be less involved with the market. The patron's support is not a wage or a fee for service, it is a gift given in recognition of the artist's own. With patronage, the artist's livelihood seems to lie wholly within the gift-sphere in which the work is made.

But if we fail to see the market here it is because we are looking only at the artist. When an artist takes a second job a single person moves in both economies, but with patronage there is a division of labor—it is the patron who has entered the market and converted its wealth to gifts. Once made, the point hardly needs elaboration. Harriet Weaver, that kindly Quaker lady who supported James Joyce, did not get her money from God; nor did the Guggenheims, nor does the National Endowment for the Arts. Someone, somewhere sold his labor in the market-place, or grew rich in finance, or exploited the abundance of nature, and the patron turns that wealth into a gift to feed the gifted.

Artists who take on secondary jobs and artists who find pa-trons have, in a sense, a structural way to mark the boundary between their art and the market. It is not hard to distinguish between writing poems and working the night shift in a hospi-tal, easier still for the poet to know he is no Guggenheim. But the artist who sells his own creations must develop a more sub-jective feel for the two economies, and his own rituals for both keeping them apart and bringing them together. He must, on the one hand, be able to disengage from the work and think of it as a commodity. He must be able to reckon its value in terms of current fashions, know what the market will bear, demand fair value, and part with the work when someone pays the price. And he must, on the other hand, be able to forget all that and turn to serve his gifts on their own terms. If he cannot do the former he cannot hope to sell his art, and if he cannot do the latter he may have no art to sell, or only a commercial art, work that has been created in response to the demands of the mar-ket, not in response to the demands of the gift. The artist who hopes to market work which is the realization of his gifts cannot begin with the market. He must create for himself that gift-sphere in which the work is made and only when he knows the work to be the faithful realization of his gift turn to see if it has cur-rency in that other economy. Sometimes it does, sometimes it doesn't.

A single example will illustrate several of these points. For years before he established himself as a painter, Edward Hopper used to hire himself out as a commercial artist to magazines with names like "Hotel Management." Hopper was an expert draftsman and the illustrations and covers he drew during those years are skillfully rendered. But they are not art. They certainly have none of Hopper's particular gift, none of his insight, for example, into the way that incandescent light shapes an American city at night. Or perhaps I should put it this way: any number of out-of-work art students could have drawn essentially the same drawings. Hopper's magazine covers—happy couples in yellow sailboats and businessmen strolling the golf links—all have the air of assignments, of work for hire. Like the novelist who writes genre fiction to a proven formula, or the composer who scores the tunes for television commercials, or the playwright flown in to polish up a Hollywood script, Hopper's work for the magazines was a response to a market demand and the results are commercial art.

During his years as a commercial artist Hopper created for himself what I am calling the "protected gift-sphere" by spending only three or four days a week at the magazines and painting at home the rest of the time. He would, of course, have been happy to sell his gift-sphere work on the market, but there were no buyers. In 1913, when he was thirty-one years old, he sold a painting for $250; he sold none for the next ten years. Then, between 1925 and 1930, he began to earn a living by his art alone.

In a sense Hopper's work for the magazines shouldn't be considered a part of his art at all but rather a second job taken to support his true labors. But the point is that even when a market demand for his "true" art developed, Hopper still preserved the integrity of his gifts. It may be hard to formulate a rule of thumb by which to know when an artist is preserving his gifts and when he is letting the market call the tune, but we know the distinction exists. Hopper could have made a comfortable living as a commercial artist, but he didn't. He could have painted his most popular works over and over again; he could have sold signed, gold-flecked photographs of "Nighthawks." . . . But he didn't.

It is not my intention here to address the problems and subtleties of the various paths by which artists have resolved the problem of making a living. There are second jobs that deaden the spirit, there are artists who become beholden to their patrons and those whose temperament prohibits them from selling the work at all. But these and all the other ins and outs of artistic livelihood are topics for a different sort of essay, one addressed to questions of arts policy or offering advice to working artists. The only point I want to add here is a general one, and that is that each of the paths I have described is most often a way of getting by, not a way of getting rich. No matter how the artist chooses (or is forced) to resolve the problem of his livelihood, he is likely to be poor.

Both Walt Whitman and Ezra Pound make good examples. Neither man ever made a living by his art. In letters, Whitman has described the "sort of German or Parisian student life" that he lived in Washington during the Civil War, and his description could be used verbatim for Pound during his years in London and Paris, living in little rented rooms wearing flamboyant but secondhand clothes, straining his coffee through a cloth in the morning, building his own furniture. (By Pound's own estimation one of the attractions of Europe was its acceptance of an artist's limited means. "Poverty here is decent and honourable," he wrote to a friend from Rapallo. "In America it lays one open to continuous insult on all sides. . . .")

At one time or another during their lives both Whitman and Pound took on some sort of secondary employ. Whitman, when he was writing the early drafts of *Leaves of Grass*, edited newspapers, wrote freelance journalism, ran a printing office and a stationery store, and worked as a house carpenter; Pound, too, hired out as a journalist. All during the First World War he was paid four guineas a month to churn out articles (two a week, year after year) for "The New Age," a Social Credit newspaper. But for both men these were essentially bread-and-butter jobs, taken out of need and quit when need was relieved.

Nor was there any significant patronage in those days, at least not in America. In 1885 a group of Whitman's admirers bought the then-crippled poet a horse and phaëton so that he would not be confined to his house; at about the same time the nearby Harleigh cemetery donated the ground upon which the poet had his tomb erected. And this just about completes the list of return gifts America offered its first poet. Pound fared only a little better. The $2,000 Dial Prize was the single significant reward that he received before he was old and confined to St. Elizabeth's Hospital. Much later there were other awards—a $5,000 grant from the Academy of American Poets in 1963, for example—but again, we cannot say we are speaking of a man made rich by his patrons.

Finally, although both Whitman and Pound realized a modest income from the sale of their works in the last years of their lives, there were no returns when these men were young and most in need. Whitman lost money on the first edition of *Leaves of Grass;* Pound's American royalties for a typical year—1915—came to $1.85.

In sum we have two poets, each of whom was clearly a major figure in his century, known and read during his lifetime, each of whom at one time or another took on secondary work in support of his art, each of whom was happy to accept what little patronage was offered to him, each of whom was an eager entrepreneur of his own creations—and each of whom was essentially poor into old age.

If we are to speak fully of the poverty of artists we must pause here to distinguish between actual penury and "the poverty of the gift." By this last I intend to refer to an interior poverty, a spiritual poverty, which pertains to the gifted state. In that state, those things which are not gifts are judged to have no worth, and those things which are gifts are understood to be but temporary possessions. In a sense, our gifts are not fully ours until they have been given away. The gifted man is not himself, therefore, until he has become the steward of a wealth which appears from beyond his realm of influence and which, once it has come to him, he must constantly disperse. Leviticus records the Lord's instruction to Moses: "The land shall not be sold in perpetuity, for the land is mine; for you are strangers and sojourners with me." Likewise, we are sojourners with our gifts, not their owners; even our creations—especially our creations—do not belong to us. As Gary Snyder says, "You get a good poem and you don't know where it came from. 'Did I say that?' And so all you feel is: you feel humility and you feel gratitude." Spiritually, you can't be much poorer than gifted.

The artist who has willingly accepted such an interior poverty can tolerate a certain plainness to his outer life. I do not mean cold or hunger, but certainly the size of the room and the quality of the wine seem less important to a man who can convey imaginary color to a canvas. When the song of one's self is coming all-of-a-piece, page after page, an attic room and chamber pot do not insult the soul. And a young poet can stand the same supper of barley soup and bread, night after night, if he is on a walking tour of Italy and in love with its beauty. Artists whose gifts are strong, accessible, and coming over into the work may, as Marshall Sahlins says of hunters and gatherers, "have affluent economies, their absolute poverty notwithstanding."

I do not mean to romanticize the poverty of the artist, or pretend to too strong a link between this state of mind and "the facts." A man may be born rich and still be faithful to his gifts; he may happen upon a lucrative second job; his work may be in great demand or his agent a canny salesman. Actual poverty and interior poverty have no necessary connection. And yet as we all know, and as the lives of Whitman and Pound testify, the connection is not unknown, either. For one thing, fidelity to one's gifts often draws energy away from the activities by which men become rich. For another, if the artist lives in a culture which is not only dominated by exchange trade but which has no institutions for the conversion of market wealth to gift wealth, if he lives in a culture which cannot, therefore, settle the debt it owes to those who have dedicated their lives to the realization of a gift, then he is likely to be poor in fact as well as spirit. Such, I think, is a fair description of the culture into which both Whitman and Pound were born. Theirs was hardly an age of patronage, as my brief list of return gifts indicates; nor was theirs a time which would have likely understood that Trobriand social code, "to possess is to give." Theirs was the age of monopoly capitalism, an economic form whose code expected and rewarded the conversion of gift wealth to market wealth (the natural gifts of the New World, in particular—the forests, wildlife, and fossil fuels—were "sold in perpetuity" and converted into private fortunes). In a land which feels no reciprocity toward nature, in an age when the rich can imagine themselves to be "self-made," we should not be surprised to find the interior poverty of the gifted state replicated in the actual poverty of the gifted. Nor should we be surprised to find artists who, like Whitman, seek to speak to us in that prophetic voice which would create a world more hospitable to the creative spirit.

III

The root of our English word "mystery" is a Greek verb, *muein,* which means to close the mouth. Dictionaries tend to explain the connection by pointing out that the initiates to ancient mysteries were sworn to silence, but the root may also indicate, it seems to me, that what the initiate learns at a mystery *cannot* be talked about. It can be shown, it can be witnessed or revealed, it cannot be explained.

When I set out to write *The Gift* I was drawn to speak of gifts by way of anecdotes and fairy tales because, I think, a gift— and particularly an inner gift, a talent—is a mystery. We know what giftedness is for having been gifted, or for having known a gifted man or woman. We know that art is a gift for having had the experience of art. We cannot know these things by way of psychological or aesthetic theories. Where an inner gift comes from, what obligations or reciprocity it brings with it, how and toward whom our gratitude should be discharged, to what degree we must leave a gift alone and to what degree we must discipline it, how we are to feed its spirit and preserve its vitality— these and all the other questions raised by a gift can only be answered by telling just-so stories. As Whitman says, "the talkers talking their talk" cannot explain these things; we learn by "faint clues and indirections."

A final story, then, of gifts and art.

In an essay called "Childhood and Poetry" Pablo Neruda once speculated on the origins of his work. Neruda was raised in Temuco, a frontier town in southern Chile. To be born in Temuco in 1904 must have been a little like being born in Oregon a hundred years ago. Rainy and mountainous, "Temuco was the farthest outpost in Chilean life in the southern territories," Neruda tells us in his memoirs. He remembers the main street as lined with hardware stores which, since the local population couldn't read, hung out eye-catching signs: "an enormous saw, a giant cooking pot, a Cyclopean padlock, a mammoth spoon. Farther along the street, shoe stores—a colossal boot." Neruda's father worked on the railway. Their home, like others, had about it something of the air of a settlers' temporary camp: kegs of nails, tools, and saddles lay about in unfinished rooms and under half-completed stairways.

Playing in the lot behind the house one day when he was still a little boy, Neruda discovered a hole in a fence board.

> I looked through the hole and saw a landscape like that behind our house, uncared for, and wild. I moved back a few steps, because I sensed vaguely that something was about to happen. All of a sudden a hand appeared—a tiny hand of a boy about my own age. By the time I came close again, the hand was gone, and in its place there was a marvellous white toy sheep.
>
> The sheep's wool was faded. Its wheels had escaped. All of this only made it more authentic. I had never seen such a wonderful sheep. I looked back through the hole but the boy had disappeared. I went into the house and brought out a treasure of my own: a pine cone, opened, full of odor and resin, which I adored. I set it down in the same spot and went off with the sheep.
>
> I never saw either the hand or the boy again. And I have never seen a sheep like that either. The toy I lost finally in a fire. But even now . . . whenever I pass a toyshop, I look furtively into the window. It's no use. They don't make sheep like that any more.

Neruda has commented on this incident several times. "This exchange of gifts—mysterious—settled deep inside me like a sedimentary deposit," he once remarked in an interview. And he associates the exchange with his poetry.

> I have been a lucky man. To feel the intimacy of brothers is a marvellous thing in life. To feel the love of people whom we love is a fire that feeds our life. But to feel the affection that comes from those whom we do not know, from those unknown to us, who are watching over our sleep and solitude, over our dangers and our weaknesses—that is something still greater and more beautiful because it widens out the boundaries of our being, and unites all living things.
>
> That exchange brought home to me for the first time a precious idea: that all humanity is somehow together. . . . It won't surprise you then that I have attempted to give something resiny, earthlike, and fragrant in exhange for human brotherhood. . . .

This is the great lesson I learned in my childhood, in the backyard of a lonely house. Maybe it was nothing but a game two boys played who didn't know each other and wanted to pass to the other some good things of life. Yet maybe this small and mysterious exchange of gifts remained inside me also, deep and indestructible, giving my poetry light.

Two Essays

HAYDEN CARRUTH

Poets Without Prophecy

Beginning with whom?—not Eliot—with Arnold perhaps?—
well, beginning rather a long time ago the meaning of the words
poem and *poet* shifted finally from a matter of substance to a
matter of technique. Today we can find vestiges of that older
way of speaking. In the country where I live people still say, when
you tell them a lie, "Oh, that's poetry," and I suppose somewhere people may still exclaim, "How poetic!" upon seeing a
sunset. We do not say these things. We consider them offensive.
For us a poem is a work of art, a composition of verbal materials, a thing, and the poet is the maker who makes it.

I don't want to suggest that we are wrong; certainly I don't
want to excuse the sentimentality and unctuousness which were
the end products of the old view. But I would like to point out
that these end products were a long time in coming—centuries,
in fact—and that there distinctly was something grand and ennobling in the idea that a poet was to be known not by his art
but by his vision; something more than grand and ennobling,
something essential. And we have lost it.

I don't know what to call it precisely. It's hard to move back
into that area of old custom without falling prey to the soft,
foolish terms it spawned so readily toward its close. But let's extend to one another the charity of understanding and agree on
an acknowledged orotundity: "the larger vision of humanity."
Once the poet was our spokesman and not our oracle, our advocate and not our secret agent, or at least he was as much the
one as the other; and if he did not speak for us, all of us, fully

283

and warmly, if his poems lacked the larger vision of humanity, we said he was deficient in one of the qualities that, virtually by definition, make a poet.

This attitude survived among the older poets of our time, though their own theories about poetry tended to suppress it; the larger vision of humanity was still a part of their poetic instinct. The *Cantos, The Waste Land,* and *Paterson* are alive with it; Frost's poems reveal an unmistakably general feeling; so do the poems of Cummings, Aiken, Ransom; Stevens veiled his concern under his marvelous verbal textures and his epistemological preoccupations, but it was there, especially in the later poems where a sense of brooding pity underlies almost every word. Even Marianne Moore, whose writing has never appealed to me, conveys a kind of coy consciousness of sodality in her least timid poems. The point is that all these poets came into the world at a time when the poet's direct responsibility to mankind at large still hadn't quite been laughed out of existence. They themselves were the ones who set off the final burst of laughter when, in order to discredit the impressionistic views of the previous age, they directed attention away from the representative role of the poet and toward his work as experimentalist, hierophant, artifex, oneirocritic, or what have you.

It should be clear that my topic is poetry and politics, though I have chosen to work my way into it by means of concepts which show political feeling as what it really is, rather than as mere partisanship.

Next came the thirties, the time when poetry was avowedly political, the time of Archibald MacLeish, Muriel Rukeyser, Alfred Hayes, and the British socialists, the time equally of the Southern Agrarians. I myself find this poetry refreshing to read today, especially the radical poetry; its motives and objectives were so forceful that often a kind of vividness was the result, against which our own verse, striving for greater richness, seems only muddy. I wonder if we aren't ready for a revival of interest in proletarian writing, similar to the Jazz Age revival which occurred a few years back. Serious attention is being given again to John Steinbeck, thanks to his Nobel Prize, and that is to the good. Others also deserve reconsideration. I nominate Malcolm Cowley and Kenneth Fearing. Nowadays they are scarcely thought of as poets, yet they each wrote a few first-rate poems.

At the same time one cannot avoid seeing that the larger vision of humanity became more specialized in the poetry of the thirties, narrowed and reduced, and that this constriction grew even tighter in our poetry of the war. We had some fine war poems, things like Eberhart's "Fury of Aerial Bombardment" and Jarrell's "Death of a Ball Turret Gunner"; they have become standard anthology pieces. Yet if we compare them with the poems of the First World War we see a great difference. In the poems of Wilfred Owen, for instance, or even in such a highly wrought work as David Jones's *In Parenthesis*, the larger vision is instinct in every word and very profoundly expressed in some; but Jarrell's gunner, whose remains are washed out of his turret with a hose, is a far more specialized figure. He does not live in our minds as a fully realizable exponent of our own suffering. The figures created by Bill Mauldin and Ernie Pyle, though shallow, come closer to this and closer to the Tommies of Owen's poetry. This isn't Jarrell's fault. He is a fine poet, and the reason for his narrowed sensibility (which I don't think he desired at all) lies in the cultural evolution of the century. There had been an attrition of poetic consciousness. Far too complicated a matter to be easily explained; yet I think we can all see the difference between Owen and Jarrell, and I think most of us can concede that it is connected with the increasing refinement of the poet as a self-appointed agent of sensibility in an insensible and ever more hostile society.

Since then this erosion of the larger view has reached a point at which poetry has become almost totally apolitical. The supreme political fact of our lives is the atomic bomb. Am I wrong? It is enormous; it occupies the whole world. It is not only what it is but also the concentrated symbol of all hatred and injustice in every social and economic sphere. Speaking for myself, I have lived in fear of it for fifteen years, fear that it will go off, one way or another, and kill me and my family, or render our lives so intolerable that we won't wish to go on. Maybe I am more timorous than most people; I believe there are actually some Americans who never think about the bomb. But poets? That would be incredible. No matter how hard they try they cannot escape being included among society's most percipient members. Yet if one were to judge by their output one would have to believe that poets are the least concerned people in the world, not only on their own account but on everyone's.

Poetry, under the editorship of Henry Rago, is as representative of the various groups among American poets as any single magazine could probably be. I have just gone through all the issues for 1961, the only recent year for which I could find a complete set on my shelves. The year produced 335 poems by 139 poets, and although I skimmed through them rapidly, it has still taken me several hours to make up a count; I didn't go so quickly that my figures are likely to be off by more than a little. In the whole year I found two explicit references to the bomb, one a passing seriocomic remark, and ten poems on the general theme of suffering in war, two of which were translations from foreign poets of an earlier time. There were a great many poems on sex in its various aspects, religion, growing old, being young, thought and feeling, the uses of knowledge, themes unintelligible to me, and painting, music, and poetry.

That's it, of course, that last—poetry. The only topic poets will admit. Time after time they say so. Robert Creeley, one of the best alive, asserts his allegiance to "the poem supreme, addressed to / emptiness. . . ." At the other end of the country, Howard Nemerov, a good academic poet, speaks of himself as

> *Dreaming preposterous mergers and divisions*
> *Of vowels like water, consonants like rock*
> *(While everyone kept discussing values*
> *And the need for values), for words that would*
> *Enter the silence and be there as a light.*

Could anything be plainer? And I believe you could find statements of this precise credo—belief in the poem as an isolated act of absolutely and solely intrinsic goodness—in 90 percent of the books published by American poets in the past ten or fifteen years. There are a couple in my own.

Not spokesmen then. But hermits, lone wolves, acolytes—building poems in the wilderness for their own salvation.

The poets will retort in two ways. First they will say that art has always been lonely work, that the artist must use his own experience, and that ultimately he must put together his vision of reality—or, as some would say, discover it—within himself. This is self-evident; but it does not require the poet to withdraw himself so far from the general experience of his time that he becomes merely a specialist pursuing specialized ends. In fact it ought to mean just the opposite: that the poet, within himself, identifies and augments the general experience in such a way that it will excite a renewed susceptibility in everyone else.

Second, the poets will say that their isolated poems are acts of an implied political significance. They will say that in evil times the individual person exerts a force for good by carrying on his private endeavor with exemplary honesty. They will say that by refining their own purity as artists and by rejecting the false values of the world they are expressing a political attitude of considerable importance and firmness, and are doing so in terms more durable than could be used in direct statements about immediate political objectives. In the past I have said this myself, and I do not think it is sophistry. But it comes close to it. Politics is practicality, and a political act is by nature an act committed in the context of immediate objectives. And isn't the "context of immediate objectives" simply a jargonistic equivalent of the "larger vision of humanity"? This context still exists, I grant you, in the very remote background of today's estranged poetry. But when the correlation between the output of *Poetry* magazine and the leading headlines of, for example, the *New York Times* is as disparate as my little tabulation for 1961 indicates, then the context has receded so far that it no longer furnishes a useful field of reference to most of the people who read the poetry.

This is the point. The larger vision has been turned over to the newspapers, to the so-called industry of so-called mass communications. I imagine there's not a single reporter covering the discussions at Geneva for whom the larger vision isn't so fully, consistently present that he must drink himself or weep himself to sleep every night. But poetry is not his job; and if he is a good reporter he knows this and steers clear of it.

The Beats are the exception to what I have been saying. At least so they seem at first, though I wonder if they aren't simply the other side of the coin. I mean the hard core of poets who still flourish their Beat credentials. Among them we find explicitly political poems in great numbers, poems designed to incite impeachments, riots, revolutions, etc. To my mind they fail. The best of these poets is Gregory Corso, an exceedingly talented poet who has written perhaps two dozen really good poems; and

287

that is enough to make anyone envious. But all these good poems are nonpolitical, most are apolitical, and the best are not particularly Beat. His most popular poem is a diatribe called "The Bomb," but for me it seems only a long composition made up partly of rant and shapeless anger and partly of attempts to exorcise the bomb in the name of some numinous human essence; it turns politics into a sort of gang war supervised by the old ladies from the settlement house. In short it contains no poetry, no imagined transmutation of experience, no single realized image to which our thought and feeling can cling. In this respect, that is, the reintroduction of poetry to politics, it seems to me that the Beats, whom we all hoped (some of us secretly) would succeed, have failed almost completely, and what success they have had has been on the wrong level.

Poets are never liberals or conservatives, they are always radicals or reactionaries; and today, of course, public life rejects these indecorous extremes. True, the far right has worked up something resembling a movement in recent years, but it remains intellectually disreputable. On the left, in spite of sporadic efforts in New York and California, those of us who are born anarchists have to agree there isn't much doing. In other words the political attitudes usually endorsed by poets are now amorphous, disintegrated, anachronistic, without programs. Yet this ought to be exactly the political condition in which poets can flourish and in which politically directed poems—and I mean *poems* in the completest sense—can be written without becoming debased by doctrinaire points of view. I cannot speak for reaction; but it is hard for me to believe that any radical poet in the country today lacks a point on which he can stand firm, a point from which, as the spokesman of us all, he can attack known injustices and stupidities. Isn't the bomb, our monstrous, inescapable, political absurdity, the place to begin? And why then isn't it happening?

Théophile Gautier, while discussing his fellow writers, said: "To be of one's own time—nothing seems easier and nothing is more difficult. One can go straight through one's age without seeing it, and this is what has happened to many eminent minds."

Yes, of our time too. We poets have gone straight through fifteen years without seeing them. One can think of a hundred reasons: the extraordinary burden of the poetry of our immediate past, the long evolution of formal preoccupations, the sociology of the culture hero; but none of these, or even all together, can suffice against the bomb, none can explain 2 poems out of 335. I think American poetry, to speak of only that element of our civilization, is stupefied by a massive neurosis—terror, suppression, spasmodic hysteria—and I cannot conceive of a therapy ingenious enough to cure it.

A Chaconnade for Everyone Named Rebecca

For all Rebeccas, yes, but I do have a particular Rebecca in mind, and she is Rebecca Thompson, born two months ago. The reason I have her in mind is this. I have been asked to write about poetry and politics, a topic upon which I have held forth so many times in the past thirty years that now I am discomfited by lack of anything new to say. I am neither a journalist nor a philosopher; I have not the stamina that permits them to go on repeating the same few ideas for a lifetime. Yet the topic is important, it is crucial, and I do not wish to shirk it. Consequently, since my own mind is empty, I choose my point of departure in Rebecca's mind and in the dance of love I find there. Where else is perfect newness, humanly speaking, combined perfectly with the perfect tradition? Rebecca is a fine old name, and I am glad to see it revived.

1. "We live in an age in which the collapse of all previous standards coincides with the perfection in technique for the centralized distribution of ideas; some kind of revolution is inevitable, and will as inevitably be imposed from above by a minority." These words were written in 1933, no matter by whom— he was not the most astute of observers. Anyway the notion was common property among the intelligentsia of the time. In the half-century since then, we have experienced its truth; the revolution has occurred. The minority from above is clearly the corporate will of our commercial megalosaurians; the technique for centralized distribution is clearly electronics; and the "ideas" are clearly our own conditioned responses. The result, as in all revolutions from the right, is massive enslavement. We are a so-

289

ciety of weakened mentalities, frightened of true ideas and dis-
trustful of language. A few of us are gripped by a crippling
nostalgia for the age of enlightenment, made all the more crippling by our knowledge of the horrendous defects of that age.
(Who does not love and hate Mme. Defarge?) A very few of us
have such a vision of our present souls as might issue in a program of salvation, which is more than crippling, a paralysis near
to death, the evident chance for such salvation being like the
eye of the needle. Who is to say whether we should cast our lot
with the very few, the few, or the many?

2. At least we have passed beyond the two great questions
that agitated poets of the time when the words I have quoted
were written, and for some years afterward too. Should poetry
stay clear of politics, for fear of pollution? Is politics even a possible topic in the lyric convention, which is all that is left of poetry in the twentieth century? We understand now that the
"purity" of poetry is a delusion, and like all delusions is both
distractive and debilitating, and we understand also that political poetry is not only feasible in our time but has been splen-
didly written already by poets whose examples obviate any
questions of technique. In short, we have today a broader vision
of poetry than was common among poets of the middle part of
our century, and we see that the "lyric convention" (though we
seldom use that term now) is a freedom, not a restraint.

3. At the same time, unhappily, we see the vision failing.
Young poets are aware of it but unable to pursue it. Their poetic sensibilities have been formed from a misappreciation of the
autobiographical fashion of recent writing in America, and their
poems are formed in the habit of egotism. It is painful to see.

4. Yet the habit has arisen from causes outside literature.
So I believe, at any rate, and the belief constitutes a grain—not
of hope, which I some time ago abjured—but of optimism, a
glint of light in the immense darkness of futurity. The failure
of young poets comes from their maleducation, a huge cultural
dysfunction that certainly is not limited to the schools—if it were,
we should have at least the chance of reform—but is pervasive
and is found perhaps under its most excruciating aspect in the
very center of the American myth, by which I mean "the home."
Poems are written for love. Poems have always been written for
love. Young poets who are unable to scan Shakespeare, who are

unable to react to any language more expressive than jour-
nalese, can hardly be expected to hear the concerned intention
of great poetry; but even if these interpretive skills were somehow, miraculously, injected into them, young poets would still
be young Americans, which is to say, sensibilities deformed by
the whole range of social environment that offers nothing but
images of fraud, fear, sensory mollification, meaningless words,
and rewarded infamy. No wonder the young poet does not know
what to do with his vestigial esthetic impulse and superincum-
bent political fear. "What's more, as a failure, a superfluous man,
a neurasthenic, and victim of the times, anything is permitted
him." So wrote Chekhov. History as usual proffers us only con-
firmations of our own tabescence. And what is permitted the
young poet today is to go to university, the seat of intellectual
desuetude, and there to join his fellows in the pretense that un-
usual line-endings and ingenious metaphors make good poems.

5. A decade ago people often asserted that all human acts
are political. It is true. It is, in fact, a truism, in spite of the desire of the modernist poets, notably T. S. Eliot, to emphasize
the imprisonment of the individual soul: no hermitage can be
so private that it severs the connectedness of humanity. But ten
years ago the truism, extended from Aristotle's definition of man
as the political animal, was usually uttered in anger, since that
was a period of social vitality and social vitality is always a man-
ifestation of anger. Moreover anger is useful, it is probably essential. (I am writing in anger at this moment, if anyone didn't
know.) But anger has its risks, chief of which is its impediment
to clear seeing. I think the political poets of the period of social
vitality did not sufficiently understand that politics is love, anger is love, and poetry is love. All human acts are loving, one
way or another. The deficient awareness of love among most,
though by no means all, angry poets of ten or fifteen years ago
is one reason why their poems fail to hold the imaginations of
young poets today.

6. Think of the state of mind of Rebecca, who has so recently come forth in the world, bringing with her the old and
only specifically human capacity, which is to love. This is not
Wordsworthian mystical obscurantism. On the contrary, it is all
that I can pragmatically conceive: the psychological development of the human foetus can be nothing, in that marvelous

environment, but a growth of love. Granted, a shattering begins at the moment of birth, and love thereafter gradually disperses into its numerous constituent elements, including anger. (This, I take it, is the meaning of the story of Pandora's box, the pun being fundamental.) But at two months, as all heeding parents know, the infant's emotive capacities are still pretty well integrated, still almost totally loving. Because of this she is beautiful.

7. What an act of daring it is to project oneself into Rebecca's mind, or as some would say, to reduce oneself to her "mental level." Yet daring is not so hard. Really it's quite easy, a psychological trick. I learned it long ago, and I am well aware that nothing in my work or life has made me exceptional in this respect. How else could I be writing this, which is so ridiculous to the world?

8. Another quotation: "Even young children understand and love distinction of soul, because it speaks from mind to mind and gives them confidence in the world." That is by Joyce Cary. (The quote under no. 1 above is from W. H. Auden.)

9. At the beginning I said that Rebecca's mind is a dance of love. Maybe it is a poem. Maybe its mode is not to be differentiated. But one thing is certain: it is an act of the imagination. What else does she possess to go with her five little wits? Another thing is certain too: it is a political act. She has not yet conceived more than the vaguest hint of loneliness. She is directed toward the other. If young poets were to ask my advice in these times of weakness and demoralization, which they mostly don't, I would say to them: "Become Rebeccas. Let the fragments of love be reassembled in you. Only then will you have true courage. And after that? Well, you know the techniques, you know the differences between poetry and propaganda—or if you don't, you can easily learn them. And then you will write political poetry in spite of yourselves."

Interview with Galway Kinnell

KATE DANIELS

Galway Kinnell was the organizer and director of the Poets Against the End of the World reading at Town Hall in New York City on May 26, 1982. Born in 1927, Kinnell is the author of numerous books of poetry and translations, including Body Rags, *and* The Book of Nightmares. *His most recent work,* Selected Poems, *won the 1982 Pulitzer Prize. During the late 1960s, he was one of the poets involved with American Writers Against the Vietnam War, along with Robert Bly, James Wright, David Ray, Denise Levertov, and David Ignatow. In the following interview, he explains why he undertook the considerable amount of time and energy involved with the organization of the May 26th reading, and also makes some specific comments on politics and poetry.*

Why did you undertake the May 26th poetry reading?

For some while I had been thinking about organizing an antinuclear poetry reading. I think there are some things that poetry can do better than other things, and on this issue, I thought poetry could deal with it directly in a way that it cannot deal with other questions, such as welfare problems and things like that. But the nuclear question is just a matter of life against death, and that is poetry's subject. It is really the heart. I felt that it would be kind of shameful for poetry, itself, if there were not some occasion of this kind. So, as the events of last spring began to take shape I decided to organize this reading.

How did you decide who to invite?

I got a little committee together because I didn't want it to be merely my personal decision even though I did have strong feelings as to who should participate. I wanted an evening that would sparkle as only poetry at its best can do. I didn't want an evening full of long diatribes; I wanted true poetry, and I wanted it read beautifully. So, basically, the people I wanted to have there were those who felt deeply about this issue, whose poetry I admired tremendously, and who would read it with vitality. Those were the only things I was thinking about. I suppose there would have been other ways to do it, such as representing the various kinds of poetry in this country, the different schools, and so forth. Or I could have chosen the people who had the longest involvement with political issues. In the end, I rejected both of those courses and did it this way.

In preparing this symposium on the May 26th reading for Poetry East, *we asked each of the poets who took part why American poets seemed to be able to achieve solidarity on the nuclear issue, but continued to remain silent, or at any rate, separated from one another, on other political issues (such as El Salvador, South Africa, Northern Ireland). You've answered the question for yourself—that the nuclear issue is one of life against death, and the true subject of poetry. But what are your thoughts about why American poets in general chose to organize around the nuclear issue? I think that historically there is an extremely antipolitical strain in American poetry, so that it surprised and even shocked me when this reading came about. I was surprised at the coming together of such different kinds of writers, and at their willingness to present themselves as public poetry figures, we might say, commenting directly and specifically on a political issue. Certainly, within the context of last spring, the decision to participate in the May 26th reading was a political action.*

I think it's true that American poetry, even poetry in general, is not very often political. But I think everyone—even poets who write the most nonpolitical poetry imaginable—believes that poetry's voice in some kind of social context should be heard. So that I believe that even somebody who doesn't write political poetry as such believes that poetry should be political.

You really believe that?

With a few exceptions, yes, I do believe that. I think that a lot of what I'm calling "nonpolitical poets" who might deplore a kind of poetry that is politically didactic, polemical, or proselytizing, take the chance in their own writing to show how poetry can be political without being embarrassing to poetry in general, as they think such obvious, political poems are. The nuclear issue is so basic that it isn't political in quite the same sense that poems about El Salvador or South Africa are. It is possible to approach the nuclear issue from a very basic point of view that has nothing to do with public policy. It has to do with one's feelings that one wants to live. So, it's a kind of issue that a so-called very political poet and a so-called very nonpolitical poet could join together on, and stand on the same stage. And I think that happened.

There seems to be a lot of debate currently about the question of whether all poetry is political, or not. There was Carolyn Forché's article in American Poetry Review *some time back that suggested it was. There was a recent article in* Ohio Review, *"The Poetry of Commitment," that rejected the idea rather vigorously. In this issue of* Poetry East, *the question of the inherently political nature of all poetry, all art, is something we come back to again and again. I'm speaking of "political" here in its larger sense, not in the sense of current events or party line allegiances. What are your thoughts on this?*

I actually agree with Carolyn Forché about poetry being political. Poetry is always some kind of affirmation of consciousness, so it is an act of life. Even a poem which is despairing can further and increase life if it *lives,* if it affirms. *King Lear* would be an example of this: what a desolate play! yet it increases life. I think of some of Berryman's most despairing *Dream Songs:* "Age and the deaths . . ." Do you know that one? It is probably a poem of the most total despair I've ever met, and yet I live more on account of knowing that poem. I believe that Berryman has forced into existence a facet of consciousness that was not ever there before.

That's interesting because it relates to some of the things that you said about solipsism in "Poetry, Personality, and Death,"* You begin the article sounding anti-solipsism, sort of bemoaning the extremely solipsistic poetry of that period, the poetry of neo-surrealism, etc. But you end

---

*From *A Field Guide to Contemporary Poetry and Poetics,* Friebert and Young, editors.

up by advocating the descent into the self, although it appears to be a descent into the self that doesn't end there. Somehow it bounces back out. So the question is, how do you determine whether this "bouncing back out" occurs, or not? I believe you used the word "transfiguration" to describe this process.

You can tell because a solidarity occurs. When a personal experience is converted into art, a solidarity occurs.

You mean a solidarity with the rest of the population of the world?

Yes. The poem is no longer bewailing a particular person's fate, but is setting forth human fate. It becomes possible for other people to read the poem and not feel that they're just observing or reading the diary of a miserable fellow who jumped off a bridge somewhere. It becomes possible for the readers to feel that they're reading something which expresses some aspect of their own experience. In that sense a solidarity occurs. The poem is no longer just personal.

Would you say that solipsistic poetry is so personal that it makes a voyeur of the reader more than anything else?

Yes, it's like picking up a diary and reading about somebody's unhappy life, or whatever. It's interesting—it may satisfy curiosity—but it doesn't speak for oneself. So, in the sense that I think poetry is experience converted into art, I think poetry is political. Every poem, no matter what it's about—El Salvador or a magnolia tree—expresses some relationship to the world and to others. In that way, every poem is political. I would say that *The Waste Land,* although it's about a man's private anguish, is extremely, perhaps unpleasantly, political. Obviously, the *Cantos* are political. In fact, I think it's actually hard to find any great modern poem that is not political. I would say that in the last twenty years there's been quite a lot of explicitly political poetry written in this country. I think of Robert Bly, James Wright. I think Wright's poem on Eisenhower landing and meeting Franco is one of the great political poems. It's just a flashing moment. When I say that all poetry is political, I mean that it may be negatively political, as well as positively so. I think that a lot of poems are harmful politically, or at least from my view they seem to be. A poem that retreats into some kind of rhymed imaginary realm is political in the sense that it is separating itself from the people and establishing another country. And that's political. Maybe it is not usefully political from the point of view of the others, but from the point of view of the writer it is probably quite useful. A merely personal poem is some kind of political abdication. The poet is saying, "I'm interested in my own experience, and that's all." That is a political act, though a negative one. Poems must have vitality, and when I speak of vitality, I mean something more than just that it lives. Yes, the poem must live, but it must live on the side of life and not live in death.

The last question is one about desire, and it refers to the ending of "Poetry, Despair, and Death." You have written: "For myself I would like a death that would give me more lives, not fewer, greater desire, not less. Isn't it possible to desire a thing, to truly desire it, is a form of having it? But if anything were stronger than fate it would not be acquiescence, but coming to want only what one already has. It would be desire, desire which rises from the roots of one's life and transfigures it." When you talk about desire there, you are talking about it in its larger, largest sense. Desire as a kind of energizing force, right?

Yes, I mean desire as a kind of life principle.

Thinking of it, then, that way, could you comment on how a lack of desire on many levels, from the material to the spiritual, might possibly account for a poetry that is not a large poetry? For instance, so much political poetry comes from other parts of the world. Clearly that has something to do with situations and contexts: lack of personal freedoms, abuses of human rights, racism, sexism, authoritarianism. Things are needed, right? There must be all kinds of desires that go unfulfilled. On the most basic level, I'm talking about material desire: that one cannot purchase the necessities of life, cannot move around in one's life as one might wish. Beyond that, there is the whole realm of nonmaterial desires: religious, spiritual, sexual. It seems obvious that such situations would affect the poetry, all the art, that such a society would produce. The situation of want, of need, of desire would be a factor in all of life, and so it would seem logical that it would show up in the poetry. But what about in a society like American society where so many of our most obvious, most immediate needs are taken for granted and are given to

297

us from the moment we're born until the last moment we're alive? Could that have anything to do with our poetry, the kind of poetry we, as Americans, produce?

That's quite a question. Are you saying that there's something in our society now and in the last thirty years, say, whereby so many of our desires have been immediately gratified that somehow that greater desire, desire as life force, has been fattened or made sluggish?

Yes, I'm suggesting something like that.

Well, who knows? is my answer! It's one of those things where one can only speculate. I do think that sense of solidarity in poetry I spoke of can be greatly narrowed if you belong to a society, the only society in the world in which you have your material needs filled, over-filled all the time. The result is that you can no longer speak of that human situation of want. You just can't because you've never experienced it.

You mean because you don't have the emotional resources, and so it becomes impossible to produce the empathetic response that would make the transformation possible?

Yes. You see, somebody like James Wright had all the resources, all the desire. He was brought up in Martin's Ferry, Ohio, during the Depression, poor, mean in a mean world. That situation gave him a certain power that allowed him to write a poetry that connected him to many other places and situations. He was able to describe what everybody feels in such poor and mean circumstances, including people in other countries. Including poor people in other countries where he'd never been and whom he'd never met. It seems possible that perhaps middle class America has been deprived of that power. And that means that middle class American poets may somehow have had that power taken away from them. But these are material desires we're talking about. I thought you were also asking about some greater, more profound kind of desire.

Yes, but it starts here. What I'm wondering is whether desire is somehow incremental, a process of accrual?

It seems likely that the general fattening we've been discussing could make desires at another level less vital. The metaphor of the heath in *King Lear* is saying something of that sort: In the court surrounded by adulation and false love, Lear becomes a tyrant, a stupid tyrant, and everything is taken away from him. Then he goes out with madmen and fools onto the heath and really experiences a kind of terrific cosmic connection. Only then is he transfigured. For the first time, he is in a position of want, of need, and he becomes able to speak for everybody in a poetry that is unmatched in English:

> Thou thinkest 'tis much that this contentious storm
> Invades us to the skin. So 'tis to thee;
> But where the greater malady is fixed,
> The lesser is scarce felt. Thoud'st shun a bear;
> But if thy flight lay toward the roaring sea,
> Thou'dst meet the bear i' the mouth. When the mind's free,
> The body's delicate. The tempest in my mind
> Doth from my senses take all feeling else
> Save what beats there. . . .
> Poor naked wretches, wheresoe'er you are,
> That bide the pelting of this pitiless storm,
> How shall your houseless heads and unfed sides,
> Your looped and windowed raggedness, defend you
> From seasons such as these? O, I have ta'en
> Too little care of this! Take physic, pomp;
> Expose thyself to feel what wretches feel,
> That thou may'st shake the superflux to them
> And show the heavens more just.
>   *King Lear,* III, iv

Poets Against the End of the World

GALWAY KINNELL
AMIRI BARAKA
JANE COOPER
DAVID IGNATOW
JUNE JORDAN
ETHERIDGE KNIGHT
STANLEY KUNITZ
DENISE LEVERTOV
PHILIP LEVINE
JOSEPHINE MILES
SIMON J. ORTIZ

On May 26, 1982, thirteen American poets gathered at Town Hall in New York City to participate in a benefit reading for the nuclear freeze movement. During the spring of 1982, much attention was focused on mobilizing public attention and support for the antinuclear issue. These efforts were organized by the June 12th Rally Committee, a coalition of activists from a variety of political parties and lay organizations. Symposia, demonstrations, civil disobedience, concerts, performances, and many other events throughout the country culminated in the June 12th rallies in New York and other large cities. In Manhattan alone, three-quarters of a million people gathered peaceably in Central Park in support of the freeze.

The May 26th reading was called Poets Against the End of the World. The writers who participated were: Amiri Baraka, Robert Bly, Jane Cooper, David Ignatow, June Jordan, Galway Kinnell, Etheridge Knight, Stanley Kunitz, Denise Levertov, Philip Levine, W. S. Merwin, Josephine Miles, and Simon J. Ortiz. Feeling that this was an important event in American literary history, *Poetry East* asked these poets to make a statement on their participation in this reading, and to say something specifically about the question of politics and poetry. All but Robert Bly and W. S. Merwin accepted our invitation.

Galway Kinnell

A new fear has risen into human consciousness. It cuts across all political viewpoints and it has nothing to do with nationality. If we could tap the feelings of someone on the streets of Kiev we would no doubt find exactly the same terror of nuclear war that we find in someone on the streets of New York. Indeed this fear may soon become a binding force among the peoples of the world, for it has to do with the very existence of us all.

This fear is not particularly personal. It is for much more than our own lives. It is a fear quite simply for everything that matters. One could describe it as the other side of love. We feel it most keenly with respect to our children—the brightness of being they carry so innocently into the fire storms that we prepare.

I don't know which poems my colleagues will read tonight. I imagine some will try to articulate this fear—the complex feelings surrounding it—sadness, disgust, despair—even resolve. Some may do so by speaking explicitly about nuclear war, others by evoking less direct manifestations of the self-destructive forces in us.

I am sure that many poems that will be read tonight undertake what may be poetry's noblest function—to affirm the sacred character of life—not human life only but all the life of the planet.

We thirteen poets here are a somewhat random assortment; we are simply the ones who happen to be on the stage this evening. There will be many other evenings and many other stages, before all us poets have spoken and the theme is worn out.

Why are we here? At the very least, if the human race is to destroy itself, it would be horrible for anyone, especially anyone who lives by the word, to accept this fate in silence.

But we are here also because we believe in poetry's power to articulate and inspire. Some of us remember a reading similar to this one, called "Poets for Peace," held here in Town Hall in 1965. It was the first of the many readings protesting the Vietnam war. Looking back we can see that those readings meant something; they may actually have had an effect. If those readings mattered then, may this one, and any readings that follow, matter even more, when the issue is the absolute one of life against death.

Introduction to "Poetry Against the End of the World"
Town Hall, May 26, 1982

Amiri Baraka

On May 26, 1982, a rather remarkable gathering of poets was brought together on the stage at Town Hall, NYC, responding to this theme. It was a remarkable gathering because of the *reach* and breadth of the group. Not only were there black and white and Latino, male and female (and I would gather hetero- and homosexual) poets, represented in a group of modest size, but there was also a general disparity of ideology and aesthetic represented. I know that certainly there were a few poets there that I myself had castigated from time to time with the *nom de guerre* "academic" and likewise other poets I have felt closer to aesthetically who have been jumped on, as I myself have been, by some of the first mentioned as perhaps "lacking discipline." Yes, the gathering contained all the correct elements necessary for at least a tongue fight, if nothing else.

The variety of ideologies I've mentioned, usually easy to perceive in the various poets' works, ranges I'm certain, from Marxism-Leninism to Anarchism, Liberalism, Pacifism, Nationalism and even some formal religion of one kind or another. Yet there we all were, some passionately, others more cautiously, rubbing up against each other backstage, and at the right moment squatting side by side squinting out into the lights at Town Hall, readying our poetry (and songs) against the end of the world.

What is obvious, I suppose, is that the theme had such strength and immediacy it could draw such a wide front of people. (Also, that the coordinators of the event were in touch with both the A and Z of the poetry world, as well as the M's.) And this is as it must be—because if we are talking about "the end of the world," that will affect us all, even the solipsists, though they might not believe it. Specifically, we were gathered to oppose world nuclear destruction or some might say, we were gathered to support efforts at world peace. To me, they are both, objectively, the same. Yet I suppose we must also mention that in one sense, all of us so displayed in some "activist" stance against world nuclear holocaust must to a certain extent bear the ubiquitous sobriquet "left," since, believe me, there is a rather sizeable group of people who either *do not know* that the entire earth society is threatened by nuclear extinction or who *do not believe* (for one metaphysical reason or another) that *most,* if not all, of us could be wiped out by mindless human actions. There is another, hopefully smaller group, that believe that in the event of nuclear war those of us in the "free world" (more metaphysics) would not only survive but be the better for the experience since such a war would result in the elimination of "our" enemies.

The very fact of such an open activist stance against nuclear war has definitely gotten all of our names written down on some prestigious shit list—those of us whose names were not on that list already! It is not merely saying that one is against nuclear war that gets one put on such lists (even Bonzo's Buddy has gone on record as being against nuclear war) it is also who one sees as being responsible for the steady deadly motion toward such catastrophe which sets one apart. Clearly, if we say, along with the bad actor, that it is the Soviet Union *alone* who is responsible, then we are backward enough to be trusted. If we say, on the other hand, that it is the U.S. *alone,* then we will get put on a U.S. government list but celebrated in the Soviet Union for aiding their war mongering. But the people in the USSR who also hold up the Soviet Union as being equally as culpable as the U.S. get the same harassment there. I think those who think *only* the U.S. is responsible are as one-sided and shortsightedly sectarian as those who think it is all the Soviets! I would prefer to be on both superpower shit lists, since neither of these governments represents the great majority of their people, and no one in their right mind could believe for a second that the masses of the U.S. and Russian people want nuclear destruction.

The point is that those poets reading against the end of the world seemingly opposed both of the superpowers' nuclear destructiveness and regardless of how far apart we might be on any number of important issues there was enough solidarity on the nuclear issue to put together an impressive united front.

There are a number of positive aspects to such a front. First of all it is important for all of us who consider ourselves conscious to oppose the obvious motion toward World War Three that the two superpowers are fomenting. For poets, writers, artists, whose words or images or whatever reach many more people than the average human voice this is critically important. It means that more people can be reached with the anti-nuke anti-war message. It also means that some of us who call ourselves artists, poets in this case, have chosen to do more with our words than merely titillate our own aesthetic and emotional sensibilities. We have taken some social responsibility, some positive stance in the real world. And I realize in a bourgeois society, especially the U.S., that such a stance is considered by the chief establishment artistic arbiters as being "anti-art." Art can only concern itself, as far as these aesthetes of the status quo are concerned, with abstraction and solipsistic vagary. To focus on the real world in one's work or one's life is to violate the basic dictates of bourgeois aesthetics and philosophy.

Such a responsible stance by poets of "reputation" means that perhaps U.S. poetry can take its place contemporarily among most of the world's poetry in being socially sensitive and responsible, dirty words usually to those spawned on the elitism of literary reaction of the "new criticism" or structuralism, etc. It means that perhaps a broader thrust of dynamic, socially relevant poetry can come to maturity in the U.S. during the 80's and beyond (if there is to be a beyond).

One hopes that the broad front that responds to the possibility of nuclear holocaust might eventually come together around other important issues, such as the struggle for democracy by the oppressed nationalities and women and hopefully one day against monopoly capitalism/imperialism itself, which is the economic and social basis for all these menaces to human life and development.

American artists must learn that art can be, as Mao Zedong pointed out, both artistically powerful as well as politically progressive. It would be particularly instructive these days to read about the destruction of the Weimar Republic, the last democratic government before the Nazi takeover in Germany. Especially informing is the role of the various artists during the Weimar period, some fighting against the rising threat of fascism with every part of their lives and art, others remaining quiet and "neutral" while the mass murderers gained control. And still others who openly embraced both the sharp move to the right and eventually fascism itself. There is still time to choose sides, and yes, it is that cut and dried. I know it is fashionable to talk about how complex human life and art are and how they cannot be "oversimplified" to the extent that one can take some clear and definable stance in the real world. But tell me now, fifty years after the concentration camps opened in Germany (1933) about the complexity of opposing fascism in those days, and what is different today? (And by the way please make certain to see *Mephisto,* the great Hungarian film that won an academy award in 1981, which tells of an artist who sells his art to the murderers—there is a great deal that can be learned from that, a great deal!)

Jane Cooper

My eyes are just level with the roof of the dining-room table. My mother and father sit at breakfast reading newspapers, while I roam between them, free. My father announces the Japanese have invaded Manchuria. My mother, who believes what they told her during World War I, that there could never be another war, looks up in hurt and alarm. My father says, "I suppose there must always be a war some place." It is a new thought to me, and ineradicable, among the many new thoughts and sensations that bombard me every day.

I am standing at the window of a Philadelphia hospital, and down below in the street boys are hawking newspapers that announce the dropping of the first atomic bomb on Hiroshima. As a

305

schoolgirl in Princeton, I have been told that local scientists may succeed in splitting the atom, but if they do, who is to say that each atom won't in turn ignite another, until the entire chain of matter and sentient being is destroyed? I think, "The world could end in my time." I think, nevertheless, that I will somehow be around to witness the end of the world. I say aloud, "I could live to see the end of the world."

It seems to me almost impossible for a poem to address the nuclear threat directly, yet—whether we like it or not—that threat is an undercurrent in all our work now.

Whenever I write with particular tenderness of the natural world or of other human beings or of animals, the threat of extinction is with me. I am aware of the fragility of tenure of our lives on earth, and with them of the earth itself.

Whenever I write out of anger or terror, there is a sense in which the terror or anger—at specific injustice, mass oppression, torture, or simply unwilled solitude—is a cry against our race toward a common suicide.

I have never thought my poems would live after me in any way I can understand. But insofar as the signature of our humanness is to make, to speak, and to remember, writing now is an affirmation of humanness, and in that sense, a protest.

The problem is perhaps not how to write of the nuclear threat but to believe anything else is worth writing about. We must hold onto that belief.

David Ignatow

Frankly, the topic leaves me speechless. I can't imagine what there is to say about a holocaust that will leave no one and nothing alive. To write about that is to actually contemplate and to look forward to the happening. At least, that is how I feel about it. I prefer not to think of the event at all, since I refuse to believe it will happen. I still believe in the sanity of the human race in the face of such ultimate disaster. I still believe that survival is the key to our thinking—man, woman and child, red, white, black, yellow-skinned or what have you. Survival is what will be uppermost in our minds in a crisis, if it ever comes to that, and

we will survive by finding a path between disaster and antago-
nism on which each of us will be able to travel to and from one
another—if not as sworn friends then at least as sworn survivors. Whether friendship will emerge from the political and
racial differences I would not predict, but at least we will understand that we cannot survive alone at the cost of the death
of others. That kind of thinking, that period in history is gone
with the election of nuclear war as the weapon.

We will have to live with one another, tolerating each other's prejudices, gripes, biases, eccentricities and anything else that
turns off one people from another, one race from another, one
religion from another. But think of the kind of world in which
we stare into the face of a person whom we would rather have
massacred the day before nuclear weapons were elected. What
an awkward situation it will be for us all: the fact that communists who can't stand the so-called belly of the imperial-
ist/capitalist swollen there before him with good, solid beef and
potatoes, and the capitalist/imperialist will have to look steadily
and passively at the communist who once planned to do away
with him. Neither will have even a sidearm in possession, but
they will be staring at each other and, who knows, perhaps begin grouchily to talk to one another, conceding in that gesture
that there has to be something human about the other who can
speak to the point, grimace, laugh (harshly), tell a crude joke on
the other, spit on the floor in contempt but then look up at the
opponent and smile helplessly that this is as far as either one of
them can go in deriding the other, negating the other physically and/or mentally, and, I dream, they will laugh at and with
each other for finding each other in this ridiculous *cul de sac* between them. Will they begin to chat a bit about living conditions, the weather, the environment, their respective leaders? Tell
each other jokes in confidence about politics, jokes that each had
withheld in private in the past but that now are harmless enough
in the face of the nuclear threat?

And since they will have already conceded that the nuclear
bomb cannot be used, won't they begin to think seriously of
dumping them all into the sea and start all over again by making just ordinary high-powered rifles and cannon? Or, miracle
of miracles, will it occur to both of them at the same time that
they don't need weapons at all from now on, since they have

307

begun to trade jokes with each other, on politics especially?

It's difficult to go beyond this vision, in the face of the present crisis, but it is the vision I'd like to hold on to as the one that gives me the most confidence that we will prevail in spite of and perhaps because of our foolishness. It's this unity in diversity and complexity that I will seek for in my poems. I dream we will begin to sense the stupidity of dying wholesale off the face of the earth when the earth has so much to offer us. I think I'm not alone in holding on to the vision I have, because I see so many of us are silent in the face of this crisis, communing with the vision of the ultimate sanity of survival, even as it makes us pull back from our righteousness and self-approval to see ourselves as fools to have threatened our very own existence in threatening that of our opponent.

June Jordan

I am for the continuance of all life and, hence, I oppose nuclear weaponry, genocide, and every form of domination. I believe that life demands an always vigilant dedication to justice and that justice depends upon the absolute support of self-determination everywhere in the world. As I am a poet I express what I believe, and I fight against whatever I oppose, in poetry.

Etheridge Knight

I participated in the "Poetry Against the End of the World" Reading Rally at the New York Town Hall for two main reasons: (1) my good friend, Galway Kinnell, asked me to, and (2) it was an opportunity for me to put my/ass/where my/words/had been. The bringing together of the "word" and the "deed" is, to me, the essential—tho not necessarily the primary—function of the poet—of all artists, really; for what is the/Big Lie/other than saying one/thing/and doing an/other. So we had to come together for a moment to sing a single truth! Life and Art are all.

All of us have issues dear to our particular hearts—libera-

tion for Blacks, Women, the Palestinians, the Irish, whales, cau-
liflower and marijuana and unborn babies, but solidarity on the
nuclear issue is paramount because it addresses Existence itself.
And I don't think any of the poets at the Town Hall that night
subscribe to the Suicide School of Poetry.

The Poet, the Poem, the People. For Art to happen (common, communication, community) there must be a move-
ment/between/the three that starts a revaluing, a revolution, a
dance. The poet as individual, and the people, as collective—or
community—*whatever* affects, or disaffects, them—be it a poem
or a pistol, is political. (It/is/true that a great number of American poets—*those artists*—are "notoriously nonpolitical"; they operate under a "western" aesthetic that assumes that the duty of
the artist is to edify, to titillate—that the great "I/am/" and a world
view that is flat and lined is where it's at. Yet good art both *en-
tertains* and *enlightens*.) Because it/is/activity, the politics of Pound
and Eliot/is/preferable to nonpolitics. And just as surely as cel-
ibacy/is/a sexist position, nonpolitics is the most rigid of all political stances. And the most dangerous. So, it is bullshit to try
to separate poetry and politics.

> "Troubled in min'—
> I'm blue—
> But my blues ain' /gonna/ stay,
> 'Cause the sun's gonna shine
> In my back door someday."

"Traditional Blues"

Good poetry is ultimately celebration. An affirmation. It's
main appeal must always be to the freedom/God/in the individual and in the people. It/is/there. Even as we berate the murderers and the muthafuckas, we must remain lovers, and singers
to life. To me, the Reading at the Town Hall was such a celebration, from Baraka having to/do/weekends in jail to Josephine Miles's grand trek from California to be there. Out of the
maggots and mortars we sometimes have to make the music. We
do, and we dance, and we will win. And, as Meridel LeSueur,
Mother Poet from Minnesota says:

"We do not have the right to ask if we will fail. Failing and

309

death are nothing in view of the stakes of the opposite. Life is against everything against. There is no winning with the bomb. It is not even a choice. Death against death. There must be no doubting the strength of life over this kind of death, given our powerful common sense, our powerful love, our powerful numbers. . . . We do not have the right to doubt our strength and each other . . ."

So. All we/got/to do is to keep/on/poeting.

Stanley Kunitz

One of my premises is that poets are better at changing themselves than at changing others. There is no gainsaying that poetry resists being put into the service of any cause, even the worthiest. Nevertheless, I have never agreed with the sentiment expressed by Auden in his eulogy for Yeats that "poetry makes nothing happen." No doubt "Ireland has her madness and her weather still," the same as before, but it also has the life-enhancing memory of Yeats. His poems have risen from the page and become features of a spiritual landscape.

Here at home poets told the ghastly truth about Vietnam long before the public had ears for it. They were in the first wave of dissent that swelled into an overwhelming flood. Although the rhetoric of the antiwar poems of that period already seems dated, it needs to be recalled that when poets for a moment drew together into a passionate community, they proved that they could still shake the world a little.

We poets are citizens too, and most of us have never seen an ivory tower. Of course, we appreciate the unparalleled freedom we enjoy to write as we please. Thank you, Founding Fathers! At the same time we cannot help regretting that only the blessed young and a handful of incorrigible elders seem ordinarily to give a damn about what our poems are saying. Will that be enough to affect the climate of an age?

"I am the truth," said Wallace Stevens, "since I am part of what is real, but neither more nor less than those around me. And I am imagination, in a leaden time and in a world that does not move of its own heaviness."

The trouble with the old order, as it approaches nuclear catastrophe, is that it lacks imagination. It fears imagination as it fears truth, for both of them threaten power, contribute to its unease. To stay in office, power must pretend to dignity and honor and compassion, or, failing these, to good fellowship. In its self-satisfaction it does not know it is pretending; for only imagination, with its sympathy for other hearts and minds, is capable of summoning up, in Abraham Lincoln's phrase, "the better angels of our nature."

The poetic imagination, in government as well as in literature, does not ignore or suppress contradictions, but instead seizes the opportunity to create out of them new accommodations, new reconciliations, and new values. The President whom most Americans deem greatest was at once eloquent and magnanimous, an archetypal man of imagination. Is the American political system still capable of producing such a moral and ennobling force? If we yearn for greatness again, we must look beyond parties and slogans for sustenance. *O for a Muse of Fire to ascend!*

Denise Levertov

The other day a woman was apologizing to me for not having done civil disobedience on a certain recent occasion. I hadn't done it either, I told her, and I saw no need to apologize. What's essential is not whether one participates in this or that form of action but that one assesses and reassesses what, habitually or on any given occasion, one *can* do, and does it. The possibilities keep changing. Over the years, sometimes one sends money, sometimes one stuffs envelopes, sometimes one makes public speeches, sometimes one goes to jail. All these things are necessary and it doesn't always have to be the same people doing the same thing again.

One thing I've found myself doing is using the fact that, as a published poet, I have an audience, and address that audience, in person and in print, on the issues that engage my political concern. Indeed, I often risk shamelessly haranguing my readers and listeners. I would never "use" poetry itself—what I *use* is whatever prestige I have. But because the issues—justice and peace and "the fate of the earth"—are always on my mind,

311

they do enter my poems, and then I have the chance *through* poetry, to stir others' minds or to articulate what readers feel but have not found words for.

It is my hope that both approaches—the prose of speeches and conversations, and the poetry that articulates engaged emotion and belief—have a political function, just as letters to Washington or demonstrations or acts of civil disobedience do; and none of these is more important than any other. At the same time I think no one should confine him or herself consistently to a single type of action. By the same token, no one should feel remorse at not having undertaken some particular activity; self-reproach is appropriate only for consistently doing nothing at all. This means that poets should never moan and groan over not having produced political poems—it may simply not accord with their muse. But in that case, they should find some other useful thing to do in relation to their political concern. Letting their admirers know where they stand is one way to help: the risk is the alienation of readers, the gain is that those readers have at least been made to think. Sometimes the penny takes a while to drop.

All I've said up to now is applicable to all "protest," "didactic," or "engaged" poetry. But it seems, as I read over what I've written, to lack urgency. And was there ever a time as urgent? Never. Never have we faced extinction, the extinction of all future, all consciousness. Sometimes I wonder how we can write at all, under that shadow. Sometimes I wonder how we can write about anything else. But maintaining a sense of what life, nature, and spirit *are* is essential if we are to find the mind's resources to circumvent the results of the twentieth century's unethical infatuation with technology and the lust for power of its "leaders." So one task of poets in the nuclear age is to remind us of all that is beautiful and lovable. Yet I am unhappy at the many poems I see which seem to bear no mark of this period in which they are written, no shadow; I feel any good poem of the 1980s should, whatever reminder and revelation of love and wonder it brings us, also carry a rumor of the undercurrent of fear, anger, and anguish that runs through our time.

Philip Levine

I go from day to day thinking about the nuclear threat as little as possible. I believe that my government is in the hands of men who would once again use such weapons, and I believe that there are other nations no better off. I have written about the bombing of Hiroshima and the bombing of America that I fear is coming. Often I have dreamed of the fall of nuclear bombs, and I know that my children have awakened terrified by such dreams. I once overheard my two younger sons when they were only boys discussing the awesome power of these weapons; they both seemed to understand that their lives, that all life, could vanish in a flash. When I allow my imagination to range over the possibilities of nuclear war, I begin to shake with a rage I can barely control. This happens to me only when I'm off guard, when something small and personal entices my mind or dams up the usual course of my thoughts. It can be something as insignificant and casual as a burned piece of meat that gives off a metallic glint or a well known face in a particular arrangement of shadows that manages to suggest what it would look like without flesh. For a moment or for much longer I am helpless before the power of my own dread, and then the rage comes on, a rage which I believe is different from the feelings which could produce a nuclear attack, but of this I am not sure.

I recall a particular photograph of generals and admirals gathered at the White House during the Nixon years; it appeared in a local newspaper, and the quality was very poor. When I looked as closely as possible I could make out nothing on the faces of the men that separated them from other men. I fetched a magnifying glass, and while the features did not dissolve I did not find what I was looking for; just a row of bland, smiling faces outdoors on a bright afternoon, each man with several rows of ribbons rising from his left breast pocket almost to the shoulder, bland average faces that seemed to mean no one any harm. These were the sort of men, I thought, who give and obey orders. I wondered if it were possible for them to find ever in their lives a man in the White House they would not obey.

The poetry which is most highly valued in this America seems unaware of any need to change the priorities of those who rule in Washington, or closer to home, in the editorial rooms of our publishers or the befuddled minds of our critics. When our poets speak of the scarcity of bread in particular houses, the lack of doctors in entire communities, the waste of human lives everywhere, they are chastised for being impure, for allowing this sustaining and destroying world to enter their imaginations and their digestive tracks, the lives of their metaphors, the dreams of their children. In these halcyon days a poet can be too full of this particular world, the public one we were all born into and the existence of which is now threatened. Keats' supposed yearning for a world without time or change, Stevens' concern with the substance of substance, Wordsworth's rapture before a natural order we are about to lose, are held up as models, as though those poets, like some gaggle of coy girls, had all the time in the world, when in fact they and their great poems moved under the death clouds that shadow us.

This year the generals and admirals with different and equally presentable faces came to Washington and asked for more and more sophisticated (that is more expensive and deadly) weapons. I saw them on television assuring the nation that we must be ready to strike first, to win the war they are building for. The Secretary agreed. The congressmen, as fresh as cheerleaders, agreed. The President nodded his dark, wise head, and the picture was gone before I could search it with my unrevealing magnifier. In truth I do not believe in the power of my poetry or any poetry I know to touch such men in a way that would prevent them from obeying the order to attack or retaliate. That is *the* problem in the light of which the irrelevance of our academic critics, the sweetness of our prize poems, the tiresomeness of my long rant are but the crackling of thorns. I hope I am wrong. I do not think the making of bread will stop these men, or the gathering of apples, or the praying of the faithful, or many other useful, essential activities. But somehow they must be stopped.

Josephine Miles

WORLD

Coming up against the end of the world,
I saw how frayed it was,
Sleazy, ill-conceived
What an ending,
Trumped up, frazzled like our fears,
And I wondered why. On what island
Or delta or forest of aloes
Could we settle the seams of our determination?

Now I must turn to look around to see
In my own shadow
Retrieving, unretrieving,
Could we find menders, could we take up the thread
Of all this ravel,
To piece together a pattern for the world?

Simon J. Ortiz

As a poet of Native American descent, I think I understand what
genocide means. I think I understand the theft of land. Life and
land, the basic elements of an ongoing human existence. I think
I understand what U.S. national policy has been since the last
century. This national policy created the atomic bomb and now
holds the world at frightened bay with its nuclear threat.

For Native American people, the fight has always been against
those who profit from our misery, loss, and death. Immeasur-
able wealth has been gained from our land and labor. Native
Americans have fought against the conscienceless interests of U.S.
capitalism longer than anybody here in this nation. We know
who built the bomb and why.

The fighters against repression and exploitation in Guatemala and El Salvador are struggling against those same economic interests that Native Americans in the U.S. have fought.
This is what must be understood by everyone who is concerned
about the continuance of life. If we don't, we will not be able to

fully comprehend what the present nuclear threat means and how it is used against us. Further, we will not understand our own oppression nor question it; we will be blind to racism, exploitation of women, workers and the poor, supremacism, elitism, etc. in the U.S. because we will not understand how those are tied to the nature of capitalism.

If poets are truly to be for life—against the end of the world—there is only one choice to be made. We must truly be against the end of the world by accepting the responsibility of looking at the motives and processes of the U.S. economic and political system. We must write about what we observe and discover. In this way, we will be living, acting, speaking "For the sake of the people, for the sake of the land," as the Aacqumeh Hanoh of the Southwest say.

Contributors

W. H. Auden is the author of *The Double Man, For the Time Being, The Age of Anxiety, Nones,* and *The Shield of Achilles,* which received the National Book Award in 1956. Auden was a playwright, editor, and essayist as well as a poet, and his selected essays, *The Dyer's Hand and Other Essays,* appeared in 1962. His *Selected Poems,* edited by Edward Mendelson, was published in 1979.

Amiri Baraka/LeRoi Jones is a poet, playwright, and social critic. His play *Dutchman* was awarded an Obie as Best American Play of the 1963–1964 season. His books include *Blues People, Selected Plays and Prose of Amiri Baraka/LeRoi Jones,* and *Selected Poetry of Amiri Baraka/LeRoi Jones.* His most recent book is a collection of essays entitled *Daggers and Javelins.*

Wendell Berry is the author of fifteen volumes of poetry, including *The Broken Ground, Clearing,* and *A Part.* He has also written several prose collections, including *The Long-Legged House, The Hidden Wound, The Unsettling of America,* and *Recollected Essays 1965–1980.* A new book of essays, *Standing by Words,* has just been published.

Robert Bly is a poet, translator, editor, and critic. The author of some twenty volumes of poetry, his books include *Silence in the Snowy Fields, Sleepers Joining Hands,* and most recently, *The Man in the Black Coat Turns.* In 1968 he won the National Book Award for *The Light Around the Body.* A translator of Pablo Neurda, Tomas Tranströmer, and Rainer Maria Rilke, Bly has also edited a number of influential poetry anthologies, including *Leaping Poetry* and *News of the Universe.*

Hayden Carruth is the author of *The Crow and the Heart, From Snow and Rock, from Chaos: Poems 1965–1972,* and *Brothers, I Loved You All.* In 1978 he was awarded the Shelley Memorial Award.

317

His essays are collected in *Working Papers* and *Effluences from the Sacred Caves.*

Jane Cooper is the author of, among other books, *Windows and Maps.* She is Poet-in-Residence at Sarah Lawrence College. In 1979 her poem "Threads: Rosa Luxemburg from Prison" was published as a benefit for the White House Lawn Eleven of the War Resisters' League.

Kate Daniels's first book of poetry, *The White Wave,* won the Agnes Lynch Starrett Poetry Award for 1983. A co-editor of *Poetry East,* her biography of Muriel Rukeyser, entitled *Muriel Rukeyser: A Life of Poetry,* is to be published in 1986.

T. S. Eliot was a poet, playwright, critic, and editor. His books of poetry include *The Waste Land* and *The Four Quartets;* his plays include *Murder in the Cathedral* and *The Cocktail Party.* His essays are collected in *Selected Essays, On Poetry and Poets,* and *Tradition and the Individual Talent.* He was awarded the Nobel Prize for Literature in 1948.

Carolyn Forché won the Yale Series of Younger Poets Award in 1976 for her first book, *Gathering the Tribes,* and the Lamont Prize of the Academy of American Poets in 1982 for her second book, *The Country Between Us.*

Michael Hamburger is the author of over twenty volumes of poetry, and is a translator of Baudelaire, Georg Trakl, Gunter Grass, and Hölderlin. His books include *Travelling—Poems 1963–1968* and *Ownerless Earth: New and Selected Poems 1950–1972. The Truth of Poetry: Tensions in Modern Poetry from Baudelaire to the 1960s* was first released in 1969.

Patricia Hampl is the author of two books of poetry, *Resort and Other Poems* and *Woman Before an Aquarium. A Romantic Education* was the winner of the 1981 Houghton Mifflin Literary Fellowship.

Lewis Hyde is a poet and essayist whose work has appeared in *Keynon Review, American Poetry Review, Paris Review,* and *The Nation.* He is the translator of *A Longing for the Light,* poems by the Nobel Prize winner Vicente Aleixandre. *The Gift: Imagination and the Erotic Life of Property* was published in 1983.

David Ignatow is the author of *Selected Poems, Poems 1934–1969, Whisper to the Earth,* and *Tread the Dark,* which received the Bolligen Prize in 1978. He is Poet-in-Residence at York College, City University of New York, and has been the recipient of a Wallace Stevens Fellowship and the Shelley Memorial Award.

Richard Jones is the author of two books of poetry, *Windows and Walls* and *Innocent Things.* He is also an editor of *Poetry East,* and with Kate Daniels edited the critical anthology *Of Solitude and Silence: Writings on Robert Bly.*

June Jordan is the author of fifteen books, including *New Poems: Poems of Exile and Return, Things That I Do in the Dark: Selected Poetry,* and *Passion: New Poems, 1977–1980.* Her prose writing is collected in *Civil Wars,* which was published in 1981.

Etheridge Knight is the author of *Poems from Prison, Belly Songs and Other Poems,* and *Born of a Woman: New and Selected Poems.* He is also the editor of *Black Voices from Prison.*

Stanley Kunitz is the author of *Intellectual Things, The Testing Tree,* and *Selected Poems, 1928—1958,* which won the Pulitzer Prize. In 1978 he published *The Poems of Stanley Kunitz 1928–1978.* His essays are collected in *A Kind of Order, a Kind of Folly: Essays & Conversations.*

Denise Levertov is the author of fourteen books of poetry, including *The Double Image, Sorrow Dance, Collected Earlier Poems 1940–1960,* and *Candles in Babylon.* Her prose books include *The Poet in the World* and *Light up the Cave.*

Philip Levine is the author of ten books of poetry, including *They Feed They Lion, The Names of the Lost, One for the Rose,* and *Selected Poems.* In 1979, *Ashes: Poems New and Old,* and *Seven Years from Somewhere* were published simultaneously, and together received the National Book Critics Award in Poetry for 1980.

Josephine Miles is both a scholar and a poet. Her poetry is collected in *Poems 1930–1983* and *Kinds of Affection.*

Howard Nemerov is the author of *Sentences, The Blue Swallows,* and *The Collected Poems of Howard Nemerov.* In addition to three novels and two collections of short stories, he is also the author of *Poetry and Fiction: Essays, Journal of the Fictive Life*, and *Reflexions on Poetry & Poetics*.

Simon J. Ortiz is the author of *A Good Journey, Going for the Rain, From Sand Creek, Fight Back for the Sake of the Land, for the Sake of the People*, and, most recently, a collection of short stories entitled *Fightin'*.

Adrienne Rich is the author of many books of poetry, including *Change of World*, which was selected by W. H. Auden for the Yale Younger Poets series in 1951, and *Diving into the Wreck*, which was a co-winner in 1974 of the National Book Award. Her most recent collection is *The Fact of a Doorframe: Poems Selected and New, 1950–1984*. *On Lies, Secrets, and Silence: Selected Prose 1966–1978* was published in 1979.

Muriel Rukeyser was the author of fifteen books of poetry, including her first book, *Theory of Flight*, which won the Yale Younger Poets Prize, and, in 1978, two years before her death, *The Collected Poems of Muriel Rukeyser*. Her other works include biographies and plays, as well as her prose book, *The Life of Poetry*.

Gary Snyder is the author of *Myths and Texts, Regarding Wave*, and *Turtle Island*. His prose book, *Earth House Hold*, was published in 1969.

Stephen Spender is the author of *Collected Poems*, published in 1955, and *Selected Poems*, published in 1964. His prose volumes include *The Destructive Element, The Struggle of the Modern, The Thirties and After: Poetry, Politics, People 1933–1970*, and an autobiography, *World Within World*.